Neuroscience and Psychology of Meditation in Everyday Life

Neuroscience and Psychology of Meditation in Everyday Life addresses essential and timely questions about the research and practice of meditation as a path to realization of human potential for health and well-being.

Balancing practical content and scientific theory, the book discusses long-term effects of six meditation practices: mindfulness, compassion, visualization-based meditation techniques, dream yoga, insight-based meditation and abiding in the existential ground of experience. Each chapter provides advice on how to embed these techniques into everyday activities, together with considerations about underlying changes in the mind and brain based on latest research evidence.

This book is essential reading for professionals applying meditation-based techniques in their work and researchers in the emerging field of contemplative science. The book will also be of value to practitioners of meditation seeking to further their practice and understand associated changes in the mind and brain.

Dusana Dorjee, PhD, is a cognitive neuroscientist in the School of Psychology at Bangor University. Her research investigates how meditation, particularly mindfulness, impacts well-being and modifies the mind and brain. Dusana is also a long-term meditation practitioner and teacher in the Tibetan Buddhist tradition of Dzogchen.

Neuroscience and Psychology of Meditation in Everyday Life

Searching for the Essence of Mind

Dusana Dorjee

LONDON AND NEW YORK

First published 2018
by Routledge
2 Park Square, Milton Park, Abingdon, Oxon OX14 4RN

and by Routledge
711 Third Avenue, New York, NY 10017

Routledge is an imprint of the Taylor & Francis Group, an informa business

© 2018 Dusana Dorjee

The right of Dusana Dorjee to be identified as author
of this work has been asserted by her in accordance
with sections 77 and 78 of the Copyright, Designs and
Patents Act 1988.

British Library Cataloguing-in-Publication Data
A catalogue record for this book is available from the British Library

Library of Congress Cataloging-in-Publication Data
A catalog record for this book has been requested

ISBN: 978-1-138-69184-1 (hbk)
ISBN: 978-1-138-69185-8 (pbk)
ISBN: 978-1-315-46197-7 (ebk)

Typeset in Times New Roman
by Apex CoVantage, LLC

Contents

Preface

This book resulted from my exploration of long-term meditation practice both as a meditator and as a scientist. In over 16 years of my meditation practice I have experienced first-hand, and also witnessed in others' meditation progression, many of the common challenges practitioners encounter in the process of developing long-term meditation practice. These seem to range from the beginner's misconceptions about what meditation is and about the overall trajectory of meditation training, to 'fossilization' of meditation practice in long-term practitioners who are not able to progress beyond a particular stage. Yet, I have also encountered advanced, highly accomplished practitioners who shared the challenges they experienced in their long-term meditation training. A common topic in their comments was that the challenges made them question fundamental assumptions about their existence, the purpose and meaning of their life, and this process in turn catalyzed their meditation progress.

Alongside this experiential learning, as a meditation researcher I have repeatedly observed over the last decade that despite the recent boom in studies on meditation, most of them apply a short-term perspective of meditation and neglect the role of meditation in the development of purpose and meaning in life. I found this somewhat perplexing given that in the traditional contexts meditation training is intended as a long-term path and the primary goal of meditation is to enable practitioners to explore deep questions about their existence. This observation suggested to me that if meditation-based approaches are to become effective tools in supporting health and well-being across the life-span, research and applications targeting long-term effects of meditation and focus on existential well-being will be of essential importance in the next phase of development in this field.

Together, my explorations both at the personal practice and scientific research levels pointed to the same implications about the potential of long-term meditation practice in meeting a fundamental human need for experiential understanding of meaning and purpose in life – existential balance. This became the overarching theme of this book. It is my hope that the book will be helpful to those teaching, researching, practicing or developing long-term meditation training.

Acknowledgements

This book would not have come into being without the inspiration of my meditation teachers, my scientific training and the support of my family. I am particularly grateful to Urgen Dolma; she showed me that genuine long-term meditation practice can lead to unwavering grace, unconditional compassion for all and deepest contemplative insight manifesting in everyday life without a need for recognition and even in the midst of severe illness. I was also very fortunate to receive many teachings from authentic meditation masters, particularly Khenchen Lama Rinpoche, in the Tibetan Buddhist lineage of Dzogchen, which I strongly connected to. My multifaceted research training enabled me to link these experiences, teachings and my personal meditation practice to the scientific discourse; this would not have been possible without a true sense of scholastic curiosity instilled in me during my graduate training in cognitive science and philosophy. Finally, I wouldn't have found the space and time to write this book without the patience and support of my family, especially my two beautiful daughters, who brought lightness, grounding and humour to the big task.

Abbreviations

BOLD	Blood-oxygen-level dependent
EEG	Electroencephalography
ERP	Event-related brain potential
MBCT	Mindfulness-based cognitive therapy
MBSR	Mindfulness-based stress reduction
MEA	Modes of existential awareness
MRI	Magnetic resonance imaging
MSRC	Metacognitive self-regulatory capacity of the mind

Introduction

With meditation based-techniques becoming increasingly popular within and outside of the therapeutic context, questions arise about the 'whys' and 'hows' of meditation in the West. Are the meditation techniques just the current 'fashionable' way to deal with stress and anxieties of modern life? Or are they tapping into some previously neglected challenges and questions about our way of living? Do meditation techniques have a firm place in Western psychotherapeutic approaches? If the meditation-based approaches are here to stay, how can we sustain the benefits of meditation beyond the eight-week course or five-day retreat? And where will the continuous meditation practice lead us? Could therapeutic approaches integrate long-term meditation training into their repertoires? Are there any challenges and risks associated with continuous meditation practice? How can we effectively move from the cushion to everyday activities and firmly embed meditation in our daily life? All these questions seem vital to the future of meditation-based approaches in psychotherapy. More broadly, the questions are pertinent to increasing numbers of those who practice or intend to practice meditation long-term, both in secular and traditional Buddhist contexts. They also have implications for our understanding of well-being across the life-span and the role of contemplative practice in it.

In the secular context, mindfulness-based approaches, the most broadly implemented meditation-based programmes, have been shown effective in depression relapse prevention, chronic pain treatment, stress reduction, coping with psychological aspects of cancer diagnosis and treatment, etc. (e.g., Hofmann et al., 2010; Piet and Hougaard, 2011; Shennan, Payne and Fenlon, 2011). They are also making their way into the mainstream – the number of schools introducing mindfulness into their curricula is rapidly growing, as is the number of businesses interested in implementing mindfulness in their organizations. Mindfulness-based approaches are also increasingly taught to support caregivers, school teachers, nurses and doctors, veterans, and they are being introduced in prisons. Alongside mindfulness, the implementation of other meditation-based techniques, particularly those developing compassion, is also on the rise, mostly in therapeutic settings. Yet, our understanding of whether the benefits of meditation training are sustained long-term, how to maintain the initial gains and what additional changes result from long-term practice is very limited.

Indeed, most of the longitudinal research studies examining the effects of meditation-based techniques evaluated only the changes before and after a meditation-based programme, and some looked at whether the effects are sustained three months after the training; very few included longer-term evaluations up to one year. Longitudinal studies investigating effects of meditation-based programmes beyond one year are virtually absent, except for comparisons of advanced meditators with novices. The methodological drawback of such studies is that we do not know the starting level differences which could have impacted on the findings after meditation training (e.g., Taylor et al., 2011). There is also very limited understanding of how formal meditation sessions (meditation on the cushion) translates and influences our feeling, responding and behaving in everyday life, and how a transfer of well-being improvements can be supported. But this 'gap' in our understanding of long-term and real-life effects of meditation is perhaps not surprising, given the nascent nature of meditation research – there are currently only a few thousand studies on meditation and most of these have been published in the last 15 years. Majority of the research until now tackled more basic questions asking whether meditation-based techniques can have any health benefits, and more recently, whether they can modulate brain functioning and structure, as well as body physiology.

However, with the increasing numbers of those receiving basic training in meditation-based techniques as well as health professionals using meditation techniques in their work, there is a need for further research which speaks to the deeper and long-term 'whys' and 'hows' of meditation practice. Better understanding of the long-term effects of meditation practice together with challenges one can encounter is needed to inform the recommendations and development of programmes for intermediate, advanced and very advanced practitioners. We already know that the magnitude of well-being related effects resulting from meditation tends to increase with more hours of formal meditation practice (e.g., Brefczynski-Lewis et al., 2007). Such initial estimates open up questions about similarities and differences in effects of formal practice on the cushion and informal practice embedded in everyday activities. They also lead to considerations about the quality of practice, which is bound to impact on the effects meditation has, yet we know very little from Western research about the impact of practice quality on the outcomes, or even about ways to measure it.

The investigation of long-term impact of meditation practice inevitably also brings up challenging questions about the relationship between secular and traditional contemplative approaches to meditation in relation to well-being across the life-span. Within the Buddhist context, where most of the meditation techniques currently used in secular meditation-based programmes originated, meditation is considered a tool facilitating the overarching goal of existential liberation from suffering. The concept of suffering is here understood at many levels, from obvious forms of physical and mental hardship to more subtle underlying patterns of anger, unhealthy attachment, ignorance, jealousy and pride. Lack of experiential understanding of one's own mind and the construed nature of reality are considered the root causes of all our suffering.

Perhaps not surprisingly, most attendees of the secular mindfulness classes join the courses seeking some relief from tangible health problems – stress and anxiety, and often chronic, psychological and physical difficulties – rather than looking for answers to existential questions about the roots of their suffering and life's meaning and purpose. Yet, there is the possibility that the secular meditation training, particularly with a more sustained practice, will open up deeper existential inquiry of how we construe who we are. There is indeed some research suggesting that mindfulness-based approaches enhance the sense of purpose and meaning in life (Garland et al., 2007). However, there isn't an established route or approach to support such deeper existential explorations arising from meditation practice within the secular context. And there is also the possibility that this is where the secular meditation techniques reach their limits.

Whether the development and support of long-term meditation practice can happen within the secular context remains an open question for now. What is perhaps needed at this stage is an initial exploration of the possible answers to 'whys' and 'hows' outlined earlier, which bridges, rather than divides, the secular and traditional contemplative approaches. In the search for the answers there is a need for sensitivity to the subtleties of the differences between secular applications of meditation and Buddhism. A particular strength of the secular programmes is their ability to present meditation practices in a form and format which is accessible and relatable for practitioners in the West. This accessibility to broad audiences and in contexts such as education or workplace also necessitates their non-sectarian and religion-neutral nature. As a consequence, the secular programmes are for the most part not intended as a full path to freedom from suffering in the Buddhist sense (Dorjee, 2010).

In contrast, traditional Buddhist approaches contain comprehensive guidance for different levels of practitioners including time-tested methods which have led practitioners to complete liberation from suffering for centuries. However, the traditional approaches have been, and still are, seeking to find the most suitable ways to make the traditional teachings culturally accessible to Western practitioners without losing their essence. Nevertheless, the long-term perspective of meditation practice which is elaborately explicated and supported in the traditional Buddhist context remains their particular strength. This aspect of the traditional approaches is pertinent to long-term practitioners of both Buddhist and secular meditation who want to go deeper in their practice. The traditional contemplative teachings are also of utmost relevance to those for whom an exposure to secular meditation opens up broader existential questions. This suggests that closer focus on the long-term perspective of secular meditation practice might actually provide an opportunity for the traditional and secular approaches to work more closely together. In addition, the richness and variety of Buddhist practices targeting different levels of meditation experience presents a lot of potential for further enrichment of Western meditation-based programmes.

Indeed, the current wide-spread interest in meditation techniques, both in their application and in research findings, is pointing to a unique potential of these techniques. Meditation training might be opening up new horizons for the development of the human potential for balance, meaning and purpose. Furthermore, from the scientific perspective, investigations using meditation techniques seem to be tapping into the most fundamental questions of philosophy and science concerning the relationship between mind, brain and body. The current interest in meditation may suggest the beginning of a new paradigm in Western thinking and scientific exploration of the human mind – a paradigm which has the phenomenological investigation of the mind and consciousness in the context of human potential for well-being, purpose and virtue at its core.

The term 'contemplative' is now increasingly more used to describe the arising scientific discipline developing this new paradigm. The research in contemplative neuroscience is at the moment the most obvious example and other disciplines such as contemplative education are emerging. The development of contemplative psychology and contemplative psychotherapy seems the natural next step in the progression and expansion of this new paradigm. The increasing focus on long-term effects of meditation in the context of human potential for well-being and purpose seems to provide a fruitful platform for flourishing and expansion of these new contemplative disciplines.

The purpose of this book is to contribute to these developments in the field of contemplative science through considerations about the theoretical and applied framework for contemplative psychology and psychotherapy in the context of cultivating long-term meditation practice in everyday life. Specifically, we will gradually explore the need for existential realization as the possible core motivation of human behaviour and action, and the main driving force behind the current exponentially growing interest in meditation. From the Buddhist perspective, the existential realization can be described as a state of balance, mental equilibrium, which arises from being able to access, recognize and sustain a foundational state of conscious awareness from which other mental events arise. In the Buddhist tradition of Dzogchen, this state is termed 'rigpa' and means realization of the ultimate nature of the mind. It is described as a non-conceptual state with naturally arising experience of even-mindedness, peace, joy, compassion, knowing and clarity. With longer-term meditation practice, the meditator can experience glimpses of this state, often preceded by other, somewhat similar and less stable, states of balance which don't encompass all the characteristics of rigpa. In the absence of the recognizing and actual experience of existential realization, the fundamental drive towards it is expressed through different types of adaptive (e.g., caring and altruism) and maladaptive (e.g., addictions) behaviour. Hence, the book proposes that the core purpose of contemplative psychotherapy is to guide clients towards adaptive expressions of the existential drive and ultimately towards understanding and sustaining the experience of existential realization.

The first chapter of the book sets the stage for this exploration by outlining a general framework of contemplative science. This framework describes changes in the mind and brain resulting from meditation training in terms of self-regulation and modes of existential awareness. Implications of this framework for development of the human potential for well-being and balance in the context of contemplative psychology and psychotherapy are also discussed. The second chapter then draws important distinctions between immediate and long-term effects of meditation practice. It also distinguishes between formal practice and informal practice in daily life. The following chapters then explore specific ways of developing and sustaining long-term meditation practice, from mindfulness, through explicit practices developing compassion, and techniques utilizing visualization. The later chapters of the book focus on more advanced meditation practices exploring deeper levels of consciousness such as insight meditations, dream yoga and abiding in the ground state of existential balance. To support integration of theory and practice, each of these chapters contains both practical guidance on how to develop and sustain the particular type of practice, and considerations about underlying Buddhist theory as well as associated mechanisms of change in the mind, brain and body physiology. Finally, the last chapter considers broader societal consequences of long-term meditation practice and outlines associated recommendations for further research and practice in the field.

The book focuses on secular meditation-based techniques derived from various Buddhist traditions and on Buddhist practices, mostly in the Tibetan Buddhist tradition of Dzogchen. This focus on Buddhism-derived and Buddhist traditions was necessary given that the vast majority of current secular meditation-based programmes and current research on meditation builds on and examines Buddhist meditation. The focus on Tibetan Buddhist tradition and particularly the Dzogchen approach was also necessitated in practical terms by my primary meditation practice experience with these approaches. Despite this clear bias in the contemplative perspective, the general framework of contemplative science presented in this book is aimed at opening the exploration in contemplative science to a range of contemplative methods across contemplative traditions. The in-depth exploration of varied Buddhism-derived and Buddhist meditation practices presented in the book is intended as an exemplification of one possible approach to considering and examining long-term effects of meditation which can be applied to other contemplative approaches.

Overall, the book highlights that the next phase of investigating and applying meditation-based techniques in the context of long-term meditation practice will undoubtedly be challenging, but also insightful and worthwhile. Importantly, the book explains how the emerging disciplines of contemplative science may enrich our understanding of human potential for well-being and balance. It is my hope that the book will encourage the readers, from health professionals through contemplative researchers and long-term meditation practitioners, to further explore long-term meditation practice in both theory and practice.

References

Brefczynski-Lewis, J.A., Lutz, A., Schaefer, H.S., Levinson, D.B. and Davidson, R.J., 2007. Neural correlates of attentional expertise in long-term meditation practitioners. *Proceedings of the National Academy of Sciences*, *104*(27), pp. 11483–11488.

Dorjee, D., 2010. Kinds and dimensions of mindfulness: Why it is important to distinguish them. *Mindfulness*, *1*(3), pp. 152–160.

Garland, S.N., Carlson, L.E., Cook, S., Lansdell, L. and Speca, M., 2007. A non-randomized comparison of mindfulness-based stress reduction and healing arts programs for facilitating post-traumatic growth and spirituality in cancer outpatients. *Supportive Care in Cancer*, *15*(8), pp. 949–961.

Hofmann, S.G., Sawyer, A.T., Witt, A.A. and Oh, D., 2010. The effect of mindfulness-based therapy on anxiety and depression: A meta-analytic review. *Journal of Consulting and Clinical Psychology*, *78*(2), p. 169.

Piet, J. and Hougaard, E., 2011. The effect of mindfulness-based cognitive therapy for prevention of relapse in recurrent major depressive disorder: A systematic review and meta-analysis. *Clinical Psychology Review*, *31*(6), pp. 1032–1040.

Shennan, C., Payne, S. and Fenlon, D., 2011. What is the evidence for the use of mindfulness-based interventions in cancer care? A review. *Psycho-Oncology*, *20*(7), pp. 681–697.

Taylor, V.A., Grant, J., Daneault, V., Scavone, G., Breton, E., Roffe-Vidal, S., Courtemanche, J., Lavarenne, A.S. and Beauregard, M., 2011. Impact of mindfulness on the neural responses to emotional pictures in experienced and beginner meditators. *Neuroimage*, *57*(4), pp. 1524–1533.

Chapter 1

The new science of meditation

Meditation is, for the most part, no longer viewed as an exotic mystical spiritual practice. Scientific research conducted over the last two decades suggests that meditation-based techniques can have health and well-being enhancing effects in a range of clinical conditions. For example, mindfulness-based cognitive therapy (MBCT) has been shown as effective as antidepressant medication in the treatment of recurrent depression (Kuyken et al., 2015). There is also encouraging cumulative evidence on the beneficial effects of mindfulness-based approaches in the treatment of anxiety (Hofmann et al., 2010). In addition, research using psycho-physiological and neuroscientific methods documented changes in body and brain functioning after only four or five days of regular meditation practice for 20 minutes a day (Tang et al., 2007; Zeidan et al., 2011). As a result, meditation is becoming a mainstream approach to health and well-being.

Nevertheless, many questions about the effects and mechanisms of meditation, particularly when it comes to long-term practice, remain unanswered. This is partially due to the health-related applications of meditation and associated research typically taking only a limited short-term view of meditation as a tool for 'fixing various health problems'. Such an approach, while useful as an initial step in the development of a new field, restricts a broader perspective of the role meditation can play in supporting human potential for health and well-being beyond a specific health complaint. As the discipline of meditation research moves to a formative stage which will define its future standing amongst other sciences and approaches, it is timely to consider questions about the broader and long-term goals of meditation practice and research. This chapter outlines the foundations of a framework for application and research of meditation which could enable us to fully harness what meditation can offer to our health and well-being.

What is the science of meditation missing?

Majority of neuroscience research on meditation has so far been investigating how meditation changes brain structures and functions underlying our abilities to focus attention and manage our emotions (Tang, Hölzel and Posner, 2015). Yet, very few studies examined how such brain changes might be relevant to our sense of self and our deeper views of meaning and purpose in life. So despite the explosion of meditation research over the last two decades, most of the studies have neglected the possible impact of meditation on our sense of meaning and purpose. This is somewhat paradoxical, given that the ultimate aim of most meditation practices is to enable the practitioner to explore such existential questions; meditation practices are usually embedded in contemplative systems which support and guide the practitioner on a spiritual path of exploring these questions.

So if the essential goal of meditation practices is in enabling exploration of life's meaning and purpose, why is this aspect of meditation mostly ignored in the current research? There might be several reasons for this and the first one could be simply the consequence of meditation research being a young scientific discipline. Due to the nascent state of the field, most of the initial studies focused on demonstrating that meditation can have measurable impact on our health and well-being. Similarly, most neuroscientific research on meditation has been aiming to show that meditation training can be associated with detectable changes in the brain which might be health-conducive. This initial research has provided useful evidence which invited more mainstream interest in both applications and further research on meditation. Indeed, the research literature on meditation currently grows by nearly a thousand studies each year in comparison to a couple dozen per year three decades ago.

Another reason why the research on meditation has so far mostly omitted the existential questions of meaning and purpose is perhaps the complexity of meditation training. Traditional approaches to meditation are greatly multifaceted: they involve cultivation of attention control and stability, practices targeting emotional well-being, reflections on values and the construal of meaning in life, etc. (Dorjee, 2013), coupled with faith-based and ritualistic practices. Understanding and capturing such rich systems of meditation training is a very difficult task. As a consequence, vast majority of research on meditation has so far focused on particular meditation techniques, such as mindfulness, separated from the complex traditional systems where they originated. This approach might have been necessary in the initial phases of meditation research, but is becoming restrictive as the field evolves towards a more mature stage and searches for its unique standing amongst other scientific disciplines. Indeed, investigation of meditation techniques as methods of training attention, improving emotion regulation or enhancing well-being to some extent falls short of clearly showing how these techniques differ from other non-meditation-based ways of training attention, emotion regulation or well-being. After all, research shows that some computer games can enhance attention (Dye, Green and Bavelier, 2009) and various positive psychology methods can make us happier (Seligman et al., 2005)!

Given that meditation-based methods are not the only ways to improve our cognitive functioning or well-being and the evidence base on meditation is still fairly limited, it is surprising how much scientific and lay interest in meditation there currently is. It is also surprising how polarizing the attitudes towards meditation techniques and associated research are – on one side of the continuum there are strong enthusiasts, on the other sworn critics, with little balance in perceptions in the middle of the range of opinions. And quite often meditation techniques, particularly mindfulness, are currently referred to as 'the latest fad' across the continuum of perceptions.

Interestingly, one possible explanation for this somewhat imbalanced pattern of views might be that meditation techniques are tapping into the existential (meaning and purpose related) aspect of our experience which remains mostly unaddressed by other psychological approaches and more broadly by our materialistic society and the culture of popularity contests. The meditation techniques seem to provide a connection for experiential exploration of our deeper sense of meaning, purpose in life and genuine happiness. Accordingly, the proponents of meditation may see meditation-based approaches as uniquely placed to address this yearning for existential connection. And the criticism of meditation might actually also be related to the same aspect of meditation – at least some of the critics highlight that current research artificially isolates meditation techniques from their contemplative systems and presents them as means to an end, be it the reduction in stress or increase in attention focus, rather than as a path to deeper existential exploration. So both opinion extremes might be actually responding to the existential dimension of meditation training which is mostly not considered in both further research and the teaching of psychological meditation-based approaches.

How can current meditation research and teaching address this important gap in our understanding and practice of meditation? It is possible that the solution will require a somewhat radical shift in the way we have been approaching meditation research and the application of meditation-based techniques so far. It might be that we need to build a 'new science of meditation' which would clearly lay out the unique subject, aims and methods of the discipline with existential dimension of meditation and its impact on our health and well-being taking central stage. As a first step, we may need to expand our perspective of meditation practices beyond the practices themselves and start taking into account the goals and progression of the whole path of meditation training. And to tackle the complexity of such a perspective, we may need to look for common broader patterns of changes in the processes of the mind, and associated changes in the brain, in long-term meditation practice (Dorjee, 2016). Whilst applying this approach, the similarities and differences in changes resulting from different meditation approaches, including mindfulness, compassion, visualization, contemplative prayer, insight practices etc., will be of particular interest. Such research and applications may give rise to a science of meditation as a discipline with strong foundations and important implications for long-term approaches to health and well-being at the individual level and beyond. We will now explore the core building blocks and principles of the new science of meditation.

The mind's capacity to self-regulate

The ability to manage attention, emotions and behaviour is necessary for our effective everyday functioning including planning, decision making, well-being and academic success. This ability is in psychology often referred to as 'self-regulation' and development of effective self-regulation is one of the key themes in education. This is not surprising given that levels of self-regulation in 2-year-olds have been found to predict their health, wealth and even levels of criminality as adults (Moffitt et al., 2011). Hence, there is keen interest amongst educators, health professionals, parents and policy makers in supporting children to develop effective self-regulation in childhood and in the enhancement of self-regulatory skills across the life-span.

Interestingly, improvements in self-regulation seem to underlie the beneficial outcomes associated with training in meditation-based approaches, particularly mindfulness (Tang, Hölzel and Posner, 2015). Some aspects of self-regulation are uniquely targeted by meditation practices, the core one being the awareness of thoughts, sensations, feelings, behaviours and their underlying processes. The awareness and observation of contents and processes in one's own mind is often referred to as introspection. It is also referred to as a metacognitive skill, meaning that this awareness can be considered as happening one level above the usual contents and processes of the mind – it is the awareness of the contents and processes of the mind which is distinct from the contents and processes observed.

Alongside the metacognitive introspective awareness which particularly helps to monitor for and notice distractions when we are trying to focus, meditation practices develop the ability to shift attention away from distraction and stay focused on the object of meditation. The object of meditation can vary from sensations associated with breathing, to sounds and visualizations of complex sacred images. Focused contemplation on a certain topic (such as impermanence of our perceptions, material things or bodies) can also train attention control and attention focus whilst the metacognitive introspective awareness monitors for distractions or divergence in thinking to other topics. These fundamental attention skills together with metacognitive introspective awareness are the basis of any meditation training. This is because without stability of these skills the mind is unsettled and any examination of its mental processes, contents, habits and their roots is easily interrupted. Such distractibility would prevent deepening of understanding and experiential exploration.

Another aspect of self-regulation specifically cultivated through meditation training aims to develop particular emotional qualities and strategies of regulating emotions. Emotions such as loving kindness and compassion are central to contemplative training in the Buddhist tradition. Some Buddhist schools equally emphasize sympathetic joy of own and others' virtue and equanimity in relating to all beings, not only those who are close and dear to us, with loving kindness and compassion (Wallace, 1999). These emotional qualities are in Buddhism intrinsically linked to understanding and conscious effort in cultivating virtue and avoiding non-virtue. This ethical dimension of practice gives distinctive direction to practice goals and the progression of meditation training (Dorjee, 2013).

Cultivation of these emotional qualities is intertwined with development of specific emotion regulation strategies which enable the practitioner to manage emotions. For example, the meditation-specific emotion regulation strategies may involve grounding of attention focus on a neutral anchor such as breath sensations when anxiety or anger arises. Other strategies may encourage 'transformation' of negative emotions into their positive antidotes, for instance, by invoking images and feelings of loving kindness in response to experiencing anger. Another approach to emotion regulation through meditation-based techniques may involve experiential examination of the nature of emotions which can lead to realization of their neutral experiential ground from which they arise.

The enhancement of attention skills and the development of certain emotional qualities and strategies is also coupled with changes in patterns of thinking and experiencing – in conceptual processing. For example, as a result of conscious cultivation of healthy emotions and well-being supporting ways of responding, we may spend less time in negative rumination about our experiences. Rumination often happens in the form of speech (expressed out loud or silently); it often brings up certain emotional feelings and sometimes also visual images or other sensations. The shift in patterns of rumination as a result of engaging in meditation practices may lead to changes in how often we access negative meanings and negative schemas associated with a distinct pattern of brain activation. For example, a recent study found that those with higher trait mindfulness, people naturally more mindful even without explicit training in meditation, are less likely to access negative word meanings (Dorjee et al., 2015). Other studies have found less activation in brain areas associated with language processing in meditators (e.g., Pagnoni, Cekic and Guo, 2008), which suggests that meditators are less prone to rumination.

The outlined changes in attention, emotion regulation and conceptual processing do not work in isolation; they interact and cumulatively contribute to the changes in self-regulation resulting from meditation. Their distinctive feature is that they specifically rely on the metacognitive (introspective) awareness of thoughts, emotions and bodily sensations which enables the development of effective self-regulation. In this way, meditation seems to uniquely target a particular propensity of the mind for metacognitive self-regulation which has been termed the 'metacognitive self-regulatory capacity of the mind' (MSRC) (Dorjee, 2016). Since most previous research on self-regulation did not consider the contribution of the introspective metacognitive awareness to self-regulation or the interactions between attention/emotion regulation and conceptual processing, our understanding of the MSRC and its role in our health and well-being is fairly limited. However, the available evidence on well-being and the health-conducive effects of meditation indirectly suggests that improvements in the MSRC might be pivotal to these beneficial outcomes. We will now look closer at possible physiological pathways mediating the impact of the MSRC on bodily functioning.

So far, all the changes in the MSRC we have discussed – including self-regulation, emotion regulation and conceptual processing – were about modifications in the mind and brain with meditation. But these changes would have little impact on our well-being if they did not affect the physiological processes in the body. This link is rarely emphasized in current research on meditation and deserves much more attention in future research. Most research has so far focused either on changes in the mind and brain or on changes in bodily functioning, but not on associations between them. The main physiological mechanisms enabling interactions between the brain and body physiology involve regulation of hormones, hence the relevant physiological pathways are often labelled as 'neuroendocrine'. These pathways involve the release of hormones in the brain, often in response to a real or imaged threat such as a speeding car or a memory of an argument. Through the blood stream these hormones travel throughout the body and can activate the release of stress hormones (most relevant here is the hormone cortisol) in the adrenal glands. The stress hormones are released into the blood stream and then travel to the brain, signalling the need for downregulation of the stress response. If the brain isn't able to downregulate the stress hormone levels, over time the heightened levels of cortisol can lead to a damage in some brain structures which have cortisol receptors (such as the hippocampus and the prefrontal cortex). This can manifest as difficulties in remembering, concentrating, decision making etc.

Research studies on the impact of meditation practice on the neuroendocrine functioning are still scarce. Initial evidence suggests that more meditation practice is associated with stronger reductions in morning levels of cortisol (Brand et al., 2012). Another study showed increases in physiological markers of parasympathetic system activity (a branch of the autonomic nervous system associated with rest and digest response in contrast to the sympathetic fight and flight response) after ten days of Vipassana meditation retreat (Krygier et al., 2013). The research evidence on the impact of secular meditation programmes on the stress physiology is mixed (O'Leary, O'Neill and Dockray, 2015) with positive effects reported in some studies but not in others. And very few studies examined the links between brain activation and body physiology more directly. As an exception, one study found close associations between increases in the activity of a brain region involved in attention control (ACC – anterior cingulate cortex) and increases in parasympathetic system response (Tang et al., 2009). There is a need for more studies of this type.

Purpose, meaning and modes of existential awareness

Aside from improvements in the metacognitive self-regulatory capacity, the impact of meditation on the sense of meaning and purpose in life is probably equally, if not more strongly, responsible for the beneficial effects of meditation. Studies outside of meditation research have repeatedly supported a positive link between health and a sense of meaning and purpose. Just like improved self-regulation is associated with better health outcomes, higher existential well-being (sense of meaning and purpose in life) is also linked to better health. For example, higher sense of existential well-being is associated with fewer depressive symptoms and less risk-taking behaviour in adolescents (Cotton et al., 2005). Another study with a larger sample of a broad age range found that adults with higher existential well-being (top tertile) had 70% lesser odds of becoming depressed than those with lower existential well-being (lower tertile) (Maselko, Gilman and Buka, 2009). And research with cancer survivors found that their existential well-being predicted their health-related quality of life (Edmondson et al., 2008).

Interestingly, in all these studies existential well-being was dissociated from religious well-being. Religious well-being describes the formal sense of belonging to a religious group and behaviour such as attendance of religious services. Higher religious well-being did not predict depressive symptoms in adolescents as strongly as existential well-being (Cotton et al., 2005). Similarly, religious well-being (unlike existential well-being) was not linked to improvements in health-related quality of life in cancer survivors (Edmondson et al., 2008). These findings provide research support to the essential importance of the sense of meaning and purpose to well-being, health and resilience which has been emphasized in existential psychology (Frankl, 1985) and humanistic psychology for many decades.

Existential well-being also overlaps with and is central to eudaimonic well-being, which can be described in terms of accomplishing one's potential, focusing on long-term goals and having a sense of meaning and purpose in life. In contrast, existential well-being is not linked to hedonistic well-being, which focuses on pleasure-based, more short-term gratification. Interestingly, the two types of well-being have also been associated with different biological health patterns. Specifically, eudaimonic well-being, but not hedonistic well-being, has been linked to lower levels of morning cortisol associated with lower stress, better sleep patterns, better immune system functioning and lower cardiovascular risks (Ryff, Singer and Love, 2004).

This mounting research evidence supporting positive links between health and existential well-being suggests that interventions which support development of existential meaning and purpose, rather than those encouraging religiousness or hedonistic well-being, can have particularly positive impact on health and quality of life. Meditation-based techniques seem very relevant here given their traditional role in supporting existential exploration and initial research evidence suggesting their effectiveness in enhancing existential well-being. For example, improvements in the sense of purpose and meaning in life have been documented after three months of Buddhist meditation retreat which combined training in attention control and stability with development of loving kindness and compassion (Jacobs et al., 2011). The study also reported that the retreat group showed increases in telomerase – higher levels of this enzyme are associated with lower likelihood of chromosomal mutations linked to disease. But of particular relevance is a finding from this study which revealed that increases in purpose in life, but not in mindfulness, mediated the increase in levels of telomerase. Since mindfulness is primarily related to self-regulation, these findings highlight the essential contribution of changes in meaning and purpose in life to health-enhancing effects resulting from meditation training.

Nevertheless, increases in the sense of meaning and purpose have also been found after secular mindfulness-based programmes even though links to health-related outcomes were less direct. For example, Carmody et al. (2008) found increases in spiritual well-being (related to meaning and purpose in life) after eight weeks of mindfulness-based stress reduction (MBSR) training and these improvements were inversely linked to decreases in psychological distress and health-related symptoms. Similarly, Labelle et al. (2015) found increases in meaning and purpose (more broadly spirituality) in cancer patients after they participated in an MBSR programme. Even though MBSR is a hallmark mindfulness-based intervention, these improvements were likely not due to mindfulness (as primarily a form of attention training) as such since MBSR training also involves development of acceptance, self-compassion and decentring which may have contributed to the existential well-being effects more strongly. It is up to future research to disentangle the contribution of the different elements of mindfulness-based programmes to such outcomes. But overall, these encouraging initial findings provide support to the expected close positive relation between meditation training and improvements in existential meaning and purpose.

The enhancements in the sense of meaning and purpose with meditation also raise further questions about how meditation training produces such effects, particularly since the meditation practices involved in the studies we have discussed did not target the existential dimension of experience directly. The possible answer to these questions may lie in the links between changes in the MSRC of the mind and shifts in our sense of who we are and our perception reality. For example, many of us derive our sense of self from our family history, the place where we grew up, our profession, sense of belonging to certain communities and groups. Such sense of self is mostly built up from experiences and memories of our life, and schemas of how we learned to perceive ourselves are often based on what others told us. Through meditation practice these typical ways of self-construal gradually loosen up; some meditation practices impact the sense of self only indirectly while other practices directly aim to shift it.

Decentring (Fresco et al., 2007) is a term used in the context of mindfulness-based approaches to describe initial modifications in the construal of self resulting from meditation practice. Decentring describes a mode of awareness arising when feelings, thoughts and emotions (mental contents and processes in general) are perceived as changeable and fleeing and the usual immersion and identification with them lessens. Such a mode of awareness can have protective effects on health and well-being, particularly because it prevents spiralling into negative rumination and identification with thoughts, emotions and cognitive schemas. Indeed, in the context of prevention of depression relapse, decentring has been suggested as the main mechanism enabling effective regulation of depressive symptoms (Bieling et al., 2012). Decentring has also been generally discussed as the main mechanism responsible for beneficial therapeutic outcomes of mindfulness-based approaches (Shapiro et al., 2006 – these authors use the term 're-perceiving' instead of decentring, but both terms very closely overlap in their meanings).

Decentring is likely only an initial, yet pivotal, step towards further changes in modes of awareness with meditation training. Since these modes of awareness pertain to our construal of self and reality which has existential implications for our sense of meaning and purpose, the term 'modes of existential awareness' (MEA) has been proposed to specifically describe them (Dorjee, 2016). More advanced MEA are virtually unexplored in Western science, but they are clearly described in traditional meditation literature. For example, the Tibetan Buddhist tradition of Dzogchen outlines a progression from initial stages of decentring towards experiential understanding of the constructed nature of self, then experiential understanding of the illusory nature of reality and finally experiential recognition of the non-construed nature of mind called 'rigpa' from which all experience of self and reality arises (Mipham, 2007).

The experience of rigpa can be fully understood only experientially, but it is often described as a non-conceptual state in which clarity, knowing, unconditional compassion and subtle joy and tranquillity arise simultaneously. It is a MEA of ultimate balance and stability which is not subject to the transient ups and downs of self-construal, thoughts, sensations and emotions. From the perspective of Dzogchen, rigpa is unchangeably always present, but whether it is accessible to us is subject to experiential insight into the deeper layers of the mind after stabilizing our thought patterns, emotions and sensations. And even after we initially recognize the nature of the mind, the accessibility to rigpa may easily shift until, with further training, we are able to maintain the access to rigpa continuously most or all of the time.

Experiential realization of the different states in the MEA progression requires long-term meditation practice grounded in an established contemplative system of meditation which has proven effective in enabling practitioners to progress to the most advanced MEA. The sequence of meditation training in the Buddhist tradition typically involves foundational training in contemplative exploration of four topics – preciousness and opportunity of human life, impermanence, the law of cause and effect and suffering. While continuing these contemplations, the practitioner then examines ethical principles of virtue and non-virtue continuously throughout further meditation training. These foundational contemplations set out the motivation for engagement in the long-term meditation practice.

The motivation for practicing meditation can vary slightly across Buddhist schools and can develop and change as practitioners progress in their meditation training – it usually ranges from the motivation of liberating oneself from suffering in the deeper sense of recognizing the construed nature of self to liberating oneself through recognizing the nature of mind so that one can support other beings on their spiritual path. Grounded in the contemplative exploration of the foundational topics, broader ethical principles and virtuous motivation, the practitioner engages in further training which first aims to enhance and stabilize attention and then develops emotional stability. After the mind has been sufficiently stabilized, the practitioner more directly engages in the exploration of deeper layers of the mind with the aim of deconstructing the notions of self and ultimately recognizing the nature of the mind. Throughout the meditation training, the practices engage different facets of the sense of meaning and purpose in life, from contemplating the purpose of human life and nature of suffering, to direct experiential knowing of life's meaning and purpose. Abiding in the nature of mind, in rigpa, is considered a culmination of this exploration which provides the ultimate experiential answers to the questions of meaning and purpose.

Existential drive, health and well-being

Humanistic conceptualizations of self-transcendence (Maslow, 1943) are perhaps closest to the accounts of MEA in Western psychology. Maslow described self-transcendence in terms of experiencing unity with something bigger than oneself which has characteristics of non-judgment, common humanity and compassion. Self-transcendence can arise as an experiential connection to a deeper truth or a sense of awe beyond the self. Some people experience self-transcendence in nature; for others self-transcendence manifests unexpectedly in challenging circumstances such as during bereavement. Maslow suggested that self-transcending experiences engage a unique holistic mode of mind called 'being cognition' which differs from the typical logical and evaluative approaches we rely on most of the time. Such characterization of 'being cognition' seems to resemble to some extent the experiential non-conceptual descriptions of MEA in the Buddhist literature. However, a progression or different degrees of 'being cognition' were not detailed in Maslow's theory. So the experiential progression of increasingly more advanced MEA developed through meditation practice seems a timely advancement of Maslow's ideas about self-transcendence.

The historically central standing of existential meaning and purpose in conceptualizations of human potential seems to converge with the current research highlighting the pivotal role of the existential psychological dimension to our health and traditional meditation approaches targeting existential exploration. These different approaches seem to highlight the same fundamental underlying principle of the human mind; cumulatively, both Western humanistic approaches and meditation traditions seem to suggest that the search for meaning and purpose in life is the fundamental driving force of the human mind. This fundamental driving force can be termed the 'existential instinct'. Meditation approaches elaborate this principle further by proposing that the ultimate sense of meaning and purpose arises from experiential understanding of the nature of self and reality. Such realization is accompanied by a profound sense of clarity, tranquillity, knowing, contentment and unconditional kindness and compassion. It can be postulated that the existential instinct manifests as yearning for realization of the ultimate state of meaning and purpose and its experiential realization can be considered the accomplishment of the essential human potential for well-being.

The postulation of the existential instinct as a fundamental principle of the human mind has broad implications for our approaches to health and well-being. Given that the existential instinct is the primary drive towards accomplishment of human potential for well-being, experiences of the most advanced levels of MEA are likely associated with the highest levels of health and well-being. Accordingly, it can be expected that misdirection of the existential instinct towards hedonistic well-being or other goals which do not support progression towards advanced levels of MEA would have detrimental effects on our health and well-being. This means that psychopathology could be conceptualized as a misdirection of or disconnection from the existential drive resulting in divergence from the course of existential exploration which is fundamental to accomplishing human potential. This proposal is similar to suggestions by Victor Frankl (1985) that lack of existential exploration or lack of finding meaning in life will result in existential crisis, psychopathology and ill health. But it also differs from Frankl's account in terms of the experiential progression of MEA, the role of self-regulation in supporting the development of MEA and associated implications for illness prevention and intervention which we will now consider in more detail.

How can the proposed framework of MSRC and MEA and the postulation of the existential instinct explain psychopathology and guide development of clinical interventions? Let's start with an initial exploration of possible implications for our understanding of addictions, depression, anxiety and psychosis. Addictions could be considered as resulting from misdirection of the existential instinct towards counterfeit pleasurable states associated with addictive behaviour (ranging from drug addictions through shopping addictions, sexual addictions or food addictions, etc.) instead of emotionally balanced positive states associated with advanced MEA. Deficiencies in the MSRC further drive the cyclic nature of addictions and underlie the lack of inhibition even in the face of recognizing one's own maladaptive addictive behaviour.

Similarly, deficiency in the MSRC also significantly contributes to the development of depressive symptomatology which is associated with diminished meta-awareness of depressive thought cycles and difficulty in breaking the cycle of negative thoughts, cognitive schemas and emotions. Mindfulness-based approaches seem to support the development of the MSRC of the mind, and accordingly have been shown effective in preventing depression relapse (Warren et al., 2016). However, in addition to the deficiencies in the MSCR, a lack of existential drive resulting in apathy behaviour or misguided existential drive leading to self-destructive behaviour is likely a major contributory factor to depression. Indeed, improvement in decentring (one of the initial MEA states in the progression of existential exploration) has been proposed as the major therapeutic mechanism of mindfulness-based approaches in treatment of depression (Bieling et al., 2012). This converges with the findings we have discussed in the previous section showing that higher levels of existential well-being have been associated with less susceptibility to depression.

Just like addictions and depression, anxiety conditions also involve dysfunctional MSRC which can manifest as anxiety-related rumination and difficulty in effectively regulating emotions. However, anxiety disorders have a strong existential dimension too which could be described as stagnation of the existential exploration. The stagnation can result from fixation on the potentially threatening aspects of examining existential questions of meaning and purpose – anxiety seems to involve an existential threat element regardless of whether it pertains to social interactions, health concerns or direct fear of death. The fixation can lead to avoidance strategies which further increase the existential stagnation. Mindfulness-based approaches have been shown to reduce anxiety which, similarly to the mechanisms underlying positive effects of mindfulness in treatment of depression, likely involve enhancement of the MSRC as well as development of decentring as a partial remedy to the existential stagnation.

Application of similar principles of diminished MSRC and dysfunctional existential drive is more complex when it comes to psychotic disorders. Lack of self-regulation is a strong contributor to the symptomatology of psychosis resulting in disorganized cognitions and difficulties in emotion regulation. The existential dimension of the difficulties in psychosis may seem less obvious, but could be conceptualized as existential confusion. This is because psychosis often involves fixation on strongly misinterpreted representations of self and reality. The same principle of existential confusion could, however, also apply to addiction, depression, anxiety and in a broader sense to non-clinical states outside of the most balanced advanced MEA states of well-being. This suggests that the difference between psychotic conditions and less dysfunctional states of existential confusion outside of advanced MEA is mostly a matter of degree than a categorical difference between illness and health. The evidence base on effectiveness of meditation-based approaches in psychotic conditions is currently encouraging (e.g., Chadwick, Taylor and Abba, 2005), but limited. One of the main questions to be addressed is whether acutely psychotic clients (and similarly acutely depressed clients) would be able to benefit from meditation-based approaches. Further, more extensive research is needed to address this and other open questions about applications of meditation-based techniques in psychopathology in order to provide conclusive answers.

Towards a long-term perspective of meditation

The pivotal role of self-regulation in psychological health is well recognized and this, together with the health-protective effects of existential well-being, highlights the importance of psychological approaches which can enhance both self-regulation and support existential well-being. It has been particularly emphasized that future healthcare must meet existential well-being needs of patients because of their strong contribution to health (Mueller, Plevak and Rummans, 2001). The emerging pattern across clinical and non-clinical evidence as well as mental conditions discussed in this chapter suggests that meditation-based approaches have a unique potential to enhance both self-regulation and existential well-being of practitioners. This is due to their impact on the enhancement of MSRC and the development of MEA with both supporting adaptive manifestation of the existential drive towards experiential realization of meaning and purpose in life.

For the unique potential of meditation-based approaches to be fully harnessed in healthcare and beyond (with implications for prevention and well-being enhancement in education, for example), the new science of meditation needs to address several essential questions. The main one pertains to acknowledgement of the core contribution of existential exploration to the outcomes of meditation training and focused investigation of this dimension of meditation practices. Another question relates to whether secular meditation approaches can go beyond the effects of self-regulation and decentring documented so far and enable practitioners to progress onto advanced MEA. This question is very pertinent if realization of the advanced MEA is essential to the accomplishment of human potential for meaning and purpose in life. Addressing these questions necessitates investigation of long-term effects of secular meditation-based approaches as well as research into long-term trajectories of health and well-being across traditional meditation systems. Such research needs to be broadened to a range of contemplative traditions to build up a complete picture of the role contemplative practices can play in realizing human potential for health, well-being and purpose in life. To encourage further exploration in the secular context as well as in Buddhist and non-Buddhist contemplative traditions, in the chapters that follow we will apply the proposed framework of MSRC, MEA and existential drive to the exploration of several meditation types from the long-term everyday practice perspective.

Summary

This chapter introduces the current status of research into meditation and outlines a 'new science of meditation' together with its implications for our understanding of human potential for well-being. After an initial brief review of the main findings of meditation research over the last two decades, the chapter discusses the lack of research attention to the impact of meditation on existential sense of meaning and purpose, particularly from the perspective of long-term meditation practice. To remedy this major drawback the rest of the chapter outlines the main pillars of the 'new science of meditation' in terms of the metacognitive self-regulatory capacity (MSRC) of the mind and modes of existential awareness (MEA). The MSRC involves interacting processes of metacognitive introspective awareness, attention regulation, emotion regulation and conceptual processing which can be enhanced by meditation training. The MEA can be described as experiential shifts in the construal of self and reality resulting from meditation training. Enhancements in the MSRC, such as improved stability and control of attention and emotion regulation, enable increasingly advanced shifts in MEA. Decentring is an example of an initial MEA which enables the perception of thoughts, feelings and sensations as transient mental phenomena rather than solid facts. The postulation of MSRC and MEA is then linked to research evidence highlighting the essential role of existential well-being (sense of purpose and meaning) to our health. This link is further considered in relation to traditional existential and humanistic approaches in psychology to emphasize the core contribution of the existential well-being to our health. This exploration culminates in the postulation of existential instinct as the fundamental driving force of human potential for meaning and purpose which is realized through continuously maintaining an advanced MEA. This non-conceptual state is associated with experience of subtle joy, clarity, knowing, tranquillity and compassion. Consequences of this proposal for our understanding and treatment of addictions, depression, anxiety and psychotic disorders are briefly discussed. The chapter concludes with a discussion of broader implications of the new meditation science for healthcare and human potential for well-being, which sets the stage for examination of specific meditation practices from this perspective in the following chapters.

References

Bieling, P.J., Hawley, L.L., Bloch, R.T., Corcoran, K.M., Levitan, R.D., Young, L.T., MacQueen, G.M. and Segal, Z.V., 2012. Treatment-specific changes in decentering following mindfulness-based cognitive therapy versus antidepressant medication or placebo for prevention of depressive relapse. *Journal of Consulting and Clinical Psychology*, 80(3), pp. 365–372.

Brand, S., Holsboer-Trachsler, E., Naranjo, J.R. and Schmidt, S., 2012. Influence of mindfulness practice on cortisol and sleep in long-term and short-term meditators. *Neuropsychobiology*, 65(3), pp. 109–118.

Carmody, J., Reed, G., Kristeller, J. and Merriam, P., 2008. Mindfulness, spirituality, and health-related symptoms. *Journal of Psychosomatic Research*, *64*(4), pp. 393–403.

Chadwick, P., Taylor, K.N. and Abba, N., 2005. Mindfulness groups for people with psychosis. *Behavioural and Cognitive Psychotherapy*, *33*(3), pp. 351–359.

Cotton, S., Larkin, E., Hoopes, A., Cromer, B.A. and Rosenthal, S.L., 2005. The impact of adolescent spirituality on depressive symptoms and health risk behaviors. *Journal of Adolescent Health*, *36*(6), p. 529.

Dorjee, D., 2013. *Mind, brain and the path to happiness: A guide to Buddhist mind training and the neuroscience of meditation*. London: Routledge.

Dorjee, D., 2016. Defining contemplative science: The metacognitive self-regulatory capacity of the mind, context of meditation practice and modes of existential awareness. *Frontiers in Psychology*, *7*, pp. 1–15.

Dorjee, D., Lally, N., Darrall-Rew, J. and Thierry, G., 2015. Dispositional mindfulness and semantic integration of emotional words: Evidence from event-related brain potentials. *Neuroscience Research*, *97*, pp. 45–51.

Dye, M.W., Green, C.S. and Bavelier, D., 2009. The development of attention skills in action video game players. *Neuropsychologia*, *47*(8), pp. 1780–1789.

Edmondson, D., Park, C.L., Blank, T.O., Fenster, J.R. and Mills, M.A., 2008. Deconstructing spiritual well-being: Existential well-being and HRQOL in cancer survivors. *Psycho-Oncology*, *17*(2), pp. 161–169.

Frankl, V.E., 1985. *Man's search for meaning*. New York: Simon and Schuster.

Fresco, D.M., Moore, M.T., Dulmen, M.H. van, Segal, Z.V., Ma, S.H., Teasdale, J.D. and Williams, J.M.G., 2007. Initial psychometric properties of the experiences questionnaire: Validation of a self-report measure of decentering. *Behavior Therapy*, *38*(3), pp. 234–246.

Hofmann, S.G., Sawyer, A.T., Witt, A.A. and Oh, D., 2010. The effect of mindfulness-based therapy on anxiety and depression: A meta-analytic review. *Journal of Consulting and Clinical Psychology*, *78*(2), p. 169.

Jacobs, T.L., Epel, E.S., Lin, J., Blackburn, E.H., Wolkowitz, O.M., Bridwell, D.A., Zanesco, A.P., Aichele, S.R., Sahdra, B.K., MacLean, K.A. and King, B.G., 2011. Intensive meditation training, immune cell telomerase activity, and psychological mediators. *Psychoneuroendocrinology*, *36*(5), pp. 664–681.

Krygier, J.R., Heathers, J.A., Shahrestani, S., Abbott, M., Gross, J.J. and Kemp, A.H., 2013. Mindfulness meditation, well-being, and heart rate variability: A preliminary investigation into the impact of intensive Vipassana meditation. *International Journal of Psychophysiology*, *89*(3), pp. 305–313.

Kuyken, W., Hayes, R., Barrett, B., Byng, R., Dalgleish, T., Kessler, D., Lewis, G., Watkins, E., Brejcha, C., Cardy, J. and Causley, A., 2015. Effectiveness and cost-effectiveness of mindfulness-based cognitive therapy compared with maintenance antidepressant treatment in the prevention of depressive relapse or recurrence (PREVENT): A randomised controlled trial. *The Lancet*, *386*(9988), pp. 63–73.

Labelle, L.E., Lawlor-Savage, L., Campbell, T.S., Faris, P. and Carlson, L.E., 2015. Does self-report mindfulness mediate the effect of Mindfulness-Based Stress Reduction (MBSR) on spirituality and posttraumatic growth in cancer patients? *The Journal of Positive Psychology*, *10*(2), pp. 153–166.

Maselko, J., Gilman, S.E. and Buka, S., 2009. Religious service attendance and spiritual well-being are differentially associated with risk of major depression. *Psychological Medicine*, *39*(06), pp. 1009–1017.

Maslow, A.H., 1943. A theory of human motivation. *Psychological Review*, *50*(4), pp. 370–396.

Mipham, J., 2007. *White lotus: An explanation of the seven-line prayer to Guru Padmasambhava*. Boston: Shambhala Publications.

Moffitt, T.E., Arseneault, L., Belsky, D., Dickson, N., Hancox, R.J., Harrington, H., Houts, R., Poulton, R., Roberts, B.W., Ross, S. and Sears, M.R., 2011. A gradient of childhood self-control predicts health, wealth, and public safety. *Proceedings of the National Academy of Sciences*, *108*(7), pp. 2693–2698.

Mueller, P.S., Plevak, D.J. and Rummans, T.A., 2001, December. Religious involvement, spirituality, and medicine: Implications for clinical practice. *Mayo Clinic Proceedings*, *76*(12), pp. 1225–1235.

O'Leary, K., O'Neill, S. and Dockray, S., 2015. A systematic review of the effects of mindfulness interventions on cortisol. *Journal of Health Psychology*, *21*(9), pp. 1–14.

Pagnoni, G., Cekic, M. and Guo, Y., 2008. "Thinking about not-thinking": Neural correlates of conceptual processing during Zen meditation. *PLoS One*, *3*(9), p. e3083.

Ryff, C.D., Singer, B.H. and Love, G.D., 2004. Positive health: Connecting well-being with biology. *Philosophical Transactions – Royal Society of London Series B Biological Sciences*, *359*, pp. 1383–1394.

Seligman, M.E., Steen, T.A., Park, N. and Peterson, C., 2005. Positive psychology progress: Empirical validation of interventions. *American Psychologist*, *60*(5), pp. 2108–2121.

Shapiro, S.L., Carlson, L.E., Astin, J.A. and Freedman, B., 2006. Mechanisms of mindfulness. *Journal of Clinical Psychology*, *62*(3), pp. 373–386.

Tang, Y.Y., Hölzel, B.K. and Posner, M.I., 2015. The neuroscience of mindfulness meditation. *Nature Reviews Neuroscience*, *16*(4), pp. 213–225.

Tang, Y.Y., Ma, Y., Fan, Y., Feng, H., Wang, J., Feng, S., Lu, Q., Hu, B., Lin, Y., Li, J. and Zhang, Y., 2009. Central and autonomic nervous system interaction is altered by short-term meditation. *Proceedings of the National Academy of Sciences*, *106*(22), pp. 8865–8870.

Tang, Y.Y., Ma, Y., Wang, J., Fan, Y., Feng, S., Lu, Q., Yu, Q., Sui, D., Rothbart, M.K., Fan, M. and Posner, M.I., 2007. Short-term meditation training improves attention and self-regulation. *Proceedings of the National Academy of Sciences*, *104*(43), pp. 17152–17156.

Wallace, B.A., 1999. *The four immeasurables: Cultivating a boundless heart*. Ithaca, NY: Snow Lion Publications.

Warren, F.C., Kuyken, W., Taylor, R.S., Whalley, B., Crane, C., Bondolfi, G., Hayes, R., Huijbers, M., Ma, H., Schwelzer, S. and Segal, Z., 2016. Efficacy and moderators of mindfulness-based cognitive therapy in prevention of depressive relapse: An individual patient data meta-analysis from randomized trials. *JAMA Psychiatry*, *73*(6), pp. 565–574.

Zeidan, F., Martucci, K.T., Kraft, R.A., Gordon, N.S., McHaffie, J.G. and Coghill, R.C., 2011. Brain mechanisms supporting the modulation of pain by mindfulness meditation. *The Journal of Neuroscience*, *31*(14), pp. 5540–5548.

Chapter 2

Long-term meditation practice

Development of a long-term perspective in personal meditation practice as well as in research on meditation invites careful considerations about many facets of long-term vs short-term effects of meditation. For example, initial research suggests that there are marked differences in the brain changes resulting from short-term, medium-term and long-term meditation practice (e.g., Brefczynski-Lewis et al., 2007). This raises questions regarding the contribution of quantity and quality of meditation practice to such effects. Is it the hours spent in meditation or the intensity and quality of the practice or both? There are also questions about how such differences in quantity and quality translate into the well-being effects of meditation within an actual meditation practice and in everyday life outside of formal meditation sessions. And finally, there is the issue of possible adverse effects of meditation, which has been mostly neglected in meditation research over the last two decades and is increasingly more salient with meditation becoming a popular mainstream practice. Discussion about adverse effects of meditation is particularly pertinent in the context of developing a long-term meditation practice. In this chapter, we will consider each of these questions in detail, but first start with an explanation of how neural plasticity contributes to the effects of meditation.

Neural plasticity, body physiology and meditation

For a long time in the history of neuroscience research findings seemed to suggest that brain does not change much in the adulthood. Brain clearly develops and changes during childhood as we learn to walk, talk, read and write and acquire a range of other skills. The brain also has an amazing capacity to re-learn skills lost due to brain damage during young age provided that other parts of the brain which can overtake the skills are intact. However, much of this brain flexibility in learning is lost after the age of 12, even though development of some brain areas continues until the age of 25. Accordingly, neuroscience researchers claimed for many decades that the modulations in the brain due to learning are very limited after the developmental brain maturation is completed.

Contrary to this long-held view, the brain research over the last two decades showed that brain can change even in adulthood when we acquire new skills. By now there are many studies in support of the overarching finding that the brain is changeable by learning new mental skills across the lifetime. For example, the research shows that the brain is modified when we learn to play a musical instrument (Herholz and Zatorre, 2012), learn a new language (Li, Legault and Litcofsky, 2014) or learn to dance (Karpati et al., 2015), etc. The training in the new skill does not need to take a long time – measurable changes have been observed after 40 hours of learning to play golf as a leisure activity (Bezzola et al., 2011) or two weeks of brief daily learning to mirror read (Ilg et al., 2008). Research into such brain changes, however, also showed that the modifications resulting from learning are reduced if the learning is not sustained. For instance, a study on learning to juggle found clear changes in brain structure after three months of practice, but these changes were largely reduced three months later after the participants in the study stopped practicing juggling (Draganski et al., 2004). Together, all these research findings highlight how our everyday choices about activities and experiences we undertake reshape our brains. The term 'neural plasticity' has been used to describe the ability of the brain to change as a result of our experience.

The specific mechanisms underlying brain plasticity are complex, but it is commonly assumed that neural plasticity is linked to growth of new neural connections between brain cells (neurons). Neurons have two types of branch-like parts which enable connections to other neurons – axons, which lead information to other brain cells, and dendrites, which receive information from other brain cells. Axons are covered in fatty substance called myelin, which gives a whitish colour to brain parts mostly consisting of axons. Dendrites, in contrast, are greyish in colour and accordingly tissue containing mostly dendrites (and cell bodies plus support cells) is grey in colour. These differences in colour are used to describe the grey matter of the brain, which is located mostly on the surface of the brain, and white matter of the brain mostly forming tracts inside the brain. Research shows that both grey and white matter volume and other properties such as tissue density can be changed by neural plasticity (May, 2011).

The relatively recent shift in our understanding of neural plasticity in the adulthood was facilitated by the development of research methods that allow investigation of changes in the brain 'online' – while human participants are engaging in thinking, talking, perceiving, sensing and feeling. We have also been for a long time able to learn about neural plasticity from research using reaction-time measures assessing speed of responses to carefully selected stimuli or their sequences; such responses are often recorded via button presses in experimental tasks (Ahissar and Hochstein, 2004). It might sound surprising, but reaction-time research can often provide as strong evidence on neural plasticity of learning as some imaging methods (Dorjee and Bowers, 2012). Importantly, new neuroscientific methods allowed research into subtle changes in the brain structure with learning. The new brain research methods which enabled these advances in the study of neural plasticity fall into two main categories: magnetic resonance imaging (MRI) and electroencephalography (EEG).

The MRI measures changes in brain tissue properties using a strong magnetic field. The MRI methods are typically divided into two main categories: structural MRI and functional MRI (fMRI). While the structural methods are able to differentiate changes in, for example, volume and density of brain areas, fMRI is based on changes in magnetic properties of iron (contained in the protein haemoglobin) in the blood flow in the brain. Only fMRI is able to detect changes online, during a task performance while participants are engaging in thinking, emotional processing etc. Both structural and fMRI measures have very good spatial resolution, enabling us to understand where in the brain changes occurred. However, fMRI is not very accurate when it comes to recording timing of the changes in brain processes. This is because fMRI is based on measuring changes in blood-oxygen-level dependent (BOLD) signals, which are typically delayed by a couple seconds after a metabolic demand in an area of the brain arises. It is assumed that if an area requires more energy (increased metabolism and oxygen demand) it is involved in the task performed. So the inference about involvement of brain areas in learning as measured by fMRI is somewhat indirect.

In contrast, EEG-derived measures can record brain activity from the surface of the brain with millisecond accuracy while participants are performing a task, so these measures have excellent temporal resolution. EEG methods measure the core activity of neurons – neuronal firing across large numbers of neurons – so provide more direct assessment of brain activity than fMRI signals derived from BOLD. However, EEG methods cannot assess specific localization of the changes in neuronal firing in the brain because of the natural curvature of the brain's surface, which results in neuronal firing being projected in different directions from the source brain areas. In addition, EEG signals, for the most part, cannot capture neuronal firing from the structures inside the brain, only on its surface. Nevertheless, EEG methods have been available to researchers for much longer than MRI; hence there is a larger body of evidence in support of specific neural EEG-based markers of attention, emotion regulation, conceptual processing etc. The EEG methods are also much cheaper than MRI and the recording equipment is easily portable, allowing for recording in various environments (e.g., in meditation retreat).

Neuroscientific research using MRI and EEG methods in investigating neural plasticity linked to meditation has clearly documented tangible changes in the brain. It supported the hypothesis that learning to meditate, just like learning other skills we have mentioned earlier, results in modifications in the brain function and brain structure. In a way, the findings regarding neural plasticity changes with meditation provide even stronger evidence of neural plasticity principles than learning to juggle, play violin, dance or play golf. This is because meditation has been stereotypically considered an elusive practice, restricted in its effects to the mind of the meditator; after all, there are no visible 'outcomes' of meditation practice other than perhaps subtle shifts in facial expression, unlike the number of balls juggled without falling for a certain amount of time.

Yet, neuroscientific studies have now documented relatively consistent modifications in at least a few areas of the brain as a result of meditation practice including the anterior cingulate cortex, insula and amygdalae (Tang, Hölzel and Posner, 2015). There is also growing evidence of neural plasticity changes with meditation from event-related brain potential (ERP) research, which is an EEG-based method measuring brain responses to particular types of probes (e.g., sad faces, happy faces or rare sounds). Research using ERPs, for example, suggests that meditation practice enhances efficient use of attention resources (e.g., Slagter et al., 2007). This is an important finding because attention is a limited capacity since in every moment there is an overload of information in our environment (people's voices and other sounds, things around us, our thoughts, emotions etc.) and we need to choose most relevant information for the task at hand. Interestingly, some of these changes in attention regulation have also been associated with health-conducive effects in body physiology such as decreases in stress hormone levels (Tang et al., 2009). The connections between bodily stress pathways and stress-related hormonal changes in the brain, discussed in the previous chapter, enable these effects. Through these connections, neural plasticity induced by meditation can enhance our ability to downregulate the stress response.

If we examine the previous research on neural plasticity changes with meditation from the perspective of the framework of meditation research outlined in Chapter 1, most of the research focused on processes of the metacognitive self-regulatory capacity (MSRC) of the mind. The majority of the studies particularly investigated changes in attention and emotion regulation linked to meditation. Much less research has been dedicated to investigation of changes in conceptual processing with meditation, which is a relatively new topic in meditation research. Similarly, research on modes of existential awareness (MEA) is very limited. Most studies that investigate neural modulations relevant to the construal of self heavily relied on attention and emotion processes which contribute to, but are not necessarily central to, the construal of self (e.g., Lutz et al., 2016). Finally, very few neuroscientific studies considered links between changes in self-regulation or existential awareness in relation to changes in health and well-being of meditators. We will consider the research findings relevant to MSRC and MEA in detail in the following chapters.

Despite the important contribution of neuroscientific studies to research on the neural plasticity of meditation, there is a need for caution in interpreting their findings. Neuroscientific evidence is often given stronger weight than evidence from other methods (such as reaction-time experiments) particularly by non-neuroscientists. This is often the case when sensationalist reports in the media discuss brain changes resulting from meditation. Directly speaking to this issue are findings from one research study (with other studies supporting the same conclusions) which examined trustworthiness of explanations containing neuroscience information as judged by neuroscience non-experts in comparison to neuroscience experts (Weisberg et al., 2008). The results showed that non-experts considered explanations containing neuroscience information, even when it was irrelevant (!), as more persuasive than explanations of equal quality but without neuroscientific references and language. This wasn't the case for experts, who disregarded neuroscience information if it wasn't relevant to the explanation.

The state and trait effects of meditation

Meditation practices, depending on their types, are expected to produce effects such as improved concentration or emotional balance. We might experience such effects while meditating or right after we have completed a meditation session. These changes could be considered shifts in a state – the term 'state' suggests that such changes are temporary, transient and closely linked to the immediate practice of meditation. Initial neuroscience findings show that these temporary changes produce measurable modulations in the brain. For example, fMRI research findings with participants without any previous meditation experience have shown clear differences in the recruitment of brain areas when the participants were engaging in a brief breath-focus meditation in comparison to unfocused attention (Dickenson et al., 2012). The particular modulation was in increased brain activity in attention control areas during the breath-focus meditation. The study thus showed that neural correlates of state difference between meditation and unfocused states are observable even in meditation novices. Another example of state shifts comes from a study, this time with experienced Vipassana meditation practitioners, which contrasted meditators' concentration while they were engaging in focused meditation with when they were engaging in neutral unfocused thinking (Cahn and Polich, 2009). The study used ERP indexes of distractibility (P3a ERP component) and found significantly diminished brain responses to distractors during meditation than during the thinking period. This finding suggested that the meditation state was associated with increased concentration and better ability to reduce distraction, as would be expected.

It is certainly reassuring that meditation can produce the expected effects while we are meditating or right after completion of a meditation practice, but do such effects transfer into times during the day when we are not actively engaging in a formal meditation practice? Such broader persistent impact of meditation is potentially of most relevance to our health and well-being since it would indicate that meditation can not only temporarily improve how we feel, but also produce lasting long-term changes. For example, could regular meditation practice modify the way we habitually cope with stressful events or how well we are able to concentrate on tasks during the day? We could expect that with repeated meditation practice we are changing neural plasticity in attention and emotion regulation areas of the brain and these changes gradually override usual (less healthy) ways of responding in everyday life. This would suggest that repeated experience of meditation states could result in more lasting 'trait' changes in our mind and brain.

A large body of research regarding personality traits such as neuroticisms or extraversion traditionally implicated that such traits are quite stable characteristics of personality across lifetime. However, recent research challenged this assumption and some studies showed that regular meditation practice can lead to shifts in personality traits. For example, a study on the effects of a three-month meditation retreat documented significant reductions in neuroticisms (characterized by distress and excessive worrying) after the retreat (Jacobs et al., 2011). The retreat involved training in attention regulation (Shamatha) and also cultivation of loving kindness, compassion, rejoicing and equanimity. Changes in personality-related traits were also found in a study with participants attending an eight-week mindfulness-based stress reduction (MBSR) course. This study reported changes in traits associated with type D 'distressed' personality – characterized by negative affectivity and inhibition of emotional expression in social interactions (not showing how we feel, which is also linked to introversion) (Nyklíček, van Beugen and Denollet, 2013). The researchers found that scores on both of the traits of distressed personality significantly reduced after the MBSR course, suggesting a trait shift. The assessments of the traits in this study also controlled for possible temporary state effects of negative affectivity.

Neuroscience research shows that effects of meditation beyond the immediate state shifts are also associated with changes in brain structure observed outside of meditation and as early as after eight weeks of meditation training. One study assessed participants' brain structure in areas relevant to stress processing before and after eight weeks of MBSR training (Hölzel et al., 2009). The participants were healthy but stressed adults. The results revealed significant reductions in self-reported perceived stress and also significant reductions in the density of grey matter in the right amygdala. These reductions in the density of amygdala grey matter were significantly related to the reductions in perceived stress scores of course participants, lending further support to the link between this structural change and well-being enhancing effects of the MBSR training. Amygdalae are brain regions involved in treat detection; increased activation of the amygdalae has been associated with anxiety disorders or post-traumatic stress disorder (PTSD). In another study with MBSR participants, structural modifications in the brain were found in regions involved in emotion regulation (increased grey matter density in posterior cingulate cortex and temporo-parietal junction) and memory (increased grey matter density in the hippocampus) (Hölzel et al., 2011).

The studies we have discussed show that meditation practice can lead to both state and trait changes in the mind and brain, but meditation-related traits are present even without any meditation training. Mindfulness is a good example of this. We will discuss definitions of mindfulness in detail in the next chapter; here it will suffice to say that mindfulness can be described as the ability to notice our emotions, thoughts and sensations in a non-reactive way and regulate our attention to these. While research studies show (see examples above in this section) that mindfulness is a modifiable state as well as a trait, they also suggest that mindfulness is a disposition all of us have to some degree regardless of whether we have been engaging in formal mindfulness practice. In other words, some people are naturally more mindful than others even without any mindfulness training.

In research, assessments of the mindfulness disposition have been used in examining brain activation which can be associated with this trait. For example, in a neuroscience study with participants without previous meditation training researchers investigated the possible relationship between mindfulness disposition and processing of emotions (Creswell et al., 2007). Participants were asked to view faces with angry or sad emotional expressions and respond to them either by labelling the emotion depicted or the gender of the face in the picture. The findings revealed that in the emotion-labelling task participants with higher mindfulness disposition (naturally more mindful) showed stronger activation in prefrontal brain areas (particularly medial prefrontal cortex) associated with cognitive control and monitoring of thoughts and emotions. More mindful participants also showed decreases in the activation of the amygdalae linked to the stress response. Interestingly, there was a negative relationship between the activation in the prefrontal areas and the amygdalae – the higher the activity in the prefrontal cortex the lower the activity in the amygdalae. This indicates a possible neural mechanism of emotion regulation with the prefrontal areas downregulating the activity in the amygdalae during affective labelling as a possible mindful emotion regulation strategy. However, the mindfulness disposition wasn't related to differences in brain activity in the gender-labelling task. These findings provided interesting insights into how mindfulness disposition could be involved in regulation of emotions, with other studies applying the same principles in investigating links between the mindfulness disposition and attention etc.

Research on dispositional mindfulness (and other meditation-related traits), however, also has some drawbacks. For instance, it is possible that findings in the study we have just discussed (Creswell et al., 2007) were influenced by other participant abilities the researchers did not assess such as general attention abilities or better emotion regulation. This could be the case since higher mindfulness is associated with better attention abilities (Malinowski, 2013). So in a way it is a case of a 'chicken vs egg' problem with dispositional attention and dispositional mindfulness – we cannot determine whether better attention naturally leads to more mindfulness or if it is the other way around. This is a general shortcoming of studies relying on associations between trait dispositions and brain activity – we cannot interpret their findings in a conclusive way because it is not possible to ascertain whether they were purely due to the disposition or other factors. Studies which involve assessments before and after meditation training are able to provide stronger evidence of changes resulting from meditation because we have a starting point of assessing participants' brain activity and therefore changes observed after the training are attributable to meditation as the only factor which changed during the training time. This can be further ascertained by inclusion of a control group in a study to make sure changes observed after meditation training are not due to other factors such as different time of the year, aging, practice with the assessment tasks etc.

Interestingly, changes in states as well as traits can interact with the dispositions we have towards meditation. For example, earlier in this section we have discussed fMRI research findings from participants without any previous experience of meditation who showed state differences in brain activation when they were engaging in breath-focus meditation and in unfocused attention state (Dickenson et al., 2012). In the same study the researchers found that those participants who were naturally more mindful (higher mindfulness disposition) also showed stronger activation in brain areas associated with attention control during the brief breath-focus meditation. This suggests that disposition to mindfulness (keeping in mind the drawbacks of dispositional research discussed in the previous paragraph) may influence how readily we engage with actual mindfulness practice and associated brain changes.

Indeed, an MBSR study provided preliminary support for this suggestion in an investigation of possible links between baseline levels of trait mindfulness and well-being gains from participation in an MBSR course (Shapiro et al., 2011). The researchers found that participants who were naturally more mindful at the start of the training showed larger improvements in well-being than those with lower mindfulness disposition. These differences in gains amongst the initially more and less mindful participants were present even when assessed one year after the MBSR training was completed. However, initial research with children points to the reverse effect. In a study with primary school children (7–9-year-olds) those with lower levels of executive control to start with showed the largest improvements in executive control (regulation of behaviour, metacognition, etc.) after mindfulness training (Flook et al., 2010). Even though the researchers did not assess mindfulness levels directly, other research suggested that executive control performance and mindfulness are positively linked (Teper, Segal and Inzlicht, 2013). These findings need to be interpreted with caution, since both the study by Shapiro et al. (2011) and Flook et al. (2010) had small sample sizes and some aspects of their statistical analyses were not very strong, but this research highlighted the importance of investigating links between mindfulness disposition and gains from mindfulness training. Further research is needed to elucidate these associations.

Overall, the available evidence suggests that meditation can lead to both temporary changes in mind and brain states and to longer-term shifts in personality traits, cognitive functioning and brain structure. Initial findings also indicate that natural dispositions towards meditation practice may impact on the beneficial effects participants experience from meditation training. These suggestions, however, should be considered with caution because findings of studies relying on questionnaire measures of mindfulness are subject to many shortcomings such as differences in interpretations of questions and ability to reflect accurately on our mental states and traits (Grossman, 2011). There is also an ongoing debate in the field about how to best measure meditation-specific states, traits and dispositions such as mindfulness to avoid some of these limitations with one possibility being reaction-time assessments instead of questionnaires (Levinson et al., 2013). These debates are far from coming to an overarching consensus at the moment. Nevertheless, the distinctions between state and trait effects of mindfulness have practical implications for our considerations of long-term effects of meditation in everyday life, both within and outside of formal meditation sessions, and we will build on these distinctions in our discussions in the following chapters.

The quantity and quality of meditation practice

The questions about state and trait effects of meditation are closely related to how often (quantity) and how proficiently (quality) we are engaging in meditation. The quantity of meditation practice seems to be more straightforward to assess – we simply need to keep track of the minutes and hours we spend in meditation practice every day, every week etc. However, keeping track of meditation practice becomes more complicated if we broaden the amount of practice to meditation on the go – informal practice we may engage in throughout the day (we will discuss the differences between formal and informal meditation practice in more detail in the next section). But why should we try to evaluate the amount of practice in the first place? The reasoning here is that the more we practice, the more we improve in our ability to meditate, which we would expect to translate into both state and trait changes. The trait changes could then have more profound impact on our health and well-being both within and outside of formal meditation practice.

Indeed, there is research, even though limited in numbers and scope, suggesting that more hours spent in meditation practice result in more beneficial effects on health and well-being. For example, a study which investigated the relationship between formal meditation practice and outcomes of MBSR training found that those participants who spent more time in formal meditation at home also showed larger increases in well-being from before to after the MBSR course (Carmody and Baer, 2008). Similarly, a study with military personnel who were experiencing pre-deployment stress found that those who spent more time in home meditation practice (as part of an MBSR course) showed larger reductions in negative affect and increases in positive affect (Jha et al., 2010). The study also found that those with more hours of practice outside of the MBSR classes showed increases in working memory capacity. This is an important finding given that stress is associated with a reduction in working memory capacity and military personnel from this study with less hours of practice did not show the protective effects of mindfulness on working memory (they showed a decline in working memory).

Amount of meditation practice has also been associated with differences in brain changes resulting from meditation. For instance, one fMRI study investigated links between the amount of long-term meditation practice and connectivity between brain areas which support attention control (Hasenkamp and Barsalou, 2012). The connectivity patterns examined were particularly relevant to disengagement from random mind-wandering as an off-task unfocused activity. The findings reported stronger connectivity of the attention networks in meditators with more hours of meditation, suggesting that more meditation practice is associated with more pronounced neural plasticity changes underlying attention control.

However, the relationship between the amount of meditation practice and associated changes in the brain is not always linear – more meditation practice does not always mean more brain activity (or less brain activity if the activity is associated with health detrimental effects). Indeed, a study which compared meditation beginners with experienced meditation with less and more hours of meditation practice found a non-linear pattern of brain activation differences amongst the groups (Brefczynski-Lewis et al., 2007). Experienced meditators in this study were practitioners in the Tibetan Buddhist tradition divided into two subgroups: the 'less' experienced subgroup with 19,000 hours of meditation practice on average and the 'more' experienced subgroup with the average of 44,000 hours of meditation. The meditation beginners received written instructions in meditation and were asked to practice meditation 1 hour per day for a week. Both beginners and experienced meditators were asked to practice concentrative meditation during the evaluations. The fMRI assessments of differences in brain activation between the beginners, less experienced and more experienced meditators pointed to an interesting non-linear pattern of differences in brain activation during the concentrative meditation. As expected, beginners showed less activation in brain areas related to sustained attention than experienced meditators with less hours of practice. However, experienced meditators with more hours of practice had less activation in the same brain areas linked to sustained attention than experienced meditators with less hours of practice. In fact, the pattern of brain activation in the experienced meditators with more hours of practice was similar to the pattern of meditation beginners. While the diminished brain activity in beginners may have been linked to them being less able to recruit attention control areas of the brain during meditation, similar brain activity pattern in the meditators with more hours of practice likely reflects effortless engagement in sustained attention which does not require strong recruitment of attention networks.

Coming back to differences in effects with quantity of secular meditation training, interestingly, the length of formal in-class meditation training does not seem to be strongly associated with positive participant outcomes, unlike home meditation practice. Indeed, preliminary research did not find a significant relationship between the amount of formal in-class training in the MBSR and mindfulness-based cognitive therapy (MBCT) and participant gains in terms of health and well-being (Carmody and Baer, 2009). The standard training in MBSR involves 2.5-hour weekly sessions delivered over eight weeks (2-hour weekly sessions in MBCT). The study looked at published research with the standard or shorter than standard duration of weekly sessions (or less than the usual eight weekly sessions) and related the overall duration of the training to the size of the effects in terms of participant improvements. The lack of a quantity of training effects in the findings from this study suggests that shorter training may be equally effective in improving participants' health and well-being and also highlights the importance of home practice which does seem to relate to participant outcomes. A contributing factor here might be the quality of engagement with the meditation practice in shorter sessions, a factor which we will consider now.

Research on quality of meditation is very limited, but initial findings suggest that qualities such as drowsiness during meditation can impact on measurable outcomes of the practice. Specifically, a study with experienced Vipassana meditators investigated brain patterns associated with distractibility by comparing ERP patterns during a focused meditation session and during a period of neutral thinking. Participants' brain responses to a simple series of tones were recorded during both meditation and thinking. White noise sounds were randomly embedded in the sequences of the tones to measure automatic reactivity of attention to distractors. The ERP findings showed that meditators' brains responded much less to the distractor sounds during meditation in comparison to the thinking period. Interestingly, meditators were also asked to rate how drowsy they felt when they were meditating right after completion of the session. The rates of drowsiness were then related to the modulation of the ERP index measuring brain responses to the distractor white noise. The results showed that only meditators who did not report feeling drowsy showed lower automatic response to the distractor sounds. In other words, they were less distracted during their meditation session. This suggests that absence of drowsiness as an indicator of better quality of meditation is linked to measurable changes in brain indexes of distractibility.

Interestingly, it has been recently suggested that quality of attention during meditation could be used as an assessment of mindfulness and is directly related to the health and well-being we experience. In one study (Burg and Michalak, 2011) participants (majority of them without prior training in meditation) were asked to observe their breath during short time periods of 20 to 80 seconds. While engaging in this meditation practice the participants pressed the left button whenever they noticed being on the breath and the right button when they lost track of their breath. They were also asked to fill in questionnaires assessing their depression and rumination levels. The findings of the study showed that participants who were better able to stay focused on their breath also reported lower levels of rumination and anxiety. Better focus on the task was also associated with higher levels of acceptance and acting with awareness as dimensions of mindfulness, suggesting a link between some aspects of questionnaire assessments of mindfulness.

A similar principle was assessed in a study (Levinson et al., 2013) with a larger sample of participants. They were asked to press count their breaths and press a button for each outbreath from the first breath to the eighth breath and a different button for the ninth breath, then start again from one. This assessed how well participants were able to stay focused on their breath as a possible measure of mindfulness. In addition, the researchers asked the participants approximately every 90 seconds about their meta-awareness – how aware they were of where their attention was. The findings indicated that those who performed better on the breath-counting task also reported higher mindfulness on a questionnaire assessment. In addition, meditators showed higher breath-counting accuracy than meditation novices, suggesting that the task was sensitive to meditation experience.

Interestingly, these assessments of mindfulness seem to tap into some aspects of attention qualities described in the Buddhist context where the cultivation of attention skills in meditation is typically outlined in terms of relaxation, stability and clarity as basic qualities of attention (Wallace, 2006). Relaxation is characterized as a balanced way of paying attention without tension or too much laxity. Stability relates to the ability to sustain attention on an object of meditation, such as breath or a sacred statue, with continuity and without losing the focus on the object of meditation. Clarity of attention in meditation describes the vividness and detail of attention focus. Buddhist teachings on calm abiding (Shamatha) build on the distinctions between these qualities of attention and present a comprehensive account of changes in relaxation, stability and vividness of attention with progression in meditation training.

For example, the teachings on Shamatha describe how at the initial stages of meditation training the practitioner often struggles with tension in the body and mind and needs to develop the quality of relaxation. The stability of attention is very limited in the initial stages, lasting only a couple of seconds before distraction draws attention away from the object of meditation. With more practice the tension in meditation practice decreases and the stability increases – the practitioner is able to stay focused on the object of meditation for longer time periods. The stability can increase further up to the point where practitioner is able to focus with minimal distraction for an hour or more. As the stability of meditation improves, development of clarity in meditation practice becomes the priority. This is achieved by increasing focus on detail and freshness in the practice, to reduce slipping into a stable but dull and drowsy meditative state.

The qualities of relaxation, stability and clarity of attention have not been systematically investigated in Western meditation research so far. This might be partially because secular meditation-based approaches which attracted most research interest over the last two decades do not aim to develop high levels of attention skills. Instead, the focus of meditation in the secular context has been primarily on health and well-being enhancing effects resulting from relatively small amounts of meditation practice. Development of higher levels of attentional stability would require more extensive regular meditation training – the accounts of Shamatha suggest that for most practitioners a year of meditation practice in retreat might be needed to achieve the highest levels of attentional balance (Wallace, 2006).

Aside from development of attention skills, there are elaborate accounts of many other qualities cultivated through meditation practice. These, for instance, include progression in development of the six Paramitas – qualities of generosity, ethical discipline, patience, perseverance, meditative concentration and wisdom (Rinpoche, 1998). Other accounts describe different degrees of emotional qualities developed in meditation – loving kindness, compassion, rejoicing and equanimity (Wallace, 1999). These, for example, can range from initial cultivation of loving kindness and compassion towards those close to us (and ourselves) to unconditional non-conceptual loving kindness and compassion towards all living beings. And from a perspective of the whole path of meditation, Buddhist teachings describe in detail the core qualities developed at each of the stages (Bhumis) towards most advanced levels of existential balance (Gampopa and Rinpoche, 1998). Cultivation of these qualities has received very little attention in meditation research so far, yet it is becoming more relevant to both research and practice with the increasing focus on long-term meditation.

Formal and informal meditation

Meditation is typically understood as a formal practice, often practiced while sitting on a meditation cushion in the half-lotus (legs partially crossed) or full lotus (legs fully crossed) position. However, meditation can be practiced in various ways, both formally and informally. Formal practice usually refers to periods of meditation practice which are purely dedicated to meditation and follow a standard approach or structure. In the secular mindfulness-based approaches formal meditation often starts with a meditation bell sound and then involves guidance by the mindfulness teacher which follows a certain progression of instructions. The formal meditation concludes again with a meditation bell sound followed by gentle stretching.

In the traditional Buddhist context, the standard progression of formal meditation sessions is somewhat different. For instance in Tibetan Buddhism, each practice session starts with prayers connecting the practitioner with the lineage of meditation practitioners. Then the practitioner develops motivation and intention for engaging in the meditation practice. After these initial contemplations, the practitioner engages in the meditation practice as such which can involve focusing on an object of meditation or examining the processes of the mind etc. for a certain period of time. The practice can follow a sequence of instructions read from a meditation practice text with longer periods dedicated to practice itself without teacher guidance. At the end of the meditation session the practitioner dedicates the merit accumulated from spending time in meditation practice 'to seal' the effects of the practice. This last part of the formal meditation session relates to the beliefs about the law of cause and effect (karma) and the importance of intentional engagement in virtuous activity.

Formal meditation can be practiced for longer or shorter periods of time during the day. In the Buddhist context, it is often recommended that the practitioner starts with shorter meditation sessions of approximately 5 minutes three or more times a day. The duration of meditation sessions gradually increases with more relaxation, stability and clarity in meditation. Longer meditation sessions for beginners are not recommended because they can lead to a build-up of tension in the body which is counterproductive to development of the quality of relaxation and hampers progress in the practice (Wallace, 2006). In the secular context, the standard format of MBSR and MBCT recommends practicing meditation for 45 minutes a day from the beginning. However, these longer sessions are supported by continuous guidance throughout the 45 minutes with relatively short periods of silence between the verbal guidance which continuously reminds the practitioner of the instructions.

Formal meditation practice does not involve sitting meditation only. Formal sessions can, for example, be conducted during movement – walking meditation is a common example in both Buddhist and secular contexts. Other routine activities such as eating can also be used as formal meditation practice across meditation contexts. In mindfulness-based approaches, eating meditation can be an opportunity to practice being in the present moment and focusing on the sensations arising as we are tasting the meal, noticing distractions and bringing attention back to the taste sensations while letting go of evaluative thinking. In the Buddhist context, eating meditation would follow the same structure as any other meditation session with initial prayers and development of motivation and intention, followed by practice of generosity and gratitude. This can, for instance, include a wish for others to enjoy nutritious food which can nourish them and support their engagement in meditation practice. The eating meditation would be concluded with dedication prayers.

Aside from formal meditation, both traditional and secular meditation training emphasizes the importance of meditation outside of formal meditation sessions. In mindfulness-based approaches practitioners are asked to select regular daily activities which they will choose to engage in mindfully – this can be taking a shower or brushing teeth mindfully, or practicing mindfulness while washing dishes or walking the dog. The mindfulness training also encourages applying mindfulness in more involved activities during the day such as engaging in a conversation or answering e-mails mindfully. During these activities the practitioners are applying the principles of mindfulness, for example, by being present with the activity rather than lost in rumination about what happened or in planning future activities. Instead the practitioners anchor their attention on the sensations in the present moment with attitudes of non-reactivity and non-judgment. These periods of informal practice can be combined with brief formal sessions a couple minutes in duration to extend the effects of meditation beyond the longer formal practice sessions.

Similarly, practitioners developing meditation in a traditional Buddhist context would be encouraged to practice both formally and informally. In this way any daily activity can be transformed into a meditation practice which would start by developing a connection with the meditation lineage and contemplating motivation and intention for the day right after waking up in the morning. All following activities during the day can be transformed into meditation, from getting dressed as a reminder of developing loving kindness and compassion for all living beings in the moment and throughout the day, through practicing mantra meditation while walking or driving to work, wishing others to have an experience of comfort while having a cup of tea etc. The informal practice during the day can also be combined with brief periods of formal meditation practice throughout the day. At the end of the day before going to sleep the practitioner reminds herself of all the virtuous activities she engaged in during the day and dedicates all the merit arising from this for liberation of all living beings (including herself) from suffering.

Both formal and informal practice intensifies in terms of quantity, and often also quality, when a practitioner enters a meditation retreat. Practicing in a retreat can range from half a day to months and years without a break. During retreat, a practitioner typically does not leave the retreat environment in order to engage in meditation with focus and without interruptions. Engagement with distracting activities such as watching TV, checking e-mail, internet or news, having conversations about non-meditation topics, etc. is purposefully limited during a retreat. The practitioner usually follows a pre-defined schedule while in the retreat, typically starting with a formal meditation practice before breakfast, then engaging in formal meditation practice until the evening. There are regular breaks for meals and other necessary activities throughout the day, during which informal meditation is practiced. In some retreats, a few formal meditation sessions are replaced by attending a meditation teaching or studying a meditation text. In some Buddhist traditions the daytime meditation practice would continue in the form of dream yoga during the night. In this way, the practitioner becomes immersed in meditation most of the time, which can boost the progress in meditative training.

While practicing in a retreat has many advantages and can significantly deepen a practitioner's meditation experience, retreat is also associated with some challenges. Intensive meditation practice can bring up challenging experiences with intensity and therefore skilled guidance by an experienced meditation teacher is a necessary pre-requisite for engagement in a retreat practice. For some practitioners, the protected retreat environment may also not provide enough everyday challenges of distraction and working with emotions which may result in stagnation in their meditation practice. Therefore, it is often recommended to combine regular retreats with formal and informal practice in everyday life. This format can for most practitioners provide a balance between the deepening of meditative experience and the transfer of meditation skills into everyday life.

Adverse effects of meditation

Meditation practice can also lead to challenging experiences which have been documented both in traditional meditation literature and in Western research. A study by Shapiro (1992) reported adverse effects experienced by 27 Vipassana meditators before, after a one-month meditation retreat and at six-month follow up. The findings showed that adverse effects were relatively common – 38% to 55% of the meditators who participated in the study reported experiencing some adverse effects at the different time points of assessment. These effects included, for example, anxiety and panic, disorientation, increases in negative affect and psychosis-like experiences. Meditators with longer meditation practice reported more adverse effects at each of the three time points, suggesting that long-term meditation practice might be associated with increased likelihood of encountering adverse experiences.

More recently, researchers investigated case studies of meditation practitioners who experienced meditation-induced psychosis. They reported on a case of a meditator who engaged in an intensive and unguided meditation practice which seemed to have induced psychotic symptoms (Kuijpers et al., 2007). The practitioner, however, had a history of mental illness and also reported several external factors which could have contributed to the psychotic onset. The study also reported on other similar cases of meditation-induced psychosis and previous history of mental illness was highlighted as a factor in more than a half of them. In addition, the study noted that physical exhaustion and effects of fasting might have also been contributing factors to the onset of psychosis. All the reported cases mentioned recovery from the psychotic symptoms from a few days to six months, with the support of medication in some cases. The study concluded that a history of mental illness as well as physical exhaustion could increase the likelihood of experiencing meditation-induced psychotic symptoms.

Investigation of adverse effects arising as part of training in secular meditation-based approaches is very limited. Initial research on adverse effects of meditation more broadly divided potential adverse effects into mental, physical (somatic discomfort and pain) and spiritual (religious delusions) (Lustyk et al., 2009). The same study suggested that participants in mindfulness-based approaches are most likely to experience, even though rarely, mental adverse effects such as psychotic symptoms, dissociative states, anxiety and depression. A brief anecdotal report on adverse effects of MBSR mentioned that particularly after the all-day retreat as part of MBSR training some participants reported symptoms of disorientation and exhaustion (Dobkin, Irving and Amar, 2012). The study suggested that such experiences might be the result of closer connection with both negative and positive experiences as a result of meditation practice. A removal of usual distractions which would prevent closer contact with experience and lack of coping skills are likely also contributing factors to the onset of such adverse effects in this context. Qualifications of the mindfulness teachers and careful pre-screening of participants attending secular mindfulness-based courses may also contribute to the likelihood of participants experiencing adverse effects, even though relevant research evidence is not available yet. Overall, a recent review highlighted the need to systematically investigate adverse effects of meditation, particularly since there is a wide-spread interest in mindfulness-based approaches (Hanley et al., 2016).

Interestingly, possible adverse effects of meditation are well-documented as part of the path of long-term meditation practice in the Tibetan Buddhist tradition, for example, based on teachings from master Dudjom Lingpa (Wallace, 2011). The adverse experiences are likely to arise with continuous sustained practice and are considered signs of meditative experience ('nyam' in Tibetan), rather than pathological states as in Western science. The traditional writings emphasize the great variety of these experiences, which is explained in the system of Tibetan medicine through imbalance of bodily elements combined with physical propensities of the practitioner. The experiences can include what from the Western perspective would be considered sensory hallucinations, paranoid thoughts, anxiety, dissociative experience, visions etc. Physical experiences of pain in different parts of the body and respiratory problems can also arise.

From the traditional Tibetan Buddhist perspective, for many practitioners such adverse experiences are an inevitable part of the path and need to be worked with in meditation practice, rather than suppressed, avoided or fixated upon. The core general guidance on dealing with such experiences is to relax in the face of these experiences, since attachment to, dissociation from and/or rumination about them can exacerbate the symptoms and lead to more lasting difficulties. The instructions regarding these experiences also emphasize the essential role of an experienced and realized meditation teacher in guiding practitioners during times when these experiences arise (Wallace, 2011). The knowledge about these states and guidance on how to work with them is typically readily available in the traditional authentic context of Buddhist meditation training.

This is where practicing within an established and time-tested system seems to be essential to development of long-term meditation practice. Secular meditation-based approaches do not take into account the whole meditative path and as a consequence also do not contain the comprehensive knowledge and a training system to deal with the adverse experiences of meditation. With the expansion of secular meditation-based approaches and, accordingly, increasing numbers of long-term meditation practitioners following secular approaches, it will soon become necessary for these approaches to develop teaching methodologies and strategies for dealing with adverse effects. Learning from traditional meditation approaches will be instrumental in this process. This is one of the reasons why the long-term perspective of meditation might necessitate bringing together the traditional and modern secular approaches to meditation.

Developing a long-term perspective of meditation

In considering health and well-being effects of meditation, a long-term view of meditation practice seems indispensable. This is because the impact of meditation on our health and well-being increases with more hours of meditation practice and most likely also with better quality of meditation practice. Repeated meditation practice can enable the temporary state effects of meditation experienced during or right after meditation to gradually translate into lasting trait shifts conducive to health. Similarly, repeated practice is necessary for meditation to have longer-term impact on brain function and structure; such effects are likely to significantly reduce if meditation practice is discontinued. In developing long-term meditation practice it is important to recognize that meditation can be practiced both in formal sessions and informally, throughout the day. Integration of meditation into everyday routine activities may particularly support maintaining continuous practice without the need of lengthy formal sessions.

Cultivation of long-term meditation practice may also bring up challenging experiences which are in the traditional meditation systems considered part of the path and a step towards further stability of the practice. Guidance of an experienced meditation teacher is essential in supporting a practitioner during these adverse experiences and also in general throughout the long-term meditation training. Such guidance is currently available only in the traditional contemplative context. With the growing numbers of practitioners trained in secular meditation-based approaches, there also seems to arise an increasing need for secular meditation-based approaches to embrace the long-term view of meditation. This has implications for supporting long-term practitioners trained in the secular context which may require closer collaboration with traditional established contemplative approaches.

Summary

Chapter 2 introduces the main mechanisms underlying changes in the mind and brain resulting from long-term meditation and associated factors such as temporary and lasting effects of meditation, quantity and quality of meditation, formal and informal practice and possible adverse effects of meditation. The chapter starts by discussing the principles of neural plasticity of the brain (changes in brain structure and function resulting from repeated practice) and their modulation by meditation. The chapter then outlines how temporary changes in the mind and brain resulting from meditation practice (state effects) could result in more lasting changes in neural plasticity and personality (trait effects) and how both state and trait changes could interact with natural dispositions towards meditation practice. These considerations lead to a discussion about the research evidence linking more hours of meditation practice with distinct patterns of changes in the brain. However, quality of meditation may also impact on the resulting changes in neural plasticity, health and well-being, even though the evidence base reporting on such effects is currently very limited. Both quantity and quality of meditation are impacted by the distinction between formal and informal practice, which is also rarely considered in the current research on meditation; therefore the next section outlines their differences in the context of embedding meditation in everyday life. The final section of the chapter discussed possible adverse effects of meditation associated with long-term practice; these are currently poorly understood by Western research, but have been clearly outlined in the traditional Buddhist meditation training.

References

Ahissar, M. and Hochstein, S., 2004. The reverse hierarchy theory of visual perceptual learning. *Trends in Cognitive Sciences*, *8*(10), pp. 457–464.

Bezzola, L., Mérillat, S., Gaser, C. and Jäncke, L., 2011. Training-induced neural plasticity in golf novices. *The Journal of Neuroscience*, *31*(35), pp. 12444–12448.

Brefczynski-Lewis, J.A., Lutz, A., Schaefer, H.S., Levinson, D.B. and Davidson, R.J., 2007. Neural correlates of attentional expertise in long-term meditation practitioners. *Proceedings of the National Academy of Sciences*, *104*(27), pp. 11483–11488.

Burg, J.M. and Michalak, J., 2011. The healthy quality of mindful breathing: Associations with rumination and depression. *Cognitive Therapy and Research*, *35*(2), pp. 179–185.

Cahn, B.R. and Polich, J., 2009. Meditation (Vipassana) and the P3a event-related brain potential. *International Journal of Psychophysiology*, *72*(1), pp. 51–60.

Carmody, J. and Baer, R.A., 2008. Relationships between mindfulness practice and levels of mindfulness, medical and psychological symptoms and well-being in a mindfulness-based stress reduction program. *Journal of Behavioral Medicine*, *31*(1), pp. 23–33.

Carmody, J. and Baer, R.A., 2009. How long does a mindfulness-based stress reduction program need to be? A review of class contact hours and effect sizes for psychological distress. *Journal of Clinical Psychology*, *65*(6), pp. 627–638.

Creswell, J.D., Way, B.M., Eisenberger, N.I. and Lieberman, M.D., 2007. Neural correlates of dispositional mindfulness during affect labeling. *Psychosomatic Medicine*, *69*(6), pp. 560–565.

Dickenson, J., Berkman, E.T., Arch, J. and Lieberman, M.D., 2012. Neural correlates of focused attention during a brief mindfulness induction. *Social Cognitive and Affective Neuroscience*, *8*(1), pp. 40–47.

Dobkin, P.L., Irving, J.A. and Amar, S., 2012. For whom may participation in a mindfulness-based stress reduction program be contraindicated? *Mindfulness*, *3*(1), pp. 44–50.

Dorjee, D. and Bowers, J.S., 2012. What can fMRI tell us about the locus of learning? *Cortex*, *48*(4), pp. 509–514.

Draganski, B., Gaser, C., Busch, V., Schuierer, G., Bogdahn, U. and May, A., 2004. Neuroplasticity: Changes in grey matter induced by training. *Nature*, *427*(6972), pp. 311–312.

Flook, L., Smalley, S.L., Kitil, M.J., Galla, B.M., Kaiser-Greenland, S., Locke, J., Ishijima, E. and Kasari, C., 2010. Effects of mindful awareness practices on executive functions in elementary school children. *Journal of Applied School Psychology*, *26*(1), pp. 70–95.

Gampopa, J. and Rinpoche, K.K.G., 1998. *The jewel ornament of liberation*. Trans. Khenpo Konchog Gyaltshen Rinpoche. Ithaca, NY: Snow Lion Publishing.

Grossman, P., 2011. Defining mindfulness by how poorly I think I pay attention during everyday awareness and other intractable problems for psychology's (re) invention of mindfulness: Comment on Brown et al. (2011). *Psychological Assessment*, *23*(4), pp. 1034–1040.

Hanley, A.W., Abell, N., Osborn, D.S., Roehrig, A.D. and Canto, A.I., 2016. Mind the gaps: Are conclusions about mindfulness entirely conclusive? *Journal of Counseling & Development*, *94*(1), pp. 103–113.

Hasenkamp, W. and Barsalou, L.W., 2012. Effects of meditation experience on functional connectivity of distributed brain networks. *Frontiers in Human Neuroscience*, *6*, p. 38.

Herholz, S.C. and Zatorre, R.J., 2012. Musical training as a framework for brain plasticity: Behavior, function, and structure. *Neuron*, *76*(3), pp. 486–502.

Hölzel, B.K., Carmody, J., Evans, K.C., Hoge, E.A., Dusek, J.A., Morgan, L., Pitman, R.K. and Lazar, S.W., 2009. Stress reduction correlates with structural changes in the amygdala. *Social Cognitive and Affective Neuroscience*, *5*(1), pp. 11–17.

Hölzel, B.K., Carmody, J., Vangel, M., Congleton, C., Yerramsetti, S.M., Gard, T. and Lazar, S.W., 2011. Mindfulness practice leads to increases in regional brain gray matter density. *Psychiatry Research: Neuroimaging*, *191*(1), pp. 36–43.

Ilg, R., Wohlschläger, A.M., Gaser, C., Liebau, Y., Dauner, R., Wöller, A., Zimmer, C., Zihl, J. and Mühlau, M., 2008. Gray matter increase induced by practice correlates with task-specific activation: A combined functional and morphometric magnetic resonance imaging study. *The Journal of Neuroscience*, *28*(16), pp. 4210–4215.

Jacobs, T.L., Epel, E.S., Lin, J., Blackburn, E.H., Wolkowitz, O.M., Bridwell, D.A., Zanesco, A.P., Aichele, S.R., Sahdra, B.K., MacLean, K.A. and King, B.G., 2011. Intensive meditation training, immune cell telomerase activity, and psychological mediators. *Psychoneuroendocrinology*, *36*(5), pp. 664–681.

Jha, A.P., Stanley, E.A., Kiyonaga, A., Wong, L. and Gelfand, L., 2010. Examining the protective effects of mindfulness training on working memory capacity and affective experience. *Emotion*, *10*(1), p. 54.

Karpati, F.J., Giacosa, C., Foster, N.E., Penhune, V.B. and Hyde, K.L., 2015. Dance and the brain: A review. *Annals of the New York Academy of Sciences*, *1337*(1), pp. 140–146.

Kuijpers, H.J., Van der Heijden, F.M.M.A., Tuinier, S. and Verhoeven, W.M.A., 2007. Meditation-induced psychosis. *Psychopathology*, *40*(6), pp. 461–464.

Levinson, D.B., Stoll, E.L., Kindy, S.D., Merry, H.L. and Davidson, R.J., 2013. A mind you can count on: Validating breath counting as a behavioral measure of mindfulness. *Frontiers in Psychology*, *5*, pp. 1202–1202.

Li, P., Legault, J. and Litcofsky, K.A., 2014. Neuroplasticity as a function of second language learning: Anatomical changes in the human brain. *Cortex*, *58*, pp. 301–324.

Lustyk, M.K., Chawla, N., Nolan, R. and Marlatt, G.A., 2009. Mindfulness meditation research: Issues of participant screening, safety procedures, and researcher training. *Advances in Mind-Body Medicine*, *24*(1), pp. 20–30.

Lutz, J., Brühl, A.B., Doerig, N., Scheerer, H., Achermann, R., Weibel, A., Jäncke, L. and Herwig, U., 2016. Altered processing of self-related emotional stimuli in mindfulness meditators. *NeuroImage*, *124*, pp. 958–967.

Malinowski, P., 2013. Neural mechanisms of attentional control in mindfulness meditation. *Frontiers in Neuroscience*, 7, pp. 1–11.

May, A., 2011. Experience-dependent structural plasticity in the adult human brain. *Trends in Cognitive Sciences*, *15*(10), pp. 475–482.

Nyklíček, I., Beugen, S. van. and Denollet, J., 2013. Effects of mindfulness-based stress reduction on distressed (Type D) personality traits: A randomized controlled trial. *Journal of Behavioral Medicine*, *36*(4), pp. 361–370.

Rinpoche, P., 1998. *The words of my perfect teacher: A complete translation of a classic introduction to Tibetan Buddhism*. Oxford: Rowman Altamira.

Shapiro, D.H., 1992. Adverse effects of meditation: A preliminary investigation of long-term meditators. *International Journal of Psychosomatics*, *39*(1–4), pp. 62–67.

Shapiro, S.L., Brown, K.W., Thoresen, C. and Plante, T.G., 2011. The moderation of mindfulness-based stress reduction effects by trait mindfulness: Results from a randomized controlled trial. *Journal of Clinical Psychology*, *67*(3), pp. 267–277.

Slagter, H.A., Lutz, A., Greischar, L.L., Francis, A.D., Nieuwenhuis, S., Davis, J.M. and Davidson, R.J., 2007. Mental training affects distribution of limited brain resources. *PLoS Biology*, *5*(6), p. e138.

Tang, Y.Y., Hölzel, B.K. and Posner, M.I., 2015. The neuroscience of mindfulness meditation. *Nature Reviews Neuroscience*, *16*(4), pp. 213–225.

Tang, Y.Y., Ma, Y., Fan, Y., Feng, H., Wang, J., Feng, S., Lu, Q., Hu, B., Lin, Y., Li, J. and Zhang, Y., 2009. Central and autonomic nervous system interaction is altered by short-term meditation. *Proceedings of the National Academy of Sciences*, *106*(22), pp. 8865–8870.

Teper, R., Segal, Z.V. and Inzlicht, M., 2013. Inside the mindful mind how mindfulness enhances emotion regulation through improvements in executive control. *Current Directions in Psychological Science*, *22*(6), pp. 449–454.

Wallace, B.A., 1999. *The four immeasurables: Cultivating a boundless heart*. Ithaca, NY: Snow Lion Publications.

Wallace, B.A., 2006. *The attention revolution: Unlocking the power of the focused mind*. New York: Simon and Schuster.

Wallace, B.A., 2011. *Stilling the mind: Shamatha teachings from Dudjom Lingpa's vajra essence*. New York: Simon and Schuster.

Weisberg, D.S., Keil, F.C., Goodstein, J., Rawson, E. and Gray, J.R., 2008. The seductive allure of neuroscience explanations. *Journal of Cognitive Neuroscience*, *20*(3), pp. 470–477.

Chapter 3

Mindfulness

Mindfulness practice has been popularized over the last three decades in the secular healthcare context as a method of improving health and well-being. There are various conceptualizations of mindfulness in both secular and traditional Buddhist contexts and also marked differences between some of them. In this chapter we will explore some of these approaches to mindfulness and consider their implications for applications and research on the effects of mindfulness in everyday life. We will start by discussing various definitions of mindfulness and approaches to cultivating mindfulness. Then we will turn to neuroscientific evidence regarding the effects of mindfulness on brain function and structure. We will also discuss the possible role of mindfulness in our health and well-being from the perspective of the framework outlined in the first chapter – in terms of self-regulation and existential well-being. Finally, we will explore how mindfulness could be cultivated in everyday life, both in formal and informal practice.

What is mindfulness?

There is no consensus on definitions of mindfulness, with various accounts presented both in secular and Buddhist contexts (Williams and Kabat-Zinn, 2013). However, there are some most commonly applied definitions which we will explore now. In mindfulness-based approaches (MBSR and MBCT) mindfulness is frequently defined as an awareness arising by purposefully paying attention in the present moment with an attitude of non-reactivity, non-judgement and openness (Kabat-Zinn, 2003; Kabat-Zinn, 2013). This definition is based on foundational work of Jon Kabat-Zinn who, together with his colleagues, developed the MBSR course in 1970s as a means to support patients with chronic health problems. The MBCT followed and was largely based on MBSR combined with elements of cognitive behavioural therapy (Teasdale et al., 2000). The MBCT was developed as a treatment particularly intended for recurrent depression (Teasdale, Segal and Williams, 1995) whereas MBSR had from the start a broader client focus in both treatment and prevention of illness.

Kabat-Zinn's definition of mindfulness influenced other conceptualizations of mindfulness in the context of mindfulness-based approaches. One of the first theoretical studies about mechanisms underlying the beneficial effects of mindfulness suggested two core components of mindfulness: attention and attitude (Bishop et al., 2004). The attention component describes the ability to notice thoughts, emotions and sensations, sustain attention on them and shift attention away from distractions. The attitude component relates to the quality of attention in mindfulness which can be characterized by non-reactivity, curiosity and openness. A few years later this model of attention was expanded by an additional component – the intention one brings to the practice of mindfulness (Shapiro et al., 2006). The intention can be simply a wish to engage in mindfulness practice in order to have better health, e.g., to reduce anxiety or have a better sleep, which is likely the case for most participants in secular mindfulness courses. Some participants though may attend the courses in order to deepen their understanding of themselves, which could be termed as 'self-exploration' (Shapiro, 1992).

Definitions of mindfulness in the Buddhist context often describe mindfulness in a narrower sense than in mindfulness-based approaches. Mindfulness (Pāli: sati; Sanskrit: smṛti; Tibetan: trenba) is here defined as a mental faculty which enables sustaining of attention on the meditative object and also entails an element of remembering to stay focused (Wallace, 1999). In Buddhism, mindfulness is typically distinguished from the mental faculty of meta-awareness (Pāli: sampajañña; Sanskrit: samprajanya; Tibetan: shizhin), which monitors for distractions and signals when the practitioner loses focus on the meditation object (Wallace, 1999). Both mindfulness and meta-awareness work together in meditation practice, enabling the practitioner to refine her attention skills. In some accounts of Buddhist psychology (Nyanaponika, 1998), mindfulness is considered a neutral mental faculty. Mindfulness becomes virtuous or non-virtuous based on the motivation and intention the practitioner brings to the mindfulness practice. For example, if mindfulness is applied in meditation to cultivate qualities such as loving kindness and compassion with the intention to become a more caring person, it would be considered virtuous. However, if mindfulness is practiced with the intention of greed, for instance to have more wealth, the mindful activity would be considered non-virtuous.

So the secular and Buddhist approaches seem to both overlap and differ in several regards. Both approaches consider attention as the central characteristic of mindfulness with the secular approaches considering mindfulness to involve a range of attention skills including meta-awareness. In contrast, mindfulness is conceptualized as separate from meta-awareness in the Buddhist approaches we have discussed. In addition, mindfulness is also described in terms of further qualities such as non-judgment, non-reactivity, acceptance and in some cases also loving kindness (friendliness) and intention for the practice in the secular context (Kabat-Zinn, 2003; Shapiro et al., 2006; Vago & Silbersweig, 2012). These qualities are not explicitly discussed as inherent to mindfulness in the Buddhist accounts. However, any training in mindfulness and meta-awareness in the traditional context typically involves cultivation of loving kindness, compassion, rejoicing and equanimity alongside development of mindfulness and meta-awareness. This can be done in separate practices alternating as part of meditation training, e.g., breath-awareness training in mindfulness and meta-awareness alternating with practices developing the emotional qualities.

Other Buddhist approaches develop mindfulness, meta-awareness and the emotional qualities of loving kindness, compassion, rejoicing and equanimity within one type of practice, as is the case of sacred visualization-based meditations in the Tibetan Buddhist tradition. In these practices the meditator trains in sustaining attention on the visualization, often while reciting a mantra, and monitors for distractions away from the visualization. At the same time, the visualizations contain elements which embody qualities of loving kindness, compassion, rejoicing and equanimity. Each visualization practice also starts with development of virtuous motivation and intention for engaging in meditation which is, again, a separate component from mindfulness, but it is cultivated in each meditation session regardless of its specific focus as a necessary pre-requisite for engagement in meditation. This shows that the majority of attitudinal qualities together with intention for mindfulness practice as described in the secular context are considered in Buddhism more general qualities of meditation practice, not inherent to mindfulness.

The broad conceptualization of mindfulness in the secular context has both advantages and disadvantages. One of its advantages is that usage of mindfulness as an overarching construct including various meditation elements might have enabled simplification of the complexity of meditation practices and their more intuitive grasp in secular healthcare and other contexts. At the same time, however, the more inclusive construct of mindfulness led to much terminological confusion in the literature

(Dorjee, 2010) with mindfulness often interpreted as the essential all-inclusive meditation practice. The secular literature on mindfulness often also uses the term 'mindfulness' without distinction as a reference to the practice, underlying psychological or cognitive processes and outcomes of the practice. Here the process could be described as the actual paying of attention combined with noticing distractions whilst applying the attitudes of non-judgment, kindness, curiosity and a particular intention for engaging in the practice. The outcome of mindfulness in this broad conceptualization is often characterized in terms of non-elaborative awareness of sensory experience or as 'direct perception' (e.g., Brown, Ryan and Creswell, 2007) which, confusingly, is a term traditionally used in Buddhism for very advanced states of realizing the nature of mind (Dorjee, 2010).

Such very broad and indistinctive descriptions of mindfulness can lead to marginalization of other meditation practices and also misrepresent the progression of practices, processes and outcomes on the path of long-term meditation training. The marginalization can arise if mindfulness is presented as the meditation practice which includes all essential ingredients of meditation. This may lead to the assumption that there is a limited need for other meditation practices specifically developing emotional qualities of compassion etc., visualization practices, mantra-based practices, devotional practices, energy practices and many other practice types frequently applied in the traditional contemplative context. The different types of practices play specific roles in long-term meditation training; they often build on each other and can also complement each other to enable a practitioner's progress on the contemplative path. The multitude of meditation practices was also developed to accommodate the variety of propensities meditation practitioners bring to their meditation practice; a skilled meditation teacher is able to accommodate these through selection of practices which are most suitable for each practitioner at each stage of their meditation progression (Rinpoche, 1998).

In the traditional Buddhist context mindfulness is considered an essential practice supporting both focused meditation and insight as the two main categories of meditation. Focused meditation practices develop attention skills and Insight (Vipassana) practices aim to cultivate experiential realization of the nature of self (in some Buddhist schools also the nature of reality). Mindfulness and metacognition skills are developed in the focused meditation training which can take on various forms – from breath-focus, through focus on sacred statues, ordinary neutral visual objects such as a pebble or recitation of mantras, to visualization of complex images. Even focused contemplations of topics such as the preciousness of human life can develop mindfulness and metacognition if they are practiced while maintaining focus on the topic and monitoring for distractions in thinking. The refined skills of mindfulness and metacognition are then applied in insight meditation together with other qualities such as virtuous intention, contemplations on impermanence and nature of suffering, emotion qualities of loving kindness, compassion, rejoicing and equanimity etc. These together with contemplative inquiry lead to the insight into the nature of self and reality, but in itself mindfulness practice cannot lead to experiential realization.

How to develop mindfulness?

As part of MBSR or MBCT courses mindfulness training involves eight weekly sessions of 2.5 hours in MBSR and 2 hours in MBCT (Segal, Williams and Teasdale, 2002) which follow a standardized progression of training. The eight sessions are typically preceded by an orientation session and/or individual interviews with those intending to take the course where participants receive detailed information about plans and practice requirements of the course. This can help manage expectations of participants and decrease dropout rates from the courses. The actual training includes practices developing mindfulness of the body (body scan), mindfulness of sounds, mindfulness of thoughts and mental habits (sitting practice) and mindful movement. Training in MBCT also emphasizes development of a decentred perspective on thoughts, sensations and emotions – perceiving them as fleeting mental events rather than solid facts. Some teachers also provide course participants with guided meditation developing acceptance and loving kindness as optional practices. All practices involve detailed verbal guidance by the teacher throughout the meditation with the amount of guidance reducing to some extent as the course progresses and participants become more familiar with the practices. Alongside mindfulness practice, MBSR and MBCT courses also contain education about stress (MBSR) and depression (MBCT), exploration of pleasant and unpleasant experiences, elements of yoga and chi-gong, sharing and inquiry into experiences arising as one progresses through the course etc. Emotional qualities such as loving kindness and compassion are not explicitly trained in MBSR and MBCT, but are considered implicitly communicated through the way the teacher relates to the students and guides practices throughout the course. Intention for engaging in the mindfulness training is also not explicitly developed as part of MBSR and MBCT courses.

Given that both MBSR and MBCT include not only mindfulness practices, but also many other elements, there is the question whether improvements in health and well-being reported from attendance of these courses can actually be attributed to the mindfulness practice as such. A recent study (Williams et al., 2014) addressed this question in a rigorous study with recurrently depressed clients. The study followed a methodologically very strong research design – a randomized controlled format which involved random assignment (to avoid biases associated with participants' treatment preferences) of participants into three groups. The first group received MBCT training together with treatment as usual and the second group received treatment as usual together with training in Cognitive Psychological Education (CPE) – a course which followed the exact length and session format as the MBCT with the exception of mindfulness practices. The third group received only treatment as usual and was considered a control group. The treatment as usual consisted of GP visits and antidepressant prescriptions, appointments with psychiatrists or psychiatric nurses, and individual help from psychologists or psychotherapists. The three groups did not differ in their treatment as usual. Participants in the MBCT and CPE groups after the completion of the formal eight-week training also attended two follow-up classes at six weeks and six months after completion of the course.

The assessments in this study on recurrent depression were conducted before and right after the MBCT and then at 3, 6, 9 and 12 months follow-up (Williams et al., 2014). Interestingly, the findings suggested that both participation in the MBCT and in the CPE significantly decreased the likelihood of depression relapse in comparison to the control group. There were no differences between MBCT and CPE groups, which suggested that the standard format of MBCT can be effective even in the absence of mindfulness practices as such. This is an important finding, which indicates that the health and well-being outcomes of mindfulness-based courses should not be directly attributed to mindfulness practice as such. However, further analyses of participants' characteristics in this study with recurrently depressed participants showed that those with childhood trauma did significantly benefit more from MBCT in comparison to CPE. So the mindfulness practice had distinctive effects in this particular group, which might be due to the decentring, acceptance and compassion elements of the training rather than attention-related core mindfulness skills (Williams et al., 2014). It is also possible that the increased attentional stability resulting from mindfulness training enabled participants to benefit from mindfulness non-specific meditation aspects of the MBCT course cultivating compassion and decentring.

There is limited research evidence on the efficacy of the standard MBSR and MBCT format versus the modified shorter format. Initial evidence suggests that shorter training delivery with fewer sessions and/ or shorter weekly sessions can lead to the same outcomes for participants as the standard longer format (Carmody and Baer, 2009). However, attendees of MBSR and MBCT courses are also required to practice meditation for 45 minutes each day over the eight weeks of training and research findings showed a positive relationship between the amount of home practice and health-related outcomes of the courses. For example, more hours of home practice have been linked to higher increases in well-being scores after MBSR training (Carmody and Baer, 2008). Similarly, more time spent in home practice has been associated with improvements in mood and working memory capacity in military personnel during the stressful pre-deployment period (Jha et al., 2010).

In the clinical context, regular mindfulness practice three or more days a week has been linked to a nearly 50% decrease in the likelihood of depression relapse in comparison to engaging in less than this amount of weekly practice (Crane et al., 2014). Aside from formal training as part of the weekly sessions and guided (recorded) home practice, participants in MBSR and MBCT are also encouraged to engage in daily informal practice of their choice such as mindful walking, mindful eating or taking a shower mindfully. Research linking the amount of informal meditation practice to course outcomes is very limited – the above study on the amount of practice and recurrent depression also assessed possible links between outcomes and informal practice, but did not find any significant relationship.

Examination of long-term effects of MBSR and MBCT has rarely been examined beyond a few months of follow up after the initial training, but initial studies reported encouraging findings. For example, a one-year follow-up of cancer patients who participated in the eight-week MBSR course showed sustained improvements in stress symptoms and reductions in cortisol levels and systolic blood pressure (Carlson et al., 2007). In addition, a three-year follow-up of participants with anxiety disorders showed maintained reductions in anxiety and panic in most of them (Miller, Fletcher and Kabat-Zinn, 1995). Another study which included a three-year follow-up, this time with fibromyalgia patients who initially trained in MBSR, showed sustained reductions in most pain symptoms, anxiety and depression, and improvements in subscales of quality of life (Grossman et al., 2007). However, the participants assessed at follow-up in this study were nearly a half of the original sample, which may have resulted in some evaluation biases such as only those who practiced being willing to fill in the evaluations at the long-term follow-up. Overall, these initial findings are encouraging, but they also raise questions regarding how to best support participants of secular mindfulness-based courses in developing and sustaining a long-term meditation practice which need to be addressed in secular mindfulness teaching.

In the Buddhist context, mindfulness is typically developed alongside metacognition in calm abiding (focused attention or Shamatha) training (Wallace, 1999). The basic principle of the practice is simple – sustaining attention on a neutral or virtuous object for gradually more extensive periods of time while monitoring for distraction and quality of attention. As we have discussed in the previous chapter, the core qualities of attention developed through calm abiding practice are relaxation (release of tension in meditation), stability (maintaining attention on an object continuously) and clarity (vividness or attention to detail as the opposite of dullness) (Wallace, 2006). The training starts with very brief periods of practice (as short as 5 minutes) two or three times a day and the practitioner gradually builds up the ability to practice in longer sessions. In the Tibetan Buddhist tradition each meditation session follows the structure we have described in the previous section – connecting with the lineage and developing motivation/intention for the practice, followed by the practice itself and then dedication of the virtue at the end of the practice.

The development of mindfulness and metacognition through mindfulness typically follows a progression of nine stages (described in detail in Wallace, 2006). These stages are outlined in the context of visualization-based practices which are the most common form of developing mindfulness in the Tibetan Buddhist tradition. The first stage is called 'Mental Placement' and is characterized by the ability to hold the visualization without distraction for a couple of seconds at best. It also takes a longer time, often 10 seconds or more, for the practitioner to realize that her attention wandered away from the meditation object. The attention and metacognition skills become more stable as the practitioner progresses to the second stage, called 'Continuous Placement'. Now the meditator is able to remain focused on the meditation object for about a minute and during that time she does not lose the meditation focus completely even though distraction arises.

The third stage, called 'Patched Placement', is characterized by the ability to focus on the meditation for between 30 minutes and 1 hour, but with periods of distraction, even though the meditator does not completely lose the meditation focus very often. Most of the time when distraction arises the practitioner is able to notice this quickly and readily bring attention back to the meditation object. The fourth stage is called 'Close Placement' and entails more stable focus for longer periods of time, mostly without major distraction. However, at this stage, when distraction due to excessive excitation is greatly decreased, the practitioner is more likely to slip into laxity, drowsiness and dullness. The practitioner may even dose off for a few seconds and then come back to the meditation object.

The fifth stage of Shamatha training is called 'Taming' and mostly involves training in overcoming the drowsiness and laxity in the practice. Up until this stage of mindfulness and metacognition training, the visualization of a meditation object lacks detail and is foggy. Meditation teachers warn that some practitioners may confuse the drowsy dull stability of meditation at this stage with advanced states of meditative stabilization (Wallace, 2006). The main remedy for the dullness and drowsiness is an increase in the clarity of meditation, which is the core of the practice at the Taming stage. Further refinement of attention skills leads to the sixth stage of 'Pacification', during which periods of major dullness and fogginess are very rare while a more subtle sense of laxity still remains. This is countered by further enhancement of clarity in the meditation practice.

'Complete Pacification' is the seventh stage of Shamatha. At this stage even subtle moments of dullness or distraction are noticed through further enhancement of the meta-awareness which supports increased clarity of the visualization. Interestingly, overreliance on meta-awareness can actually interfere with stability of attention at the next stage of 'Single-Pointed Placement'. This is because the practitioner is now able to focus continuously for long periods of time and even subtle distractions or dullness arise very rarely. Hence, monitoring for distraction and quality of practice can itself become a distraction at this stage of enhanced stability and clarity of attention.

The final stage of Shamatha, called 'Balanced Placement', is characterized by the ability to sustain attention without distraction and with clarity continuously for hours. According to Wallace (2006) there is a particular point in the practice when Shamatha is achieved which can be associated with an experience of ecstatic joy resulting from changes in the energies of the body. This experience is transient and is not the aim of training in the Shamatha practice. After the achievement of Shamatha, the practitioner's mind settles in a more stable and subtle state of tranquillity and joy. In the traditional teachings of Shamatha this is the point when the mind is able to fully engage in further inquiry into the nature of self and reality. Some other teachings suggest that full achievement of Shamatha is not required for effective engagement in the Vipassana practice. However, the stability and clarity of mind achieved at the fourth or fifth stage of Shamatha training seems to be the very minimum for progression into the insight practices. Without such stability and clarity the mind is too susceptive to distraction to be able to sustain attention long enough and with enough clarity to support the development of insight.

Training in Shamatha aimed at achieving the highest levels of calm abiding would be typically conducted in a retreat environment. Based on traditional writings, for most practitioners it would take about a year of training in retreat to progress through the stages of Shamatha to the highest levels of balance in mindfulness and metacognition (Wallace, 2006). Whilst this is obviously not possible for many non-monastic practitioners in the West, regular daily practice in Shamatha supported by occasional retreats could also support the development of higher levels of mental stability needed for effective engagement in Vipassana practice. Such training would require not only a commitment to the daily practice, but also adjustments of lifestyle to reduce distractions of various kinds and unhealthy habits (e.g., smoking and drinking alcohol excessively) which can be detrimental to health and well-being. Such lifestyle changes would support cultivation of mindfulness and metacognition not only in the formal daily sessions but also off the cushion in regular daily activities.

Guidance of an experienced meditation teacher who is knowledgeable about the stages of Shamatha training both in theory and own practice is indispensable if one intends to progress into advanced stages of Shamatha. Such guidance may help the practitioner to avoid common pitfalls of stagnation in the training by mistaking mediocre states of stability with advanced stages of Shamatha or even advanced insight. Similarly, the guidance is essential in case of adverse experiences which are in the traditional context considered as part of the path and need to be worked with in a skilful way. Research suggests that such experiences are more likely to arise with long-term meditation practice (Shapiro, 1992).

While in the traditional cultural context of Buddhism there are standard approaches to the training and assessment of meditation teachers, such comprehensive systems of teacher training and evaluation are for the most part not available in the West. This creates a knowledge gap in the Western culture which can easily cause confusion for Buddhist meditation practitioners in determining whether a teacher might be qualified to guide them to the more advanced stages of Shamatha and Vipassana. A simple questioning about the lineage, training and retreat experience of meditation teachers can be helpful in determining the authenticity of their teaching qualification.

For example, in the Tibetan Buddhist tradition it would be expected that a qualified teacher would have received teachings and extensively practiced under the guidance of an established experienced meditation master. In addition, they would have at minimum completed a cycle of preliminary practices either in a three-year meditation retreat or through regular daily practice over several years. An accomplished master would have done meditation training far beyond this initial level of training, including training in further cycles of meditation practices which can vary according to the specific Buddhist school and lineage they trained in. These can, for instance, include cycles of advanced contemplative practices in refining energies of the body such as the Six Yogas of Naropa, or practices with closer focus on Vipassana such as Mahamudra (Kagyu lineage) or Dzogchen (Nyingma lineage).

Qualified guidance of a mindfulness teacher is important in the context of secular meditation training as well. With the fast growing interest in mindfulness-based approaches, training and proper qualifications of mindfulness teachers are of increasing importance. There are several established mindfulness training organizations based at universities in the UK and the USA. In the UK, there is a framework of recommendations to guide teacher training and continuous development (Crane et al., 2012); however, there is no formal regulatory body to safeguard mindfulness training standards. So the burden of ensuring that practitioners receive training from a qualified mindfulness teacher remains on practitioners themselves in the form of questioning the teacher's meditation background and mindfulness training history. In this process basic familiarity with the typical training requirements might be helpful; for example, standard academic training in mindfulness-based approaches at UK institutions would require at least two years of study and practice preceded by at least one year of personal mindfulness practice combined with continuous mindfulness practice and regular mindfulness teaching supervision.

Several avenues of secular mindfulness teacher training seem to require further development from the perspective of supporting mindfulness practitioners in cultivating long-term meditation practice. One of these pertains to qualifications of mindfulness teachers to guide practitioners beyond the eight-week course towards not only sustaining but also further development of their meditation skills. It is possible that the expansion of meditation practice beyond standard MBSR and MBCT training may require a transition into practicing in an established traditional contemplative system. There is currently no clear guidance on how secular mindfulness teachers could handle requests for longer-term mindfulness practice guidance from their course attendees. Another aspect of secular mindfulness teaching which needs further development relates to the adverse experiences in meditation which are more likely to arise with long-term practice. Currently, the application process for attendance of MBSR and MBCT courses involves pre-screening of participants for history of mental illness or current difficulties which could exacerbate as a result of attending MBSR or MBCT training. Further research will be needed to enhance our understanding of the interactions between history of mental health problems and risk of adverse experiences during secular mindfulness training. Both within and outside of the clinical context, support of long-term practitioners of secular mindfulness will require development of clear guidance on dealing with adverse meditation experiences linked to long-term practice in the secular context. It also remains an open question whether secular mindfulness practice which is not strongly grounded in traditional contemplative approaches and motivational/intentional qualities can lead to progression into advanced stages of Shamatha and Vipassana or whether stagnation in practice is inevitable after a certain stage.

Neuroscience of mindfulness

Even though neuroscience research on mindfulness produced interesting findings and some converging evidence over the last decade, inferences from the research results to neurocognitive mechanisms of mindfulness are in many studies problematic. This is because in a lot of cases the term 'mindfulness' is used without distinction for a broad range of meditation studies investigating both secular and Buddhist meditation. For example, a latest review article on neuroscience of mindfulness (Tang, Hölzel and Posner, 2015) combined findings from studies on mindfulness-based approaches with results of studies with Zen meditators, Insight meditators and Tibetan Buddhist Dzogchen practitioners. The review concluded that there is some overlap in brain activation across these studies in regions such as anterior cingulate cortex or anterior insular cortex – this overlap was attributed to the effects of mindfulness. However, such inferences are questionable given the vast differences in types of practices and length of meditation training participants underwent across the different traditions. And even if we look at modulations in brain function and structure in studies which only investigated mindfulness-based approaches, we could not be sure that any overarching pattern of findings is solely due to mindfulness. The reason for this is that the effects of mindfulness in these studies are inseparable from other therapeutic elements of mindfulness courses such as development of self-compassion or decentring. Nevertheless, it is possible to partially bypass these difficulties by zooming in onto studies which investigated the core elements of mindfulness related to different facets of attention.

One of the first studies to investigate neurocognitive changes in attention resulting from MBSR training specifically focused on three attention networks: orienting, alerting and conflict monitoring (Jha, Krompinger and Baime, 2007). Orienting relates to the ability to direct attention and selectively attend to relevant information in the environment; alerting is linked to the ability to sustain a state of vigilance and detect changes in that state; and conflict monitoring prioritizes amongst competing information and tasks. The three networks are associated with different neural substrates (Petersen and Posner, 2012). The findings of the study on the effects of MBSR on the three networks showed improvements in orienting of attention from before to after the MBSR course, suggesting that secular mindfulness training can improve the ability to guide attention and focus more narrowly on the object of meditation (Jha, Krompinger and Baime, 2007).

The same study (Jha, Krompinger and Baime, 2007) also included evaluations in a group of experienced meditators from before to after a one-month retreat during which they trained mostly in focused attention. In contrast to the MBSR course participants, the experienced meditators showed improvements in the alerting network from before to after the retreat. This finding indicated that longer meditation training may further enhance both sustained attention and the ability to notice distractions while focusing on a meditative object. The differential effects in the MBSR group and the experienced meditator group also suggest that improvements in attention abilities may follow a specific pattern of changes with orienting of attention enhanced before alerting attention. Interestingly, this lends partial support to the traditional accounts of Shamatha training where the initial stages of training require repeated redirecting of attention and narrowing of attention focus which could be associated with orienting attention, whereas further progression in Shamatha training targets more subtle abilities of noticing distraction to meditation focus.

In line with these findings, a study which focused on assessment of attention changes in meditators from before to after retreat in Shamatha reported improvements in sustained attention (MacLean et al., 2010). Specifically, the participants were meditators who participated in a three-month retreat during which they trained in breath-focus meditation and also in visualization-based practices and meditations developing loving kindness and compassion. Improvements in their attention were assessed in a reaction-time task before and after the three-month retreat and also compared with a control group of matched meditators not training in a retreat. The findings suggested that the retreat participants were able to perform better on a sustained attention task which required subtle perceptual discrimination, possibly due to enhanced abilities of vigilance and clarity in perceptual discrimination. These findings suggest that the retreat training may have particularly improved the metacognitive element of attention cultivated in Shamatha which would be expected in the more advanced stages of Shamatha training.

However, a study on the effects of MBCT on attention changes in recurrently depressed patients showed that even secular mindfulness training might improve sustained attention abilities (Bostanov et al., 2012). This would contradict the pattern of progression in attention training with meditation proposed in the two previous studies we have discussed (Jha, Krompinger and Baime, 2007; MacLean et al., 2010). Yet, closer investigation of the experimental task used in the study on MBCT reveals that the effects obtained may be better described in terms of improvements in attention orienting and focused attention than sustained attention. Specifically, the study evaluated ERP brain responses (late contingent negative variation (CNV) component) to distractor white noise sounds while participants were asked to practice a breath-focus meditation. The findings revealed negative CNV after MBCT training which indicated that the MBCT participants were less distracted by the white noise than before MBCT training and also in comparison to control participants who did not receive MBCT training. Even though the researchers interpreted the findings in terms of sustained attention and concentration abilities, the task seems to have primarily engaged orienting attention supporting selective attention to the breath and was perhaps less demanding on vigilance and metacognitive awareness. So the results might be actually aligned with the expected progression of improvements in attention skills expected in Shamatha training.

Findings in all the studies we have mentioned in this section so far may have, however, been impacted by several factors. One of the factors is the actual motivation and effort to perform well after meditation training; this pertains both to training in the secular and traditional meditation context. In other words, those who receive meditation training may expect that their attention improves with meditation training and as a result may 'try harder' during the testing session after meditation training. The contribution of increased effort to results reporting improvements in attention after mindfulness/meditation training was partially supported in a study which tried to manipulate the motivation of participants to perform better (Jensen et al., 2012). While one group of participants was tested before and after eight weeks of standard MBSR training, the control group, which did not receive meditation training, was tested at the same two time points but further divided into two control subgroups at the second time point (post-test). One of the control subgroups was told that if they showed improved performance at the second time point they would receive a financial reward. The other control subgroup was not offered any financial reward. Comparisons of results in reaction time-based attention tasks between the MBSR group and control participants who received financial reward did not reveal any significant differences in performance. Both the MBSR group and the reward control subgroup performed better than the control subgroup which did not receive a financial reward. These findings indicated that the motivation to perform better might be a significant contributing factor to results reporting improvements in attention after meditation training.

Another possible factor which could have impacted on the findings in the studies we have discussed relates to the multifaceted nature of training in mindfulness-based approaches which involves not only training in mindfulness and metacognitive awareness, but also in acceptance and self-compassion, and in the case of MBCT also in decentring. The same point can also apply in many cases to Buddhist retreat training; for example, the study on the three-month Shamatha retreat mentioned that the meditation training also involved visualization practices and practices developing loving kindness and compassion (MacLean et al., 2010). So it is difficult to infer with certainty whether the attention effects reported in these studies were mostly due to the attention training which is at the core of mindfulness and metacognitive awareness skills or also due to other elements of the mindfulness/meditation training.

To dissociate the effects of the other practices from actual training in mindfulness and meta-awareness, Moore et al. (2012) conducted a study which involved only 3-hours of initial instruction in mindfulness followed by daily 10-minute-long practice of breath-focus for 16 weeks. With the exception of the initial session, the study did not involve regular group meetings and in this way eliminated group practice and sharing of experience in a group as contributing factors to possible changes in attention. The study also only provided instructions on the practice of breath-focus (practiced with an attitude of non-reactivity), thus eliminating possible impact of other meditation practices on the results. Changes in attention were evaluated using ERPs in an established task (Stroop task) which assesses attention control. While there were no significant effects after eight weeks of practice, differences between the meditation and control groups emerged at 16 weeks. The meditation group showed significantly more negative amplitudes of ERP responses associated with focused attention and also reduced responses indexed by an ERP component (P3b) sensitive to allocation of attention resources. Together these findings suggested that the brief daily meditation training improved focused attention and attention control abilities of the participants. This result is noteworthy both given the selective training in breath-focus (and no other meditation practice) and given the short amount of daily practice participants were asked to do. In addition, attention effort was less likely to contribute to the findings since no effects were obtained at eight weeks and no differences in behavioural (reaction time and accuracy) performance of the meditation and control group participants were found at any of the three time points.

Looking closer at the attention mechanisms involved in mindfulness and meta-awareness training, one model described a cycle of attention processes including sustaining attention on a meditation object, distraction, noticing of distraction and shifting attention back to the meditation object (Hasenkamp et al., 2012). This progression of attention processes was supported by an fMRI investigation in which experienced meditators practiced a breath-focus meditation and reported moments when they got distracted. The researchers analyzed brief time sequences preceding and following the distraction reports. The analyses revealed a distinct pattern of brain activation associated with sustained attention on the breath, distraction and noticing distraction plus shifting of attention back to the breath (Hasenkamp et al., 2012).

Another model proposed further elaboration of these stages by disengaging from the distraction. The model also suggested that each of the stages can be associated with activation of a specific attention network, progressing respectively from alerting network to default mode network, salience network, executive network and orienting network (Malinowski, 2013). We have described the orienting, alerting and executive (conflict-monitoring) networks earlier in this section; the default mode network is usually activated during moments of distraction (off-task activity) and the salience network supports monitoring for and noticing distraction. However, none of the networks work in complete separation from the other networks and there is also certain neural overlap between them. There is particularly extensive discussion about the overlap and differences between the executive, orienting and salience networks without a broad agreement amongst researchers.

As we have seen in this section, research in neuroscience of mindfulness produced many interesting findings over the last decade and a half. The main tasks for future research in this area are entangled with the definitional challenges of the concept of mindfulness. If mindfulness is defined in terms of attention, meta-awareness and non-reactivity, such research should primarily focus on investigating these aspects of mindfulness. If mindfulness is defined more broadly, including intention and a range of emotional qualities such as acceptance, kindness etc., the investigations become more complex and it also becomes more difficult to distinguish between contributions of the different dimensions of mindfulness to the outcomes. For instance, one of the recent reviews on neural mechanisms of mindfulness included factors such as exposure, memory mechanisms (extinction and reconsolidation of memories), reappraisal (changes in ways we think about experience) and perspective on the self (Hölzel et al., 2011). These seem to be possible mechanisms mediating outcomes of mindfulness-based approaches and other types of meditation training which include mindfulness. However, it is not straightforward to link the mechanism to the development of mindfulness as such, without other practices or aspects of training in MBSR, MBCT or different aspects of more traditional training. Accordingly, clarifying the construct of mindfulness together with other contributing factors and practices in the varied contexts in which it is applied would greatly facilitate further research in the neuroscience of mindfulness.

Mindfulness, self-regulation and existential well-being

Chapter 1 introduced a framework for further research on meditation which suggested that meditation practice modifies the metacognitive self-regulatory capacity (MSRC) of the mind and modes of existential awareness (MEA). Both the MSRC and MEA are further modulated by the motivation/intention we bring to meditation practice and by the context of meditation practice (secular or religious, monastic or other ordained, informal or retreat etc.). Within this framework, mindfulness would be considered a practice targeting the development of MSRC, particularly attention and meta-awareness skills together with an attitude of non-reactivity (Dorjee, 2016). Such characterization of mindfulness is more narrow than the conceptualizations of mindfulness in MBSR or MBCT because it does not equate mindfulness with intention of meditation practice, a mode of awareness or a range of emotion qualities such as acceptance, kindness etc. The definition of mindfulness in terms of changes in non-reactive attention and metacognition as the core processes of MSRC is at the same time broader than some Buddhist accounts of mindfulness (mentioned earlier in this chapter) which single out meta-awareness as a separate mental faculty.

If mindfulness is defined in terms of non-reactive attention and meta-awareness, this highlights the essential contribution of mindfulness to any meditation practice. At the same time, such a definition points to the central role of mindfulness in the development of self-regulation as one of the two core pillars of well-being. Indeed, mindfulness is indispensable in both Shamatha practices, which aim to develop attention stability and control, and in Vipassana practices, which apply refined non-reactive attention and metacognition abilities in examining the nature of self, mind and reality. Research findings suggest that training targeting mindfulness as such (non-reactive breath-focus without other elements included in MBSR and MBCT) can enhance core capacities of attention orienting and attention control as would be expected (Moore et al., 2012; Malinowski et al., 2015), whilst the current evidence on the effects of MBSR and MBCT on core attention-related self-regulatory skills is currently mixed (Lao et al., 2016).

However, training in mindfulness (defined in terms of non-reactive attention and meta-awareness) is most likely insufficient in producing strong health-conducive changes in emotion regulation and well-being. For such effects to emerge, mindfulness practice needs to be applied together with, or as part of, practices targeting development of acceptance, adaptive emotion regulation strategies and emotion qualities of loving kindness, compassion, rejoicing and equanimity. This is supported by findings from studies mentioned above which applied training in mindfulness without other elements such as group therapy, practices of acceptance, inquiry into mental habits, education about stress or cultivation of decentring which are present in MBSR and MBCT. Indeed, the studies on selective effects of mindfulness (Moore et al., 2012; Malinowski et al., 2015) found improvements in orienting and attention control of practitioners, but they did not find enhancements in their well-being or emotion regulation. Such effects are further supported by findings from clinical research which reported that both mindfulness and self-compassion mediated outcomes in recurrently depressed participants who trained in MBCT, and self-compassion particularly mediated the decoupling between reactivity of depressive thinking and poor patient outcomes (Kuyken et al., 2010). This highlights the importance of not equating the effects of mindfulness with the effects of MBSR or MBCT since mindfulness practice may not be solely responsible for the health and well-being enhancing effects of these interventions.

A similar point can be made about the relationship between mindfulness and MEA. The stability and control of non-reactive attention together with meta-awareness as the core components of MSRC developed in mindfulness practice can be considered essential pre-requisites for shifts in MEA. However, mindfulness cannot be equated with these changes in existential awareness which arise as a result of multiple factors including the development of mindfulness, motivation/intention for practice, development of emotional qualities of loving kindness, compassion, rejoicing and equanimity together with targeted experiential exploration of the mind in the process of inquiry. Interestingly, cultivation of decentring, which is one of the initial shifts in MEA, is considered the core mechanism underlying the beneficial effects of MBSR and MBCT on anxiety and depression (Bieling et al., 2012; Hoge et al., 2015). Yet again, this is likely the result of complex training in MBSR and MBCT, not mindfulness practices as such.

Hence, an essential task of future research on mindfulness seems to be in disentangling the contribution of mindfulness and other elements of training in MBSR and MBCT to the well-being supporting effects of these interventions. This would enable us to better understand the complex interplay between mindfulness as a core meditation practice enhancing attention stability, attention control and meta-awareness and other meditation practices. Based on such understanding, we might be better able to tailor meditation-based training to enhance the health and well-being of people with varied pre-existing propensities and conditions. This finer-grained approach to mindfulness research and application may lead to further understanding of the role mindfulness plays in long-term effects of meditation, both in terms of its supportive effects and limitations.

A day of mindfulness practice

The preceding discussion shows how both traditional and modern accounts of mindfulness consider mindfulness a part of any meditation practice. Therefore, development of mindfulness is integral to the myriad of different meditation practices and is often considered one of the first steps in meditation training. Accordingly, mindfulness can be developed in many different ways, breath-focus being a common approach in secular meditation-based programmes and Theravada Buddhist schools. Other approaches include visualizations-based practices and mantra recitation, focusing on a visual object (either sacred object or any neural object such as a point on the ground or a pebble), focusing on sounds etc. Mindfulness can also be developed in more discursive meditation practices, for example, in focused contemplation on a certain topic (e.g., preciousness of human life or nature of suffering) as long as the contemplations involve elements of sustained attention on the topic, monitoring of distraction and non-reactive control of attention which helps return attention back to the topic of meditation. However, discursive mindfulness meditation of this type is unlikely to lead to high levels of stability described in the Shamatha training due to elaborative verbal (even if silent speech) nature of these practices.

Mindfulness practice can be embedded into our everyday activities to support the connection between the effects of our formal practice and everyday functioning and to increase the quantity and quality of our mindfulness practice. Exploring ways to spend a usual day mindfully, we can start in the morning right after we wake up by remembering the motivation/intention for the day. This is particularly important in the Buddhist context where motivation/intention gives direction to all meditation practice. After setting the motivation for the day, we can do a brief mindfulness practice which can take on different forms depending on the context of our practice. In the secular context, the practice might simply involve attending to the sensations in our body, for instance by doing a brief body scan as we are still lying in the bed or as we sit up. In the Tibetan Buddhist context, the mindfulness practice might be a set of visualization and mantra practices, often those focusing on taking refuge and cultivating compassion for all beings. The meditations can also include brief contemplations on topics such as impermanence, opportunities of the day to develop our meditation practice and reminders about different forms of suffering and a path towards liberation from suffering. Some practitioners may prefer, and be able to engage in, a longer and more formal meditation session on the cushion. Whatever the duration of this initial morning practice, whether 5 minutes or 1 hour, developing a regular routine of waking up in a more settled meditative way may contribute to our well-being.

The initial more formal mindfulness practice right after we wake up may be followed by informal practices while we are engaging in the morning routines. Almost any of these activities can be turned into a mindfulness practice if we stay in the present moment focusing on the activity at hand while regularly monitoring sensations, emotions and thoughts in our mind and body. This would involve noticing when we are getting tense and feel pressed for time and pausing for a moment, or noticing moments of contentment and savouring those. It might be helpful to select a couple of activities from the morning routines during which we engage in mindfulness – it might be tooth brushing, making a tea or coffee, having breakfast or getting dressed. Meditators practicing in the Buddhist context may apply a slightly different approach, where, for example, they use everyday routines as reminders of contemplative topics such as impermanence or motivation for the day, or they can recite silently a mantra or do visualizations during some of the morning activities. They may also mindfully engage in loving kindness and compassion practices which we will discuss in the next chapter.

These practices can continue while commuting to work and can become a useful way to turn a dull everyday activity into a refreshing mental practice. At work, mindfulness can be practiced while working by staying present with the task at hand and reducing distractions if possible. Some of the distractions may be inevitable, other distractions are self-initiated – for example, many of us repetitively check e-mails while engaging in a task even when it is not necessary. We can also practice meta-awareness by noticing when we start to ruminate about past or future activities which are not relevant to the task at hand, and then gently return our attention back to the task. A Buddhist practitioner can also use moments of distraction as a reminder of some aspect of their practice, whether it is a contemplative topic such as loving kindness or impermanence or devotional practice. It can also be particularly helpful to build in a brief break every hour, or at any other regular interval that is possible, and use these breaks for short 2–5-minute meditation practices. These could involve mindful stretching, mindful attention to the breath or the body, listening mindfully to sounds or, in the Buddhist context, doing a brief visualization or compassion practice. The key element of mindfulness practice here is to remember these little meditation breaks, staying present while doing the meditations and monitoring for distractions.

Lunch break can be another opportunity to practice mindfulness, from walking mindfully while getting the meal, to eating the meal mindfully instead of multi-tasking while eating or eating the food while planning the tasks for the afternoon. Depending on what is possible, lunchtime might be also an opportunity to engage in a short practice of 3–10 minutes which might be refreshing and help us engage our attention during the afternoon in a more balanced and less tense and exhausting way. During the afternoon, we can apply the same principles as in the morning: staying present on tasks, reducing distractions and introducing short mindfulness practice breaks. For example, we can use a coffee break for a brief mindfulness practice – start by walking down the corridor while noticing the movement of our body and placement of our feet, staying present while making the tea, noticing the smell and taste of the tea while drinking etc. We can also try to include brief afternoon breaks to check for tension in our body and relax or stretch if needed. A meditator practicing in a traditional meditation context can use the tea break for gratitude practice or to do focused practice on a sacred object, mantra or visualization.

The commute from work can again be used to settle the mind and body, perhaps returning to the mind and body in the present moment after a busy afternoon. Or it can be an opportunity to do other calm abiding practices on the go, by focusing on sounds or any neutral visual object in the environment. Buddhist practitioners can use the time to refocus on contemplative topics of their practice, do devotional practices or visualizations. After returning home, preparation of an evening meal and talking with family can also be opportunities to stay in the moment and practice mindfulness without the need to ruminate about what happened at work or plan for the next day. Engaging with a family in a mindful way may simply mean giving them full attention and being aware of our responses and their feelings, thoughts, expressions etc. Meal time can again be an opportunity to practice focus on the senses and also being fully present with others. In the Buddhist context the meal time can be also an opportunity for practicing generosity, gratitude, loving kindness and compassion together with a brief visualization meditation.

In the evening, mindful approach can enable us to be more aware of our choices of spending the time. We may notice that we have a habit of watching TV programmes or doing some activities which are not necessary or helpful to our well-being. We may change our choices instead. We can also choose to do further formal meditation practice, a brief one or longer one, according to what is possible and how we want to engage with our meditation practice. It might be that mindfulness practice helps us to get to sleep in the evening or it might be that we practice for spiritual reasons and the formal practice in the evening is an opportunity to reflect and to do a deeper meditation practice. A Buddhist practitioner would typically end the day by reflecting on her practice during the day and dedicating virtue accumulated during the day for further progress on the path and for liberation of all beings from suffering.

Mindfulness from a long-term practice perspective

Mindfulness is currently the most popular and most investigated meditation practice. Yet, interpretation of cumulative findings from studies on mindfulness is greatly undermined by the lack of differentiation between mindfulness and other contemplative practices, in addition to the lack of distinction between effects of secular mindfulness-based approaches which have many therapeutic elements and effects of mindfulness practice as such. In neuroscience research, review studies often combine results from secular MBSR and MBCT training with findings from meditators trained in various Buddhist schools. This makes the conclusions of such studies about overarching brain patterns associated with mindfulness problematic. Nevertheless, findings from research which tried to dissociate effects of mindfulness practice from other contributory factors documented improvements in attention control, orienting of attention and efficient use of attention resources in general. However, such training restricted to mindfulness practice did not result in significant improvements in emotion regulation and well-being. This suggests that not only mindfulness but also other practices and factors contribute to the health-enhancing effects of MBSR and MBCT or traditional meditation training.

From the perspective of the framework proposed in Chapter 1, mindfulness could be considered an essential element of any meditation practice and training in mindfulness particularly targets the development of non-reactive attention and meta-awareness. However, mindfulness is not to be equated with MEA such as decentring which arise only if mindfulness is practiced together with training in other qualities including compassion combined with the development of motivation/intention and contemplative inquiry. According to this framework, future research needs to carefully distinguish between the outcomes of mindfulness practice and outcomes of mindfulness-based approaches which include many other therapeutic elements. Such refinement of our theoretical understanding of mindfulness may support more focused research on mindfulness and other practices. It may also support development of methods and approaches which support long-term meditation practice with implications for how meditation-based techniques are applied in healthcare, education and other areas.

Summary

Chapter 3 is the first to consider a specific meditation practice from the perspective of developing long-term meditation practice embedded in everyday activities. Mindfulness, as a necessary pre-requisite for other meditation practices, is the most suitable starting point for cultivating long-term meditation. The chapter considers the similarities and differences between secular and Buddhist notions of mindfulness and particularly focuses on questions about long-term meditation practice resulting from secular training in mindfulness-based approaches. It is highlighted that different conceptualizations of mindfulness may also be linked to different neurocognitive underpinnings of the practices. Finally, the chapter discusses how the new framework of contemplative psychology outlined in Chapter 1 could provide the necessary theoretical grounding for conceptualizing therapeutic effects of long-term mindfulness practice, leading to new possibilities for contemplative psychotherapy.

References

Bieling, P.J., Hawley, L.L., Bloch, R.T., Corcoran, K.M., Levitan, R.D., Young, L.T., MacQueen, G.M. and Segal, Z.V., 2012. Treatment-specific changes in decentering following mindfulness-based cognitive therapy versus antidepressant medication or placebo for prevention of depressive relapse. *Journal of Consulting and Clinical Psychology, 80*(3), pp. 365–372.

Bishop, S.R., Lau, M., Shapiro, S., Carlson, L., Anderson, N.D., Carmody, J., Segal, Z.V., Abbey, S., Speca, M., Velting, D. and Devins, G., 2004. Mindfulness: A proposed operational definition. *Clinical Psychology: Science and Practice, 11*(3), pp. 230–241.

Bostanov, V., Keune, P.M., Kotchoubey, B. and Hautzinger, M., 2012. Event-related brain potentials reflect increased concentration ability after mindfulness-based cognitive therapy for depression: A randomized clinical trial. *Psychiatry Research, 199*(3), pp. 174–180.

Brown, K.W., Ryan, R.M. and Creswell, J.D., 2007. Mindfulness: Theoretical foundations and evidence for its salutary effects. *Psychological Inquiry, 18*(4), pp. 211–237.

Carlson, L.E., Speca, M., Faris, P. and Patel, K.D., 2007. One year pre–post intervention follow-up of psychological, immune, endocrine and blood pressure outcomes of mindfulness-based stress reduction (MBSR) in breast and prostate cancer outpatients. *Brain, Behavior, and Immunity, 21*(8), pp. 1038–1049.

Carmody, J. and Baer, R.A., 2008. Relationships between mindfulness practice and levels of mindfulness, medical and psychological symptoms and well-being in a mindfulness-based stress reduction program. *Journal of Behavioral Medicine, 31*(1), pp. 23–33.

Carmody, J. and Baer, R.A., 2009. How long does a mindfulness-based stress reduction program need to be? A review of class contact hours and effect sizes for psychological distress. *Journal of Clinical Psychology, 65*(6), pp. 627–638.

Crane, C., Crane, R.S., Eames, C., Fennell, M.J., Silverton, S., Williams, J.M.G. and Barnhofer, T., 2014. The effects of amount of home meditation practice in mindfulness based cognitive therapy on hazard of relapse to depression in the staying well after depression trial. *Behaviour Research and Therapy, 63*, pp. 17–24.

Crane, R.S., Soulsby, J.G., Kuyken, W., Williams, J.M.G., Eames, C., Bartley, T., Cooper, C., Evans, A., Fennell, M.J., Gold, E. and Mardula, J., 2012. *The Bangor, Exeter & Oxford Mindfulness-Based Interventions Teaching Assessment Criteria*. Unpublished manuscript.

Dorjee, D., 2010. Kinds and dimensions of mindfulness: Why it is important to distinguish them. *Mindfulness, 1*(3), pp. 152–160.

Dorjee, D., 2016. Defining contemplative science: The metacognitive self-regulatory capacity of the mind, context of meditation practice and modes of existential awareness. *Frontiers in Psychology*, 7, pp. 1–15.

Grossman, P., Tiefenthaler-Gilmer, U., Raysz, A. and Kesper, U., 2007. Mindfulness training as an intervention for fibromyalgia: Evidence of postintervention and 3-year follow-up benefits in well-being. *Psychotherapy and Psychosomatics*, *76*(4), pp. 226–233.

Hasenkamp, W., Wilson-Mendenhall, C.D., Duncan, E. and Barsalou, L.W., 2012. Mind wandering and attention during focused meditation: A fine-grained temporal analysis of fluctuating cognitive states. *Neuroimage*, *59*(1), pp. 750–760.

Hoge, E.A., Bui, E., Goetter, E., Robinaugh, D.J., Ojserkis, R.A., Fresco, D.M. and Simon, N.M., 2015. Change in decentering mediates improvement in anxiety in mindfulness-based stress reduction for generalized anxiety disorder. *Cognitive Therapy and Research*, *39*(2), pp. 228–235.

Hölzel, B.K., Lazar, S.W., Gard, T., Schuman-Olivier, Z., Vago, D.R. and Ott, U., 2011. How does mindfulness meditation work? Proposing mechanisms of action from a conceptual and neural perspective. *Perspectives on Psychological Science*, *6*(6), pp. 537–559.

Jensen, C.G., Vangkilde, S., Frokjaer, V. and Hasselbalch, S.G., 2012. Mindfulness training affects attention: Or is it attentional effort? *Journal of Experimental Psychology: General*, *141*(1), p. 106.

Jha, A.P., Krompinger, J. and Baime, M.J., 2007. Mindfulness training modifies subsystems of attention. *Cognitive, Affective, & Behavioral Neuroscience*, *7*(2), pp. 109–119.

Jha, A.P., Stanley, E.A., Kiyonaga, A., Wong, L. and Gelfand, L., 2010. Examining the protective effects of mindfulness training on working memory capacity and affective experience. *Emotion*, *10*(1), p. 54.

Kabat-Zinn, J., 2003. Mindfulness-based interventions in context: Past, present, and future. *Clinical Psychology: Science and Practice*, *10*(2), pp. 144–156.

Kabat-Zinn, J., 2013. *Full catastrophe living, revised edition: How to cope with stress, pain and illness using mindfulness meditation*. London: Piatkus.

Kuyken, W., Watkins, E., Holden, E., White, K., Taylor, R.S., Byford, S., Evans, A., Radford, S., Teasdale, J.D. and Dalgleish, T., 2010. How does mindfulness-based cognitive therapy work? *Behaviour Research and Therapy*, *48*(11), pp. 1105–1112.

Lao, S.A., Kissane, D. and Meadows, G., 2016. Cognitive effects of MBSR/MBCT: A systematic review of neuropsychological outcomes. *Consciousness and Cognition*, *45*, pp. 109–123.

MacLean, K.A., Ferrer, E., Aichele, S.R., Bridwell, D.A., Zanesco, A.P., Jacobs, T.L., King, B.G., Rosenberg, E.L., Sahdra, B.K., Shaver, P.R. and Wallace, B.A., 2010. Intensive meditation training improves perceptual discrimination and sustained attention. *Psychological Science*, *21*(6), pp. 829–839.

Malinowski, P., 2013. Neural mechanisms of attentional control in mindfulness meditation. *Frontiers in Neuroscience*, *7*, pp. 1–11.

Malinowski, P., Moore, A.W., Mead, B.R. and Gruber, T., 2015. Mindful aging: The effects of regular brief mindfulness practice on electrophysiological markers of cognitive and affective processing in older adults. *Mindfulness*, *8*(1), pp. 78–94.

Miller, J.J., Fletcher, K. and Kabat-Zinn, J., 1995. Three-year follow-up and clinical implications of a mindfulness meditation-based stress reduction intervention in the treatment of anxiety disorders. *General Hospital Psychiatry*, *17*(3), pp. 192–200.

Moore, A.W., Gruber, T., Derose, J. and Malinowski, P., 2012. Regular, brief mindfulness meditation practice improves electrophysiological markers of attentional control. *Frontiers in Human Neuroscience*, *6*, p. 18.

Nyanaponika, 1998. *Abhidhamma studies: Buddhist explorations of consciousness and time*. New York: Simon and Schuster.

Petersen, S.E. and Posner, M.I., 2012. The attention system of the human brain: 20 years after. *Annual Review of Neuroscience*, *35*, p. 73.

Rinpoche, P., 1998. *The words of my perfect teacher: A complete translation of a classic introduction to Tibetan Buddhism*. Oxford: Rowman Altamira.

Segal, Z.V., Williams, J.M.G. and Teasdale, J.D., 2002. *Mindfulness based cognitive therapy for depression: A new approach to preventing relapse*. New York: Guilford Press.

Shapiro, D.H., 1992. A preliminary study of long-term meditators: Goals, effects, religious orientation, cognitions. *The Journal of Transpersonal Psychology*, *24*(1), p. 23.

Shapiro, S.L., Carlson, L.E., Astin, J.A. and Freedman, B., 2006. Mechanisms of mindfulness. *Journal of Clinical Psychology*, *62*(3), pp. 373–386.

Tang, Y.Y., Hölzel, B.K. and Posner, M.I., 2015. The neuroscience of mindfulness meditation. *Nature Reviews Neuroscience*, *16*(4), pp. 213–225.

Teasdale, J.D., Segal, Z.V. and Williams, J.M.G., 1995. How does cognitive therapy prevent depressive relapse and why should attentional control (mindfulness) training help? *Behaviour Research and Therapy*, *33*(1), pp. 25–39.

Teasdale, J.D., Segal, Z.V., Williams, J.M.G., Ridgeway, V.A., Soulsby, J.M. and Lau, M.A., 2000. Prevention of relapse/recurrence in major depression by mindfulness-based cognitive therapy. *Journal of Consulting and Clinical Psychology*, *68*(4), p. 615.

Vago, D.R. and Silbersweig, D.A., 2012. Self-awareness, self-regulation, and self-transcendence (S-ART): A framework for understanding the neurobiological mechanisms of mindfulness. *Frontiers in Human Neuroscience*, *6*, p. 296.

Wallace, B.A., 1999. The Buddhist tradition of Samatha: Methods for refining and examining consciousness. *Journal of Consciousness Studies*, *6*(2–3), pp. 175–187.

Wallace, B.A., 2006. *The attention revolution: Unlocking the power of the focused mind*. New York: Simon and Schuster.

Williams, J.M.G., Crane, C., Barnhofer, T., Brennan, K., Duggan, D.S., Fennell, M.J., Hackmann, A., Krusche, A., Muse, K., Von Rohr, I.R. and Shah, D.,

2014. Mindfulness-based cognitive therapy for preventing relapse in recurrent depression: A randomized dismantling trial. *Journal of Consulting and Clinical Psychology*, *82*(2), p. 275.

Williams, J.M.G. and Kabat-Zinn, J., 2013. *Mindfulness: Diverse perspectives on its meaning, origins and applications*. Abingdon: Routledge.

Chapter 4

Compassion and related qualities

Development of compassion is central to Mahāyāna Buddhism – one of two major approaches within Buddhism which includes Tibetan Buddhism, Zen Buddhism, Chinese Buddhism and some other traditions. Mahāyāna schools recognize various levels of compassion and outline a progression of realization a practitioner goes through when engaging in the long-term practice of compassion. In this traditional context cultivation of compassion together with qualities of loving kindness, rejoicing and equanimity could be considered as the bridge between calm abiding Shamatha practices and Vipassana practices developing insight into the nature of self and reality. Meditations on compassion and the related qualities are typically practiced alongside training in mindfulness and meta-awareness, but after their development and refinement these qualities are maintained and ever present throughout the Vipassana training. In Tibetan Buddhism, the highest level of compassion, unconditional non-conceptual compassion, is considered an integral part of experiencing the most advanced levels of insight.

In the Western context of meditation-based therapeutic approaches, compassion is the core concept in compassion-focused therapy (Gilbert, 2005). Self-compassion (Neff, 2003) is another construct which builds on traditional Buddhist accounts of compassion, even though it primarily emphasizes the importance of developing a compassionate attitude towards our own experience, thoughts, feelings and habits. Within MBSR and MBCT courses, compassion training is not explicit; foundational qualities of compassion are cultivated implicitly in the way the teacher engages with the participants in the courses and provides meditation guidance. However, some MBSR teachers provide their course attendees with optional guided practices in loving kindness, which is a quality related to compassion.

In this chapter, we will in detail explore the theory, applications and mechanisms of compassion and related practices of loving kindness, rejoicing and equanimity starting with definitions and descriptions of these in the Buddhist and Western scientific contexts. This will be followed by an outline of specific meditation practices which cultivate compassion and related qualities in the Buddhist context. We will then discuss possible neurocognitive mechanisms of compassion and loving kindness. Considering the potential of these practices in supporting our well-being more broadly, we will then examine their place in the framework of metacognitive self-regulatory capacity (MSRC) and modes of existential awareness (MEA) outlined in Chapter 1. The chapter will conclude with practical suggestions on how to embed these practices in both formal and informal meditation in everyday life from a long-term perspective of meditation training.

What is compassion? A Buddhist perspective

While in the Western context we may think about compassion as an emotion, Buddhist languages including Pāli, Sanskrit and Tibetan (Ekman et al., 2005) don't have a word equivalent to what we mean by 'emotion'. So compassion is not considered an emotion in the Buddhist psychology (Pāli: Abhidhamma; Sanskrit: Abhidharma). Buddhist considerations about the mind and behaviour are firmly grounded in ethics and a long-term view of health and well-being. Accordingly, the states, faculties and processes of the mind are first and foremost defined in terms of whether they lead to harm (non-virtue) or genuine happiness (virtue). In this way, Mahāyāna Yogacara Abhidharma of the Tibetan Buddhist tradition recognizes anger, craving, ignorance/delusion, pride, afflictive doubt and afflictive views (Goleman, 2003) as the main afflictive states. In contrast, examples of wholesome mental states include conscientiousness, regard for consequence, non-attachment, non-hatred and diligence. Compassion, together with mental states of loving kindness, sympathetic joy and equanimity are core wholesome mental states which are emphasized and explicitly developed as part of the Mahāyāna Buddhist path. They are together termed 'the four immeasurables' (Pāli: appamaññā; Sanskrit: apramāṇa; Tibetan: tsad med zhi).

Compassion in the Buddhist Mahāyāna context can be described as connecting with suffering (of others and oneself) and a genuine wish for freedom from suffering. The connecting element of compassion involves courage to see suffering rather than avoidance or denial of it which can be the habitual initial response. We can have a tendency to avoid connecting with suffering because we associate the experience of pain, sadness and heaviness with it. However, compassion has a different quality; the sense of sadness which arises in compassion is intertwined with a sense of hope and readiness to help. It is also connected with the recognition of the ordinary way of being as a way of suffering with its deeper roots in the afflictions of the mind and a key to freedom from suffering in recognizing the nature of our mind. Compassion also has the qualities of freshness, authenticity and opportunity for change. It motivates us to do what we can to help in the face of suffering.

In the West, compassion can sometimes be perceived with a sense of cynicism which may arise from us perceiving the notion of helping alleviate suffering whenever we see it as an idealistic and ignorant attitude since it seems clearly unachievable. This view is grounded in a somewhat limited notion of both suffering and the possible help we can provide to those who suffer. In the Western culture suffering is typically considered as a lack of resources – not having enough food, shelter or care. From the Buddhist perspective these obvious forms of suffering extend much further to mental suffering of affliction where even those of us who have all the necessities of existence can experience deep suffering of existential confusion, anger, greed, unhealthy self-focus etc. With an attitude of genuine compassion we more readily engage in the usual ways of reducing suffering such as contributing to charitable causes or providing food, shelter and care whenever we can. From the Buddhist perspective our ways of helping can extend beyond these, into meditation practices in which we intentionally connect with the suffering and wish for freedom of suffering. Another way of helping is teaching others ways to reduce their suffering through meditation.

Importantly, genuine compassion has an unconditional quality and needs to be applied with wisdom. Some may engage in compassion and help others because it is a social expectation or because they want to appear altruistic and compassionate. This means that the motivation underlying their compassionate behaviour is superficial and compassion has pretentious, rather than an authentic, quality. This highlights the essential contribution of motivation/intention to genuine compassion in the Buddhist context. And even with a positive intention, compassion can lead to misguided and misplaced action if it is not applied with wisdom. For example, in Buddhism compassion is cultivated towards all beings; even those who have harmed or are harming us or others. The logic here is that they are doing so from an afflictive state of mind which will lead to suffering for them in the future. This assumption is based on the law of cause and effect as a fundamental principle of Buddhism. However, having compassion for those who are doing harm does not mean that we should passively watch them engaging in harmful activity; instead, the wise compassionate action may mean stopping the harm while keeping the compassionate stance and not succumbing to anger towards them. So while compassion is applied broadly to all beings in Buddhism, action arising from compassion needs to be guided by wisdom.

In the Tibetan Buddhist tradition, different gradients of compassion are distinguished (Rinpoche, 2004). The first gradient of compassion, the one most commonly practiced, is grounded in the dualistic differences between self and the other, but it arises out of authentic concern and care which make it genuine compassion. This type of compassion involves providing for others when they need food, medical care, shelter etc. The second gradient of compassion builds on the first gradient but extends it further by looking deeper into the causes of suffering. It recognizes the afflictive mind as the cause of suffering and understands ways to lessen suffering through meditation training. Accordingly, in addition to the immediate help, this gradient of compassion involves a heartfelt yearning for those who are suffering to reach a state of mind free from suffering and not to have to suffer again. Finally, the third gradient of compassion can be termed as non-referential, which refers to its all-encompassing nature. This highest level of compassion is non-dual and arises automatically as a non-conceptual quality of relating to others in the mind of advanced practitioners all the time and towards all beings. This type of compassion is inherent to the highest level of existential awareness and arises effortlessly when the practitioner recognizes the nature of mind without the need of common meditation practices such as contemplation, visualization or mantra recitation.

Compassion is in Buddhism usually practiced as part of a progression of practices starting with loving kindness, then compassion followed by rejoicing and equanimity. Loving kindness can be described as a wish for genuine happiness for oneself and all beings. The ultimate happiness is here understood as a state of balance, free from afflictions and suffering associated with them. It is not happiness in the ordinary hedonistic sense of owning things or gratification from pleasure; this type of ordinary happiness is in the Buddhist context considered part of the suffering cycle where we develop unhealthy attachment to impermanent sources of suffering such as possessions or ordinary relationships etc. When practicing loving kindness we cultivate a yearning for experiencing genuine lasting happiness which is not dependent on our personal circumstances and transcends hedonistic happiness. We also understand that meditation practice is the path to reaching such happiness which is free from ending and sorrow; in Buddhism this is the state of enlightenment, when we realize the nature of our mind and abide in pristine awareness.

Sometimes when we practice loving kindness, we can become ungrounded; this is where the next practice in the sequence of the four immeasurables, compassion, brings us back to the reality of suffering and this can help us stay focused on our meditation practice. However, it can also happen that our practice of compassion slips into excessive sadness and grief if we don't practice in a balanced way. This tendency is then countered by meditation on rejoicing, in which instead of suffering we bring to our mind all the wholesome actions of others and our own virtuous activity. The human mind has a natural tendency to notice threat and remember negative experiences, possibly for evolutionary reasons- it can help us avoid the same source of danger the next time. However, this negativity bias can under normal circumstances also distort the percep-tions of our life if we don't make an effort to counter it by focusing on the positive aspects of our experience. This is why rejoicing enables us to pay attention to the virtuous acts of self-less kindness others have shown to us or others, or those we have shown to others. From a Buddhist per-spective, by rejoicing we are also sowing the seeds of our own happiness and even sharing in the virtue arising from such actions even if we have not done them ourselves.

The final quality developed as part of the four immeasurables is equa-nimity, which further expands the scope of training in loving kindness and compassion. Equanimity does not mean that we develop indiffer-ence to others. In fact, it is the opposite of indifference: it means that we cultivate loving kindness and compassion widely to all sentient beings. We naturally have the tendency to favour those who are close to us, our family and friends. It might be easier for us to develop loving kindness and compassion towards them because we feel extra affection for them. Equanimity helps us expand the perspective of loving kindness and com-passion to people we don't know, and even those who are causing suffer-ing to us. The logic here is that we recognize that all beings, whether they are close to us or not, wish for happiness. And just like others, we all also get misguided and confused in our search for happiness, and often strive for things and achievements which cannot provide genuine happiness to us. In this process we often also engage in afflictive mental states which create further suffering to us. This is generally the case for those who are causing harm as well. In addition, they will experience further suffering as a result of their current harmful actions. Understanding the cycle of suffering in this way leads to development of loving kindness and com-passion towards all sentient beings. In turn, the practice of equanimity releases the divisive perceptions between us, those close to us and others, which brings us closer to realization of a non-dual state of mind.

Development of compassion together with loving kindness, rejoicing and equanimity is a stepping stone for cultivation of bodhicitta, which is sometimes described as the mind of enlightenment. Bodhicitta is often divided into relative and absolute. The relative bodhicitta describes genuine yearning to reach enlightenment as the highest state of existential well-being – a state of freedom from suffering. At the same time, there is a heartfelt wish to help others to reach that state since we recognize the shared nature of suffering which all beings experience. As part of relative bodhicitta this strong intention translates into actual meditation practice as a path to the state existential balance. In the Buddhist tradition of Dzogchen, absolute bodhicitta is the realization and sustaining of the actual state of existential balance which means ultimate freedom from our suffering and its roots. In this state we are also able to help other beings most effectively to reach freedom from suffering.

What is compassion? A Western scientific perspective

In the Western psychological context, compassion arises as a response to empathy, which is the capacity to share other people's feelings (Singer and Klimecki, 2014). Empathy is based on our ability to take on other people's perspectives and resonate with how they feel. Based on one scientific theory, we can respond to this initial sharing of thoughts and emotions in two ways – either by empathic distress or by compassion. Empathic distress is a negative aversive response to empathic sharing; it is a response characterized by more self-focus, stress and a wish to withdraw as a result of negative experience arising from empathic sharing. In contrast, compassion is a response to empathic sharing which has a stronger focus on the other rather than the self and is associated with positive emotions such as sympathetic concern. Compassion is an approach-oriented response linked to pro-social behaviour and willingness to help.

The pro-social aspect of compassion was investigated in a study that examined the impact of compassion training on the willingness to help. This was assessed in a computer game which measured the rates of helping and the results showed an increase in responses of help after the compassion training in comparison to memory training (Leiberg, Klimecki and Singer, 2011). Importantly, the researchers dissociated effects of helping behaviour motivated by abiding to social norms from genuine altruistic helping behaviour by introducing non-reciprocity trials in the study (no reward for helping). They found that the more time participants spent in compassion training, the higher the rates of genuinely altruistic (non-reciprocal) helping they showed. This suggests that long-term compassion training may particularly encourage development of unconditional helping behaviour.

The role of compassion in supporting the development of positive emotions in response to witnessing difficulty has also been investigated in more detail. In a study which evaluated the impact of compassion training on perceptions of others' distress (Klimecki et al., 2012), participants were asked to watch videos which showed other people in distress. Before compassion training these videos induced negative emotions in participants. However, after compassion training, the experience of negative emotions significantly reduced and participants reported more positive emotions. This could be attributed to the approach, rather than withdrawal, orientation towards others' distress which is associated with compassion.

The shift towards positive emotions and approach-oriented behaviour suggests that compassion could be considered an adaptive emotion regulation strategy – a way of managing our emotions which is conducive to our well-being. Previous research showed that reappraisal could be considered the primary adaptive emotion regulation strategy; reappraisal involves a change in thinking about a distressing experience. For example, somebody who loses a job may initially perceive this in a negative way, but after a while start considering the situation as an opportunity to set up their own exciting business. Reappraisal describes this shift in thinking, which has been shown to reduce stress and has a positive impact on health. Both compassion and reappraisal could be considered adaptive emotion regulation strategies, but it is not clear whether the mechanisms by which they produce beneficial effects are similar or quite different.

One study investigated the mechanisms of compassion and reappraisal by directly comparing the impact of these two strategies on ratings of positive and negative emotions in experienced Tibetan Buddhist meditators (in the Nyigma school, which emphasizes compassion training) who viewed distressing videos of others (Engen and Singer, 2015). The meditators were asked to modulate their emotions either by compassion or by reappraisal while viewing the videos. The findings revealed differential mechanisms of compassion and reappraisal: based on participants' ratings compassion resulted in an increase of positive emotions while reappraisal led to a decrease in negative emotions. The added benefit of compassionate emotion regulation which is linked to approach-oriented behaviour may suggest that it can be a particularly useful strategy in helping professions. However, the findings of this study need to be interpreted with caution given that the participants were very experienced meditators with extensive training in compassion meditation and this may have impacted on their readiness to use compassion in regulating their emotions.

Similar findings of increases in positive mood have also been found after secular loving kindness training (Hofmann, Grossman and Hinton, 2011). For example, one study employed a brief loving kindness practice (7 minutes long) and investigated whether this short meditation could have impact on a sense of connection and positivity towards strangers (Hutcherson, Seppala and Gross, 2008). The brief loving kindness practice involved participants connecting with the love of loved ones and then sending love and compassion to strangers. Participants evaluated how connected and positive they felt towards people depicted in pictures they were viewing. The findings indicated increases in ratings of connectedness and positivity towards strangers after the brief loving kindness practice. Some participants in the study had meditation experience, but not extensive, and findings showed the same pattern when meditators practicing loving kindness and compassion were excluded.

Another study on loving kindness investigated the impact of more extensive secular loving kindness training on positive emotions, personal resources and life satisfaction (Fredrickson et al., 2008). The loving kindness programme consisted of six 1-hour-long sessions delivered over seven weeks. In addition, participants were asked to practice guided loving kindness meditations at home for 10–30 minutes at least five times a week. The findings indicated improvements in positive emotions after the loving kindness programme as well as increases in self-reported purpose in life and mindfulness and a decrease in illness symptoms (together considered as personal resources). Interestingly, amongst the outcomes was also a reduction in anger after the programme. These changes in personal resources were predictive of life satisfaction and reductions in depression symptoms in participants. This study particularly highlighted how loving kindness practice could be one of the approaches to increase non-hedonic (not short-term pleasure-based) positive emotions which are associated with better well-being outcomes. Cumulatively, a recent meta-analytic review of findings from this and other studies suggested that loving kindness meditation seems to have moderate impact on reduction in depression symptoms, increases in mindfulness and in compassion (Galante et al., 2014). The review highlighted both the potential for loving kindness meditation in mental health treatment and the need for better designed studies.

In the Western therapeutic context, the orienting approach and positive affect qualities of compassion and loving kindness are applied as part of compassion-focused therapy and self-compassion therapy. Compassion-focused therapy (CFT; Gilbert, 2009) highlights the importance of compassion in supporting clients with high levels of self-criticism and shame which are often associated with early sensitization to experiences of threat. CFT builds on Buddhist psychology, attachment theory and Western neuroscientific understanding of affective systems. With regard to neurobiology, CFT particularly emphasizes the need for balance between the threat-focused system, resource-seeking system and soothing/safeness system. Imbalance between the three systems in favour of the threat-focused and resource-seeking system combined with early experiences sensitizing these systems can lead to psychopathology. In addition, the theory of CFT suggests that Western society in general encourages over-stimulation of the resource-seeking and threat-focused systems. The goal of compassion practices is to stimulate the soothing/safeness system associated with feelings of contentment and kindness, which can support more adaptive affective functioning.

In CFT, compassion is defined as a set of attributes and skills. The compassion attributes include a caring attitude towards lessening distress, sensitivity to distress, being emotionally moved by distress, being able to tolerate and stay with (rather than avoid) distressing experiences, being able to understand others' point of view or own feelings and thoughts and non-judgment. The compassion skills include compassionate attention (to positive qualities in others and oneself), compassionate reasoning (thinking which is kind and supportive), compassionate behaviour (exposure to frightening thoughts and feelings with kindness and in a gentle way), compassionate imagery (of ideal compassion, compassionate self), compassionate feeling and compassionate sensations (in the body). In CFT the therapist works with the client using practices to cultivate the compassionate attributes and skills in order to activate the safeness/soothing system and rebalance the over-activated threat-focus and resource-seeking systems. In this way, the primary focus of compassion in CFT is on compassion towards the self and the focus isn't on pro-social behaviour as in the conceptions of compassion discussed above (Singer and Klimecki, 2014).

Another approach to therapeutic applications of compassion focuses on the construct of self-compassion, which consists of the three facets of self-kindness, common humanity and mindfulness (Neff, 2003). Self-kindness is the opposite of harsh criticism and means being understanding and kind to ourselves when faced with difficulty. Common humanity refers to the perception of our experience as part of the human condition, just like others', rather than from an isolationist perspective. Finally, mindfulness describes the ability to hold and stay with painful experiences without over identifying with them. As the term 'self-compassion' suggests, the focus of this construct is on developing compassion towards oneself which differs from some Western conceptions of compassion (Singer and Klimecki, 2014) and from the Buddhist understanding of compassion. However, the facet of common humanity has an element of connectedness with others and recognition of the shared nature of human suffering. The third facet of self-compassion, mindfulness, seems to be closer in its meaning to the construct of decentring as the ability to step back from our experience and perceive it in a less self-focused way.

There seem to be several points of difference between the Western and Buddhist conceptions of compassion, even though each of the Western accounts builds on Buddhist psychology. The first point of departure is the scope of compassion – whilst in the Buddhist context compassion has broad focus on all sentient beings, in the Western context the focus of compassion is more immediate and concrete, on the suffering we are experiencing or those around us are experiencing. There also seems to be a difference with regard to the recognition of different degrees of compassion – the Buddhist tradition recognizes a basic focus on the obvious forms of suffering, as well as a deeper focus on the roots of suffering and the deepest unconditional continuous compassion as a non-conceptual stance towards all sentient beings. In contrast, the Western conceptions focus on the basic forms of suffering without the more encompassing focus beyond the observable. Finally, compassion in the Buddhist tradition is cultivated as part of the progression on the spiritual path towards freedom from suffering, and accordingly, compassion practice closely connects to motivation/intention for the practice and more advanced insight practices investigating the nature of self, mind and reality. Compassion in the Western context has been conceptualized in a narrower sense without a clear connection to existential well-being.

Developing compassion and related qualities in the Buddhist context

In the Buddhist context, there are many different forms of practices which cultivate compassion and related qualities. Here we will focus on the three most common approaches to developing and working with compassion. The first approach we will discuss involves the foundational training in the four immeasurables which is a sequence of practices starting with loving kindness, progressing into compassion and then rejoicing and equanimity (Wallace, 1999). Then we will discuss two other meditation practices which build on the core training in the four immeasurables. These are, for example, practices which work with the four immeasurables as antidotes to common afflictive emotions such as anger or attachment, and the practice of Tonglen, which is often also called the practice of giving and taking.

Training in the four immeasurables typically starts with the practice of loving kindness in which the meditator gradually develops a vision of genuine happiness for oneself, others and then all sentient beings. The vision of genuine happiness is grounded in the Buddhist understanding of happiness as explained earlier in this chapter. The actual practice may start with a contemplation on what we could consider to be genuine happiness for ourselves: we could imagine what it would feel like to achieve the state of complete existential balance. Alternatively, the meditation on loving kindness can start by considering happiness for others; for some people this might be easier since many of us, particularly in the Western cultures, get caught up in a cycle of self-criticism which may make it more difficult to start the practice of loving kindness with ourselves. Whether the development of loving kindness towards others is the first or the second step in our practice, it will involve contemplation on the genuine happiness of those who are close to us, our family and friends. We can simply think of them, bring them to our mind, and develop a strong wish for genuine happiness for them. We connect fully with this feeling and extend it to all those who are close to us.

In the next step of the loving kindness practice we expand the scope of our contemplation to those people who are neutral to us, those whom we don't have a close relationship with, whom we don't like or dislike. We can think of strangers in a supermarket or people we see while walking down the street whom we don't have any particular connection to. In this step of the meditation we try to extend the feeling of loving kindness to them as well, wishing them to reach a state of genuine happiness. We can then explore the differences in the quality of loving kindness we develop to those who are close to us and those we do not know and consider what the source of the differences is. We may find the quality of loving kindness is very similar or the same in both cases. The differences might be associated with the extra affection and attachment we have towards those who are close to us. However, this affection and attachment has a different quality from genuine loving kindness.

The following step in the loving kindness practice can be particularly challenging because it involves development of loving kindness towards those who are doing us and others harm. This may at first seem illogical, but again, coming back to the understanding of loving kindness as a wish to achieve a state of freedom from afflictions, the attitude of loving kindness towards people who are engaging in harmful behaviour will become more obvious. It means that by wishing loving kindness to them we wish their minds to be free from the afflictions from which their harmful behaviour arose. If their mind is free from afflictions, they will no longer harm others.

In the last step of the practice we further expand the wish for genuine happiness to all beings in their all forms, depending on our beliefs. With practice, we can at this stage generate a state where we feel unconditional loving kindness in the broadest sense without having to think specifically of different life forms of beings. We can rest in that state which has elements of joy and happiness, but also even-mindedness and contentment. If we become ungrounded in our practice, and instead of genuine happiness slip into a frivolous state without clarity or balance, compassion practice can help us find grounding again and refocus our practice on the fundamental qualities of lasting happiness.

Practices of loving kindness and compassion are sometimes described as two sides of the same coin. While loving kindness focuses on the vision, on the wish for genuine happiness, compassion focuses on the reality of suffering and the wish for freedom from suffering. In the practice of compassion we can progress in the same way as in the practice of loving kindness. We first develop compassion for ourselves or for those who are close to us, whichever is the easier step for us to start with. We zoom in onto the different forms of suffering we and others experience, from physical suffering through emotional suffering and mental suffering. We can also try to look deeper at the sources of these different forms of suffering and contemplate their roots. While connecting with the suffering, we also develop the courage, hope and sincere wish to help in whatever way we can to reduce this suffering. In this way we don't slip into sadness and grief when seeing the suffering, but transform it into positive qualities and a wish for change.

In the next steps of the meditation we develop compassion for those who are neutral to us and then to those who are doing or have done harm to us or others. Similarly to the practice of loving kindness, we work on the principle that they are suffering when engaging in afflictive states and they are also creating sources of their further suffering. This reasoning leads to development of compassion for them. In the following step of the meditation we try to extend the compassion to other beings, in their different forms. We can think of the suffering of animals, for example, and cultivate compassion towards them. Finally, often with further practice we try to expand the perspective of our compassion to all beings in all their forms and abide in a non-conceptual state of compassion. The aim of long-term practice of compassion is for this state to become the undertone of all our activity, in and outside of meditation.

The practice of compassion is followed by meditations on rejoicing. In the practice of rejoicing we bring to our mind wholesome activities we have done and also wholesome activities of others. While recalling these events, the feelings of loving kindness and compassion which were inherent to these wholesome events arise in our mind in the moment of remembering and fill us with sympathetic joy. This practice is particularly helpful in countering feelings of sadness which can arise if we overemphasize the exposure to suffering and don't engage enough in the stages of compassion associated with hope and other positive emotions. The practice of rejoicing can also support long-term practitioners in avoiding slipping into dullness in their practice which can happen with repetition of the same meditation routine and result in stagnation of progression on the path. Rejoicing can bring clarity and freshness to the practice, and also remind the meditator of the intentions and broader view of the path.

In the last meditation in the sequence of the four immeasurables, equanimity, we further explore the similarities and differences in the quality of loving kindness and compassion towards different categories of people and beings. We try to focus on the underlying core similarities in the quality of these states across the different subjects of our meditations. This core quality could be described in terms of grounded joy and affection combined with tranquillity and an unconditional wish to help. The differences might have a different quality of extra affection which has an element of attachment conditioned by familiarity and preferences.

The four immeasurables can be regarded not only as practices cultivating the particular emotional qualities we have just described; they also contribute to the long-term meditation path beyond their primary role in development of compassion and associated states. For example, when we cultivate loving kindness we invite the vision of genuine happiness which is grounded in the core Buddhist teachings of the Four Noble Truths (Gethin, 1998) and Four Thoughts that turn the mind to Dharma (Rinpoche, 2013). Based on these teachings, the only form of lasting happiness results from mind training, which releases unhealthy attachments and purifies the mind from afflictions. A state of genuine balance and happiness is free from these and has the stability ensuring they do not arise again. Loving kindness practice reminds us of the possibility of lasting happiness and the way to achieve it.

Similarly, the gradients of compassion practice we have described earlier present different levels of insight into the nature of suffering: from understanding suffering in the most obvious way, through relating the observable suffering to its deeper roots in our mind, up to an experiential realization of a state which is free from suffering and from which the non-conceptual state of compassion arises continuously (Rinpoche, 2004). And both the practice of loving kindness and the practice of compassion entail an element of recognizing the law of cause and effect (karma) based on which harmful actions in the present perpetuate further cycle of suffering for those engaging in such actions. This is also the case for the practice of rejoicing where unconditional joy at others' virtue results in our own virtue. Finally, the practice of equanimity further expands the insight aspect of meditations on the four immeasurables by examining the artificial conditioned notions of like and dislike for friends, family, strangers and enemies. In this way, the practice of equanimity supports the development of genuine bodhicitta, which in the Mahāyāna path serves as a catalyst towards striving for the highest levels of existential well-being.

The practices of the four immeasurables are also the basis for other meditation-based techniques which can be applied both in formal meditation sessions and in informal ways in everyday life. One of these techniques uses the four states of loving kindness, compassion, rejoicing and equanimity as direct antidotes towards afflictive emotions as they arise in our mind stream. In this way, loving kindness can be applied as an antidote to anger, compassion can counter unhealthy attachment, rejoicing can reduce jealousy and equanimity can neutralize self-focused pride. Specifically, in a formal meditation session, we can contemplate on the experience of anger and bring to mind a genuine wish for happiness for us and others which can put the reasons for our anger into perspective. We may realize that the reason for our anger is actually fairly negligible in the big picture, or we may find the reason for the anger is deeper and our response can take into account the broader trajectory towards lasting happiness for us and others. When we are faced with unhealthy attachment, for example to material things or recognition we crave, we can remind ourselves of deeper sources of suffering and develop compassion towards ourselves and others who have the same experience. Meditation on compassion can help us bring the cravings into perspective and use them instead as a motivation for our further meditation practice.

Similarly, rejoicing can be an excellent antidote to feelings of jealousy when we witness others' success. Here it is important to remember to rejoice in wholesome activity and apply rejoicing in the context of broader understanding of virtue and non-virtue. Finally, when we experience success ourselves, equanimity can be a useful antidote to exaggerated self-focused pride. In this type of pride there is a sense of overemphasis on our achievement and denigration of others which lacks equanimity. To counter this imbalanced state, we can contextualize our success and remember all those who supported us in the achievement, without whom we would not have been able get where we are. We can then contemplate on our success and pride in the context of genuine loving kindness and compassion and explore how the feeling of pride compares to them and how it feeds into our sense of existential well-being.

Tonglen (Tibetan: gtong len or tonglin), the meditation on giving and taking, is another common technique which builds on and expands the practices of loving kindness, compassion, rejoicing and equanimity. It is a simple but powerful practice based on the principle that whenever we have a wholesome experience we wish all beings would experience the same, and whenever we experience suffering we wish that we and also all sentient beings who are suffering would not have to suffer any longer. The practice, just like the practice of compassion or loving kindness, can have different gradients. At the basic level, for example, whenever we have a nourishing meal or enjoy a warm drink which gives us a feeling of contentment and ease, we think of other beings and wish them to experience the same. And when we are ill, we think of others who are in the same moment feeling just like we are feeling and wish that not only us but also they would not be ill.

As we progress in our meditation practice, we can combine the basic practice of Tonglen with deeper meditations on genuine happiness and causes of suffering. In this way, when we engage in meditation and develop glimpses of unconditional loving kindness and unconditional compassion, we wish that all sentient beings would experience these balanced wholesome states. And when we are ill or witness suffering, we wish that both the obvious suffering and its deeper causes in the afflicted mind would be purified for us and for all sentient beings. At the most advanced levels of meditation practice, we sustain a state of connection with all beings all the time and the division between us and others will appear as only temporary and artificial. As a result, we continuously abide in a state of unconditional loving kindness and compassion for all beings and there is no need for explicit wishes for happiness and freedom from suffering in particular situations because the state of our mind naturally radiates these all the time.

Neuroscience of compassion and loving kindness

One line of research over the last decade showed that the pattern of neural activation associated with empathy and empathic distress is different from the brain activation linked to compassion (Singer and Klimecki,

2014). Specifically, fMRI studies on empathy repeatedly suggested activation in the anterior middle cingulate cortex and anterior insula (Lamm, Decety and Singer, 2011). In contrast, fMRI research on compassion indicated increases in activation of the medial orbitofrontal cortex and ventral striatum (Klimecki et al., 2012). These differences in brain activation patterns have been attributed to the differential emotional response to empathy and empathic distress which typically results in negative affect in comparison to compassion, which results in positive affect. Further supporting these distinctions, the same findings were reported in meditation novices who were trained first in empathy and then in compassion (Klimecki et al., 2014). In addition, the compassion-specific pattern of brain activation was confirmed in meditators experienced in compassion practice (Engen and Singer, 2015).

However, the outlined differences in brain activation between empathy and compassion are not uniformly supported across research studies. For example, an fMRI study with experienced meditators did not find the empathy/compassion dissociation (Lutz et al., 2008). In this study meditators' brain responses were recorded while they were practicing loving kindness/compassion meditation and listening to negative, positive and neutral sounds. The findings showed greater activation in the insula in response to negative sounds than positive sounds in experienced meditators in comparison to novices. Increased activation in the insula was also linked to higher intensity of meditation as reported by both meditators and meditation novices. This result contradicts the findings from studies comparing empathy and compassion in novices where activation in the insula was primarily associated with empathy (Lamm, Decety and Singer, 2011), but in the current study with experienced meditators the specific location of the activation in the insula may have been slightly different (Lutz et al., 2008). In addition to these findings, a comparison between loving kindness/compassion meditation and rest indicated increased activation in other regions including the amygdala and temporo-parietal junction (TPJ) to all sound types in meditators. This finding was interpreted in terms of increased orienting, consideration and mental activity in meditators in response to emotional information which might also be linked to approach-oriented behaviour.

All the neuroscience findings which we have discussed so far were recorded while participants were engaging in a loving kindness/compassion practice. Hence, these modifications in brain function were a mix of state effects associated with the immediate meditation practice and trait changes resulting from long-term meditation practice. This raises the question whether any of these changes would also be observable if the participants were not asked to meditate while viewing emotional videos or listening to emotional sounds. To address this question, an fMRI study assessed changes in patterns of brain activation in participants after secular Mindful Attention Training (MAT) compared to secular Cognitively-Based Compassion Training (CBCT – based on Tibetan Buddhist compassion practices) (Desbordes et al., 2012). All participants were new to meditation at the start of the training. Before and after the meditation training both groups of participants (and an additional active control group) were asked to view pleasant, unpleasant and neutral images while their brain responses to these pictures were recorded. There were no meditation instructions before the pictures were viewed.

The findings from the study (Desbordes et al., 2012) showed decreases in the activation of the amygdalae in the mindfulness (MAT) group after the training in response to all three types of stimuli whereas the group which trained in compassion (CBCT) showed a trend towards increased activation in the right amygdala to negative stimuli. In So, the results also suggested that different types of meditation can impact brain responses to emotional stimuli differentially. While mindfulness training seemed to decrease reactivity to all types of emotional signals, compassion training seemed to increase orienting towards negative stimuli. Importantly, the increase in right amygdalae activation in the compassion group was associated with a decrease in depression scores in participants. This suggests that compassion training may increase exposure to negative stimuli without this having a negative impact on our emotional well-being; so the increased sensitivity to negative stimuli was in this study associated with a reduction in self-reported depression symptoms. Overall, these findings were interpreted as an indicator of differential trait shifts in the processing of emotional information resulting from mindfulness and compassion training which are observable outside of actual meditation states.

While these results suggest that compassion can lead to functional changes in the brain, research evidence on possible changes in brain structure with compassion meditation is virtually absent. However, one structural MRI study investigated possible changes in grey matter volume which could be associated with loving kindness meditation (Leung et al., 2012). The researchers compared the brain structure of meditators in the Theravada tradition who have been practicing loving kindness meditation for more than five years with brain structure of meditation novices. The findings revealed increased grey matter volume in the right angular and posterior parahippocampal gyri in meditators. The finding of structural changes in the right angular gyrus, which is part of the TPJ, is aligned with the fMRI results from the study with meditators who were listening to emotional sounds (Lutz et al., 2008). The TPJ is involved in cognitive empathy, which involves reasoning about others' mental states. The structural changes in the posterior parahippocampal gyrus are unique to this study and the researchers suggested that they might reflect changes in emotion regulation as a result of loving kindness practice.

Other studies have found functional changes in brain activity during loving kindness meditation which were somewhat different from those reported in studies on compassion. For example, an fMRI study examined differences in strength of connections between different brain regions in experienced meditators and meditation novices while both groups were engaging in loving kindness meditation (Garrison et al., 2014). The meditators were trained in the Theravada tradition and had on average 752 hours of loving kindness practice. The findings suggested less activation in meditators in the posterior cingulate cortex/precuneus (PCC/PCu) regions, which might be a finding non-specific to loving kindness meditation, simply reflecting less mind-wandering in meditators. However, the findings also revealed increased connectivity between the PCC/PCu and the left inferior frontal gyrus in meditators whereas the novices showed more connectivity between PCC/PCu and other regions including posterior insula and parahippocampal gyrus. The researchers interpreted this finding as suggesting stronger focus on the loving kindness meditation in meditators and more self-related processing in meditation novices. However, the study also reported decreased activation in the TPJ in meditators and this was interpreted as less self-related thinking in this study; yet the previous study we have discussed interpreted larger grey matter volume in a region of TPJ as a possible positive consequence of cognitive empathy (Leung et al., 2012).

Very few studies investigated links between compassion/loving kindness practices and physiological changes. One interesting study explored a possible link between telomere length and loving kindness practice (Hoge et al., 2013). Telomeres are end parts of chromosomal sequences and their length has been associated with health outcomes – longer telomeres have been associated with less susceptibility to chronic illness. Importantly, stress has been shown to cause shorter telomere length. The study by Hoge et al. (2013) found that women who were experienced meditators in loving kindness practice had significantly longer telomeres in comparison to control participants. This result was robust even after controlling for possible interfering factors such as age and BMI and suggested that loving kindness practice may have protective effects on health which impact the cellular level of biological risk. This effect was specific to women and the overall sample including male participants showed only a trend towards significance.

Overall, the emerging picture of findings from neuroscience research on compassion and loving kindness is intriguing, but also full of inconsistencies. Whilst it is clear that compassion and loving kindness practices can result in tangible changes in the brain, and possibly also in body physiology, the exact pattern of these changes is not clear at this stage. One neuroscience approach highlights possible dissociations between empathy associated with empathic distress and compassion (Singer and Klimecki, 2014), but findings from other studies (e.g., Lutz et al., 2008) do not support this dissociation. Some studies have also reported opposite findings for changes in TPJ in loving kindness meditators with both increases and decreases in TPJ being interpreted in terms of positive effects of loving kindness meditation (Leung et al., 2012; Garrison et al., 2014).

One of the most interesting findings in the neuroscience literature on compassion is perhaps increased activation in the amygdalae during compassion practice whereas a downregulation in this region is typically observed with mindfulness practice. Amygdalae are regions of the brain involved in threat detection, so the increased activation may seem contradictory to the positive affect associated with compassion; however, it has been shown that the increase in amygdala activation is in the context of compassion practice linked to better mental health (Desbordes et al., 2012). Finally, no studies have so far directly compared brain patterns associated with different types or gradients of compassion. One study reported a distinct pattern of changes in brain function when meditators engaged in unconditional compassion meditation (Lutz et al., 2004), however these findings were not compared to other types or gradients of compassion. Further research is needed to elucidate the neurocognitive and psychophysiological mechanisms of compassion and related states.

Compassion, self-regulation and existential well-being

We will now examine the contribution of compassion and related states to our well-being from the broader perspective of the mechanisms of meditation involving metacognitive self-regulation and existential awareness introduced in the first chapter. Compassion, loving kindness, rejoicing and equanimity are typically developed alongside calm abiding training (Shamatha). This is because they can counter difficulties associated with self-judgment and reactivity which can arise in meditation training which primarily cultivates concentration, attention control and meta-awareness. As such, training in the four immeasurables contributes to the development of processes underlying the metacognitive self-regulatory capacity (MSRC) of the mind.

However, aside from supporting the development of attention skills, compassion and related practices also selectively cultivate emotional qualities and emotion regulation strategies which enhance the MSRC further. For example, the practice of the four immeasurables develops the qualities of compassion and loving kindness that have been shown to increase positive emotions and approach-oriented unconditional pro-social behaviour (Leiberg, Klimecki and Singer, 2011). With long-term practice, this may to translate into a trait-like response to others' suffering even outside of formal meditation. In addition, practices like Tonglen and working with the four immeasurables as antidotes to afflictions develop specific emotion regulation strategies that can be applied in everyday life to cope with emotions as they arise.

The practices of the four immeasurables likely also modify the conceptual systems, even though no studies so far investigated such changes. Modulations in conceptual processing with these practices could involve shifts in thinking schemas about how we perceive our own suffering and others' suffering and how we relate to it. With more advanced practices of compassion, the changes could also include shifts towards more holistic, non-conceptual meanings and less engagement of the construed propositional meanings and schemas (Dorjee, 2016). This is because more advanced compassion practice encourages experiential connection with the felt sense of compassion rather than basic compassion, which arises from contemplations and reasoning about suffering. In this way the practice of compassion and related qualities further enable progression towards more advanced shifts in MEA.

Indeed, one of the core distinctions between advanced shifts in existential awareness is the experience of a compassionate state as a separate or inherent quality of existential awareness. Specifically, the non-conceptual experience of substrate consciousness from which all mental activity arises is often accompanied by the experience of compassion, but this quality is experienced as separable from, rather than intrinsic to, substrate consciousness. In contrast, pristine awareness (rigpa), which is the most advanced mode of existential awareness recognizing the nature of self, mind and reality, includes unconditional non-conceptual compassion as its inseparable and integral dimension. This type of compassion naturally radiates without effort when a practitioner abides at this most advanced level of existential awareness. However, even at basic levels of compassion training, these practices prepare the foundations for experience of non-dual pristine awareness by diminishing the boundaries between near and far, and the self and the other.

Compassion and related practices have a particularly strong potential to enhance our well-being given that they support both the self-regulatory and existential well-being mechanisms underlying our overall well-being. In comparison, Shamatha practices developing mindfulness and meta-awareness mostly target the cultivation of the attention aspects of self-regulation and their impact on the development of existential awareness is limited. Building on these, compassion and related practices cultivate explicit emotion qualities and emotion regulation strategies. Hence, both mindfulness and compassion practices are essential to long-term meditation practice, with compassion having broader reach and impact on MEA.

A day of compassion practice

With the variety of practices developing compassion, loving kindness, rejoicing and equanimity, there is a multitude of ways we can introduce compassion meditations into our everyday routines. In addition, everyday life provides many opportunities for us to develop and refine compassion and related qualities on the go, more so perhaps than a protected retreat environment. We can start the practice of compassion right after we wake up by including considerations about compassion into contemplations about the motivation/intention for the day. In the Buddhist context this would include a sincere wish to engage in meditation practices throughout the day so that we can better help ourselves and other beings and relieve suffering whenever we can. In this way, compassion is an integral drive behind our intention and meditation practice throughout the day.

Then as we engage in the morning routine we can further reinforce the compassionate intention – when we are getting dressed we can remind ourselves of the intention to engage in the activities during the day in ways which reduce our and others' suffering. As we are preparing the morning meal we can think of others and do a brief practice of Tonglen, wishing that all those who are in need of a meal or drink would have it. The practice does not need to be restricted to working with positive emotions only. If we feel stressed or tense as we are rushing through the morning routine, we can remind ourselves that we are not the only ones feeling this in this moment and make a wish for us and for others that we would feel more relaxed and settled.

As we are commuting to work, we often think about tasks which are waiting for us and this in itself can cause us stress. When we notice this, we can again recognize that we are most likely not the only people having these thoughts in this moment and we can wish for ourselves and others to release the stress and turn our attention to meditation practice instead. We can look around and notice those who are sharing the commute with us or notice the people we are passing. As we are noticing them, we can wish them to be happy, without expecting them to know that we are unconditionally wishing them happiness or expecting anything in return. This can also remind us to wish that we too would experience genuine happiness and consider for a moment what genuine happiness means for us. This can be as simple as silently saying, 'I wish you to be happy, I wish myself to be happy', or we can focus more closely on the experience of genuine happiness and extend this feeling as a wish to those around us and then all beings beyond what we can perceive immediately.

As we engage in the interactions in the morning, we can keep coming back to the phrases of wishing others and ourselves happiness or simply return again and again to the experience of loving kindness and try to sustain that subtle state while engaging in work tasks. It is important to keep the practices of loving kindness and compassion authentic. When we practice loving kindness and compassion, it doesn't mean that we will be walking around with a smile on our face all the time and talk to everybody in an exaggerated sweet manner. Such a way of relating to others is pretentious and lacks the genuine qualities of loving kindness and compassion. Rather, as we go through the morning we recognize moments of happiness and generate a genuine wish of happiness for others unconditionally, and when we experience suffering or witness others' difficulties we genuinely wish them to be free from this suffering and if possible try to actively help.

The lunch break can be an opportunity for a short formal practice in the four immeasurables. In the Buddhist context this can involve remembering phrases such as: 'May all beings be happy, may they be free from suffering, may they have happiness which is free from sorrow, may they rest in equanimity free from attachment and aversion'. During this practice we can connect with the underlying experiential quality of each of the four immeasurables or we can visualize those close to us, those we are neutral to, those we have difficulty with and then all sentient beings. While having a meal, we can engage in the eating meditation, but again expand it to include elements of loving kindness and compassion, wishing all those who don't have a meal as we do to have it. We can also think of the food we are consuming as nourishing us so that we can engage in the practices of loving kindness and compassion.

In the afternoon, as we continue with our work tasks, we can try to apply antidotes whenever a difficulty arises. For example, if we experience frustration, we can remember that many other people have the same experience in the moment and we can also remind ourselves of the bigger picture, of what is really important for our genuine happiness. We can also recognize the suffering which is part of experiencing frustration and anger and make a wish to be free from the suffering. This may help us create a healthy distance from the current difficulty. Frustration and anger are often associated with narrowing of our space of thinking; our focus is restricted to the problem. If we briefly remind ourselves of loving kindness and compassion, this can help us expand the scope of our focus and release the immediate tension associated with frustration and anger.

In contrast, if we experience a moment of pride at achieving at work, we try to contextualize this. We remind ourselves of all those who contributed to the achievement and this may reduce our attachment to the achievement and reduce the likelihood of us slipping into distorted self-centredness. In this way we can antidote unhealthy attachment and practice equanimity towards our achievement. We can also try to explore the significance of our achievement more deeply, in terms of its contribution to our and others' genuine happiness or reduction of suffering. And when we witness others' deserved achievements, if we notice glimpses of jealousy arising in our mind stream, we can remind ourselves of rejoicing and the virtues associated with it. We may notice that a genuine sharing of others' joy of achievement can also bring joy to us.

As we commute home from work, we can continue our practice of loving kindness and compassion, wishing genuine happiness and freedom from suffering to all the people we pass by on our way. As we engage in the evening routines, perhaps preparing an evening meal, we can make a wish for all people to have somebody to prepare a meal for them when they need it. We can also try to sustain the compassionate and kind mind-set while interacting with family and friends, perhaps bringing more care, patience and interest to the interactions with them. While we are watching TV, we can practice loving kindness and compassion too. For example, news often contain many reports of others' suffering and struggling; we can use this as an opportunity for practicing unconditional loving kindness and compassion for them. Then before we go to sleep, we can do brief formal meditation practice on the four immeasurables again and also review our day and rejoice in all the wholesome activities we have done. In the Buddhist context, we would end the day with a dedication of all the virtue we have accumulated during the day for our progress on the path so that we can more efficiently help other beings. We would also dedicate the virtue for the benefit of all beings, so that they would experience genuine happiness and be free from suffering.

Compassion from a long-term practice perspective

As shown in this chapter, practices of compassion and related qualities are pivotal to the contemplative process on the long-term path of meditation. This is because they deeply connect with other core aspects of meditation training including development of compassionate motivation/intention for engaging in long-term meditation in order to cultivate genuine happiness and reduce our and others' suffering. Compassion and loving kindness also support development of mindfulness and meta-awareness by enabling a gentle, non-judgmental and understanding approach to dealing with distraction, lack of relaxation, stability or clarity in our practice. Finally, compassion contributes to and supports the development of contemplative insight, with the highest levels of non-conceptual compassion being inseparable from the highest states of existential balance. Accordingly, the practice of compassion and related qualities develops, expands and gets refined with long-term meditation training. In this way, the practices of compassion, loving kindness, rejoicing and equanimity are an indispensable part of any long-term meditation practice.

Summary

Chapter 4 explores the role of compassion and related qualities of loving kindness, compassion, rejoicing and equanimity in long-term meditation practice. The chapter starts by considering the meaning of compassion in the Buddhist context and then examines how the Buddhist accounts of compassion differ from Western scientific theories and applications of compassion practices. This is followed by an outline of three types of meditation practices which develop and/or work with compassion and the three related qualities. These practices are the meditations on the four immeasurables, the practice of Tonglen and working with antidotes to afflictive emotions. We then examine the current evidence base on the neural underpinnings of compassion and loving kindness practices. Next, we consider the place of practices cultivating compassion and related qualities in a broader framework of meditation training as developing the metacognitive self-regulatory capacity (MSRC) of the mind and modes of existential awareness (MEA). Finally, the practical and theoretical considerations are integrated using examples of how compassion practice can be embedded in routine everyday work and life activities throughout the day.

References

Desbordes, G., Negi, L.T., Pace, T.W., Wallace, B.A., Raison, C.L. and Schwartz, E.L., 2012. Effects of mindful-attention and compassion meditation training on amygdala response to emotional stimuli in an ordinary, non-meditative state. *Frontiers in Human Neuroscience*, 6, p. 292.

Dorjee, D., 2016. Defining contemplative science: The metacognitive self-regulatory capacity of the mind, context of meditation practice and modes of existential awareness. *Frontiers in Psychology*, 7, pp. 1–15.

Ekman, P., Davidson, R.J., Ricard, M. and Wallace, B.A., 2005. Buddhist and psychological perspectives on emotions and well-being. *Current Directions in Psychological Science*, 14(2), pp. 59–63.

Engen, H.G. and Singer, T., 2015. Compassion-based emotion regulation up-regulates experienced positive affect and associated neural networks. *Social Cognitive and Affective Neuroscience*, 10(9), pp. 1291–1301.

Fredrickson, B.L., Cohn, M.A., Coffey, K.A., Pek, J. and Finkel, S.M., 2008. Open hearts build lives: Positive emotions, induced through loving-kindness meditation, build consequential personal resources. *Journal of Personality and Social Psychology*, 95(5), pp. 1045–1061.

Galante, J., Galante, I., Bekkers, M.J. and Gallacher, J., 2014. Effect of kindness-based meditation on health and well-being: A systematic review and meta-analysis. *Journal of Consulting and Clinical Psychology*, 82(6), p. 1101.

Garrison, K.A., Scheinost, D., Constable, R.T. and Brewer, J.A., 2014. BOLD signal and functional connectivity associated with loving kindness meditation. *Brain and Behavior*, 4(3), pp. 337–347.

Gethin, R., 1998. *The foundations of Buddhism*. Oxford: Oxford University Press.

Gilbert, P., 2005. *Compassion: Conceptualisations, research and use in psychotherapy*. London: Routledge.

Gilbert, P., 2009. Introducing compassion-focused therapy. *Advances in Psychiatric Treatment*, 15(3), pp. 199–208.

Goleman, D., 2003. *Destructive emotions: How we can overcome them? A scientific dialogue with the Dalai Lama*. New York: Bantam Books.

Hofmann, S.G., Grossman, P. and Hinton, D.E., 2011. Loving-kindness and compassion meditation: Potential for psychological interventions. *Clinical Psychology Review*, 31(7), pp. 1126–1132.

Hoge, E.A., Chen, M.M., Orr, E., Metcalf, C.A., Fischer, L.E., Pollack, M.H., DeVivo, I. and Simon, N.M., 2013. Loving-Kindness Meditation practice associated with longer telomeres in women. *Brain, Behavior, and Immunity, 32*, pp. 159–163.

Hutcherson, C.A., Seppala, E.M. and Gross, J.J., 2008. Loving-kindness meditation increases social connectedness. *Emotion*, 8(5), pp. 720–724.

Klimecki, O.M., Leiberg, S., Lamm, C. and Singer, T., 2012. Functional neural plasticity and associated changes in positive affect after compassion training. *Cerebral Cortex*, *23*(7), pp. 1552–1561.

Klimecki, O.M., Leiberg, S., Ricard, M. and Singer, T., 2014. Differential pattern of functional brain plasticity after compassion and empathy training. *Social Cognitive and Affective Neuroscience*, *9*(6), pp. 873–879.

Lamm, C., Decety, J. and Singer, T., 2011. Meta-analytic evidence for common and distinct neural networks associated with directly experienced pain and empathy for pain. *Neuroimage*, *54*(3), pp. 2492–2502.

Leiberg, S., Klimecki, O. and Singer, T., 2011. Short-term compassion training increases prosocial behavior in a newly developed prosocial game. *PLoS One*, *6*(3), p. e17798.

Leung, M.K., Chan, C.C., Yin, J., Lee, C.F., So, K.F. and Lee, T.M., 2012. Increased gray matter volume in the right angular and posterior parahippo-campal gyri in loving-kindness meditators. *Social Cognitive and Affective Neuroscience*, *8*(1), pp. 34–39.

Lutz, A., Brefczynski-Lewis, J., Johnstone, T. and Davidson, R.J., 2008. Regulation of the neural circuitry of emotion by compassion meditation: Effects of meditative expertise. *PLoS One*, *3*(3), p. e1897.

Lutz, A., Greischar, L.L., Rawlings, N.B., Ricard, M. and Davidson, R.J., 2004. Long-term meditators self-induce high-amplitude gamma synchrony during mental practice. *Proceedings of the National Academy of Sciences of the United States of America*, *101*(46), pp. 16369–16373.

Neff, K., 2003. Self-compassion: An alternative conceptualization of a healthy attitude toward oneself. *Self and Identity*, *2*(2), pp. 85–101.

Rinpoche, D.P., 2004. *Trainings in compassion*. Ithaca, NY: Snow Lion Publications.

Rinpoche, K.K.G., 2013. *This precious life: Tibetan Buddhist teachings on the path to enlightenment*. Boston: Shambhala Publications.

Singer, T. and Klimecki, O.M., 2014. Empathy and compassion. *Current Biology*, *24*(18), pp. R875–R878.

Wallace, B.A., 1999. *Boundless heart: The four immeasurables*. Ithaca, NY: Snow Lion Publications.

Chapter 5

Visualization in meditation practice

Visualization-based meditations are a common type of contemplative practices across contemplative traditions. One of the reasons why they are so commonly used might be their multifaceted nature and effects – visualization-based practice can at the same time train mindfulness and meta-awareness skills, cultivate compassion and other whole-some emotional qualities and also develop contemplative insight. Yet, in comparison to research on mindfulness or compassion, very few studies investigated the effects of visualization-based meditation. In addition, the limited research which is available is mostly focused on the impact of these practices on attention, ignoring the possible broad impact of visualization-based meditation on a variety of processes and outcomes.

In this chapter, we will examine visualization-based practices more closely, particularly based on examples of meditations in the Tibetan Buddhist tradition. We will first briefly discuss Western psychological understanding of mental imagery and its implications for mental health before outlining what visualization-based practices are and how they are applied as part of long-term meditation training in Buddhism. We will then explore in detail a generic example of visualization-based meditation practice in the Tibetan Buddhist tradition. This will be fol-lowed by a discussion about neuroscientific evidence on brain changes associated with visualization-based meditation. We will then discuss the role of visualization-based practices in the broader framework of meditation training in terms of their possible impact on metacognitive self-regulation and shifts in modes of existential awareness (MEA). Finally, we will explore how visualization-based practices could be readily integrated into everyday activities throughout the day.

What is visualization-based meditation?

The defining feature of visualization-based meditation practices is their employment of mental imagery. From the Western psychological perspective mental imagery can be described as sensory experience arising without external information. Interestingly, both psychological and neuroscientific research on mental imagery has shown that mental imagery relies on the same processes and mechanisms as actual perception stimulated by external objects (Pearson et al., 2015). Mental imagery can also impact our mental functioning in a way similar to actual perceptions; it is particularly comparable to the effects of weak (blurry) perceptions. Furthermore, mental imagery can impact on our physiology just like perception as exemplified in a study which examined changes in pupil dilation in response to mental images of different brightness (Laeng and Sulutvedt, 2013). Participants in the study were asked to imagine bright and dark objects such as a 'sunny sky' or 'dark room' and the researchers found that their pupil dilation responded accordingly – with pupil constriction to bright imagery and pupil dilation to dark imagery. Similar effects were obtained when participants imagined shapes of different brightness they were previously shown.

Given the powerful perception-like effects of imagery including physiological changes, it is perhaps not surprising that recent research highlighted the pivotal role of mental imagery in clinical conditions (Hackmann and Holmes, 2004). For example, it has been shown that a strong element of fearful mental imagery is present in anxiety disorders (such as images of snakes or anxiety-associated events). Similarly, depression seems to be associated with a reduced ability to imagine positive events or feelings and intrusive imagery is one of the prominent symptoms in post-traumatic stress disorder (PTSD). Mental images can also drive addictive behaviour and hallucinations in schizophrenia can be considered a case of mental imagery with mistaken external information attribution.

Just like imagery can be considered one of the main aspects of symptomatology in varied clinical conditions, it can also be used in treatment of these conditions countering the misattributions or deficits in mental imagery. Indeed, imagery exposure has been used in therapeutic contexts for several decades; it involves controlled imagery of fearful situations (e.g., boarding a plane for someone with a fear of flying) while applying new ways of coping with the fearful response to the imagined event. Another mental imagery technique which has been applied as part of cognitive behavioural therapy is imagery rescripting, which involves replacing a negative intrusive imagery with either less threatening imagery or positive imagery (Holmes, Arntz and Smucker, 2007). Recent research suggested that imagery-based techniques can be particularly effective when dealing with emotional content in therapy, more so than talking therapy. For example, when study participants were asked to complete neutral scenarios in a positive way by either imaging a positive event or verbally thinking of a positive event, the imagery condition showed stronger increases in positive mood than the verbal condition (Holmes, Lang and Shah, 2009).

Overall, the cumulative scientific evidence on the mechanisms and clinical relevance of mental imagery points to its powerful perception-like effects on our cognition and well-being. It is therefore perhaps not surprising that visualization-based practices have been applied for many centuries in the context of meditation training as a means of refining attention, modifying cognitive schemas, fostering positive emotions and enabling existential insight. Because of their multifaceted effects, visualization-based practices are not easily classified into a specific meditation type category. A recent study suggested that meditation practices can be divided into attention family, constructive family and deconstructive family (Dahl, Lutz and Davidson, 2015). While practices in the attention family aim to support the development of self-regulation of attention through training in mindfulness and meta-awareness, meditations in the constructive family foster wholesome thinking schemas and emotional qualities such as compassion and loving kindness. In contrast, the deconstructive family of practices supports the cultivation of experiential understanding of thinking and emotional patterns as well as insight into the nature of self and reality. Visualization-based practices can belong to any of these categories or cut across them depending on their emphasis and specifics.

For example, mental imagery is an important aspect of training in the four immeasurables which involve imagining a person close to us, a neutral person, a harmful person and all sentient beings. Similarly, practices of Tonglen (giving and taking) have a strong element of imagery when sharing wholesome experiences and experiences of suffering with others. These meditation techniques would perhaps primarily belong to the constructive family of practices, but they also entail elements of attention training and elements of insight as discussed in Chapter 4. Imagery is also an important element of many foundational Buddhist contemplations such as practices of the Four Thoughts that turn the mind to Dharma. As part of these practices, the meditator would, for example, imagine consequences of long-term engaging in anger or afflictive attachment. These practices would perhaps again primarily belong to the constructive family, but also entail elements of attention training when a practitioner tries to stay focused on a particular contemplative topic and monitor for distractions in thinking. There is also an aspect of insight about the nature of our existence, albeit limited and mostly intellectual, arising as a result of contemplating on topics such as impermanence and causes of suffering.

However, imagery is the primary focus of two particular groups of meditation practices in the Tibetan Buddhist tradition with the main group involving visualization of deities and the other group working with energies in the body. The deity visualization meditations are at the heart of Tibetan Buddhist meditation training because they develop several aspects of meditators training at the same time. They are considered particularly effective because they can simultaneously develop attention stability and control together with meta-awareness, emotional qualities of loving kindness and compassion as well as insight. Specifically, the deity practices involve visualizations of complex images representing various qualities of existential balance (enlightenment) such as unconditional compassion or advanced modes of existential awareness. The visualization is accompanied by recitation of a mantra specific to the deity and also represents the core qualities embodied by the image of the deity.

The second group of visualization-based practices is based on a theory of energy (Tibetan: lung) which flows through the body. By engaging in meditation practices which work with these energies the practitioner can enhance her existential insight and progress towards more advanced states of existential awareness. The meditations working with energies are usually practiced in retreat under careful guidance of an experienced meditation master who can assess whether a practitioner is ready to engage in this type of meditation training. Given the traditionally secret and highly individual nature of this type of visualization-based meditation training, we will not consider this group of practices in detail here. However, a recently published study suggested that these types of practices can have measurable impact on body physiology – specifically, the Tibetan Buddhist practice of tummo, which aside from its core spiritual purpose aims to increase bodily temperature, was indeed associated with significant increases up to 38.3 degrees Celsius (Kozhevnikov et al., 2013). Importantly, these large effects were only observed when the practice was accompanied by specific targeted visualizations, but not without this element of the practice.

Importantly, all deity visualizations and energy practices are firmly grounded in the contemplations on the Four Thoughts that turn the mind and the practices of the four immeasurables which together shape the motivation/intention for engaging in the deity practice. Meditators are typically required to practice these foundational contemplations together with the four immeasurables before they are ready to start practicing deity visualization or engage in energy practices. In addition, the practitioners should have at least basic intellectual and partial experiential understanding of the illusory construed nature of reality before they start with deity visualization, so that they understand the construed nature of the visualizations and do not reify them.

With regard to the attention aspect of the deity practices, the practitioner aims to visualize the image continuously, thus training stability of attention while at the same time monitoring for distraction, which develops meta-awareness. The meditator brings attention back to the visualization when distraction is noticed, thus cultivating attention control. At the same time, the mantra recitation engages verbalization, hence limits distractions due to overt or silent speech and that further amplifies the effect of the visualization. Just like with any other type of Shamatha practice, long-term training in deity visualization follows the progression of nine stages with increasing levels of stability and clarity of visualization. At the advanced stages of training the practitioner is able to hold the visualization for an hour or longer with vividness and clarity of detail and without major distraction.

Deity visualization has a clear wholesome quality; it does not focus on a neutral meditation object such as breath-focus, neutral sound or a pebble. Visualizing deity has the quality of connecting with wholesome qualities of existential balance represented in the image of an enlightened being, a Buddha in various forms depending on qualities they predominantly embody. In this way, deity meditation aims to support the practitioner in development of emotional qualities such as compassion and loving kindness applied with equanimity to all beings as enlightened beings would. Various aspects of these qualities are represented by different aspects of the images. For example, images of White Tara, a female Buddha, depict her with six eyes representing her ability to continuously perceive the suffering of all beings in their various forms with all their afflictions. Mantra recitation which accompanies the visualizations further enhances and expresses the quality of the deity.

The insight aspects of deity visualization involve the nature of the deity and ways in which the visualization of the deity is created and dissolved. Just like the ordinary reality as most of us perceive it, the deity which we visualize is considered to be illusory in its existence. This is based on the understanding that we construe our reality and develop afflictive attachment to it from which suffering arises. Abiding in the pristine awareness of the mind which is unconstrued and without afflictions is the only state which is free from afflictive construal of reality. Our ordinary reality is considered an illusory afflictive construal of our mind. In contrast, the deity we visualize is considered also illusory, but the purest construal our mind can produce. This is because it arises from pristine awareness, a state of existential balance, with the intention to alleviate suffering of sentient beings. As explained in Tibetan Buddhist teachings, for most practitioners the notion of pure awareness is hard to comprehend or experientially realize, whereas they can more easily relate to personalized representations of qualities of the Buddha mind. Therefore deity practice can for many meditators present a path of progression in their contemplative training which would otherwise stagnate.

In many of the deity visualization practices, the meditator not only visualizes a deity as separate from them, but also tries to visualize themselves as a deity, and then visualize other beings as deities and the surroundings as pure Buddha lands. This step in the visualization practice enables to the practitioner to realize the core assumption in Tibetan Buddhist practice that all sentient beings naturally have pristine awareness but do not recognize this. So in terms of pristine awareness presence, all beings are no different from beings who abide in pristine awareness (Buddhas; in Tibetan Buddhism this term is applied for various deity forms and for all practitioners who achieved enlightenment), which is the state of existential balance. The difference is that unenlightened beings lost connection with pristine awareness and are not able to access it or stabilise glimpses of pristine awareness; thus their mind is full of afflictive views and emotions. When we visualize ourselves and others as deities we remind ourselves of the pristine awareness which is present in our mind and minds of all sentient beings and in this way we try to connect with it.

When visualising oneself or others as a deity, it is essential that the practitioner grounds this practice in the illusory nature of the visualization. This is why many teachers recommend that only practitioners with certain levels of understanding and experiential knowledge of the illusory nature of reality engage in deity meditation. Otherwise, the deity practice may result in over-identification with the deity and solidify states marked by lack of recognition of the construed nature of the deity. For this reason, practitioners were traditionally introduced to deity practices only by an experienced and accomplished master who assessed their readiness for engaging in this type of meditation practice. The initiations would be combined with teachings explaining how to engage in the deity meditations. In the current era in Western countries, initiations to deity practices are often offered without such assessment and those attending these initiations often have very limited understanding of the practices combined with a lack of foundational understanding of the motivational/ intentional grounding of the practices. This is one of the drawbacks associated with presenting meditation practices which were traditionally only practiced as part of a complex meditation system in separation from it. To counter this approach, increasing numbers of Buddhist organizations are starting to offer comprehensive programmes of meditation study, rather than separate retreats or teachings. Hopefully this trend will grow and will be adapted by meditation teaching organizations and teachers more broadly.

Developing visualization-based meditation practice in the Buddhist context

Just like any other meditation in the Tibetan Buddhist tradition, each visualization-based meditation focusing on a deity starts with developing motivation/intention for the meditation. The contemplation on motivation/ intention at the beginning of the practice would focus on impermanence, the nature of suffering, the principle of cause and effect and the current opportunity to engage in meditation practices which can reduce our suffering. We would then remember the shared nature of suffering across all sentient beings and develop compassion, which further drives our motivation/ intention to engage in the meditation practice. Those more advanced in their practice bring to their awareness the authentic motivation/intention of bodhicitta as a genuine wish for achieving the highest levels of existential balance and helping others on their path to existential balance.

The practitioner would then proceed onto the next step in the meditation practice which for advanced practitioners involves resting in the most advanced state of existential awareness they are capable of generating. In this part of the practice the practitioner reminds herself of the construed and therefore illusory nature of reality. This may involve at the basic level an intellectual reminder and contemplation about the inherently empty nature of self and then resting in the awareness of awareness which is a practice of being simply aware of being aware without focus on a particular object. This practice is a precursor of insight meditations in which the practitioner experientially explores the nature of self and the nature of reality from the space of awareness of awareness. More advanced practitioners can during this part of the visualization-based practice abide in a non-conceptual state of realizing the construed (empty) nature of self or in the state of pristine awareness. Importantly, this step in the visualization-based practices is an indispensable part of the meditation which grounds the practice in the understanding of the illusory nature of the self and prevents the possibility of clinging on to the visualizations as ordinary reality.

From this non-conceptual state the practitioner creates the visualization of the deity, often starting with a syllable symbolizing the deity which then transforms into the deity and surroundings. Tibetan Buddhist teachings outline that through this process of generating the deity the practitioner purifies the experience of birth in this lifetime (Kongtrul, 2002), so it is an essential step. Every aspect of the deity visualization, including clothing, facial expressions, adornments and surroundings, has many layers of symbolic meaning beyond the actual depictions. For example, the adornments of the deity or the objects they hold in their hands may represent unity of wisdom and compassion, or qualities of the six Paramitas (generosity, ethical discipline, patience, perseverance, meditative concentration and wisdom) etc. At the deepest level of meaning the visualization can represent the non-duality of pristine awareness (Mipham, 2007).

During the main part of the meditation the practitioner sustains attention focus on the visualization while monitoring for distractions and returning the attention back to the visualization. At the same time, the meditator recites the mantra of the deity and the visualization of the mantra letters can also be part of the overall deity visualization. The visualization often involves a cycle in which the deity sends blessings to all beings and in this way, for example, purifies the afflictions in their mind and relieves their suffering. The practice may involve visualization of external deities as well as visualizing oneself as the deity. At the start of the training in visualization-based meditation the practitioner may alternate between looking at a picture of the visualization and trying to remember the details, then looking away and recreating the image in their mind (Tsogyal, 1999). There might be a need to shift between the image viewing and visualization quite often at the initial stages of the practice, but this will lessen with more training. At the beginning of the training in deity meditation the clarity of the visualization can be fairly poor, lacking detail and vividness. However, with repeated practice at the advanced stages of proficiency, the meditator tries to hold all the details of the visualization with clarity and for increasingly longer periods of time without losing focus.

The increasing levels of proficiency in long-term practice of the visualization-based deity meditation are not only associated with the usual signs of progression in Shamatha practice – increased clarity and stability of meditation – they are also accompanied by phenomenological shifts in terms of connection with the qualities of the deity. These can, for example, manifest as an experience of gradients in the progression of compassion training, from basic levels to the non-referential experience of compassion. At the same time, the practitioner may notice gradual shifts in her existential awareness – experiential deepening of the realization of emptiness (construed nature) of self as well as the illusory nature of reality. This demonstrates how visualization-based practice can work at the attention, emotion and insight levels at the same time. Yet, there is also a sense of the sequential nature of the progression at these three levels where increased levels of stability and clarity enable enhancements in development of emotion qualities such as compassion and these then together serve as catalysts for existential insight and progression in MEA.

After sustaining the deity visualization for a certain amount of time, the practitioner gradually dissolves the visualizations in the opposite order to the one applied at the beginning of the practice when the visualization was created. This process of dissolution is symbolic of purifying the experience of death (Kongtrul, 2002). The dissolution of the seed syllable of the deity is typically the last step in the visualization followed by abiding in the awareness of awareness, emptiness of self or pristine awareness based on the capacity and proficiency of the practitioner. This again serves as a reminder of the illusory nature of the visualization, which is construed, yet in comparison to our usual perceptions of reality pure in its nature. Some teachers recommend these non-conceptual phases of the visualization-based practice to be equally long as the time spent in creating, maintaining and dissolving the visualization.

After the silent non-conceptual phase practitioners often visualize themselves as the deity and visualize others and surroundings as deities and the pure land just like in meditation. This visualization is sustained in breaks between formal meditation sessions. The purpose of this visualization is to remind ourselves repeatedly, throughout the day, of the essential pure nature of our mind and our experiences even though it can be superficially morphed into various construed forms and afflictions. At the end of the formal visualization-based meditation session we remind ourselves of the wholesome states cultivated during the practice and dedicate the merit with a wish that the practice would support us in progressing on our path towards existential well-being so that we can be free from suffering and help others achieve the same.

Neuroscience of visualization-based meditation

Activation of brain areas during visualization seems to closely resemble the activation of the brain during actual perception of the visualized object (Kosslyn, Ganis and Thompson, 2001). So, for example, when we are looking at a picture of the deity or visualizing it, the brain parts activated during both processes are very similar. There are, however, slight differences in the robustness of the overlap between different brain areas involved in visual perception and imagery. These areas include a hierarchy of brain regions progressing from early visual areas such as V1 of the occipital cortex to highest levels of visual processing in the ventral temporal lobe (Pearson et al., 2015). This progression of visual areas is referred to as a hierarchy because the early visual areas specialize in low-level processing of features such as edges or location of shapes on the retina whereas high-level visual processing involves more abstract representations, for example of what objects as wholes look like. So the hierarchy follows a trajectory of increasing abstractness and meaningfulness of the visual representations.

Interestingly, research studies have reported strong overlap in activation of higher level visual areas in both perception and visual imagery, whereas the brain activations in early visual areas seem to follow the same patterns but differ in intensity with imagery producing weaker patterns. This could be due to closer proximity and more neural connections between higher level visual areas and regions of the medial temporal lobe which encode memories including remembered images. However, greater clarity and vividness of imagery has been linked to activation in early visual areas V1 and V2 (Cui et al., 2007). Importantly, these lower visual areas not only send but also receive information from higher visual areas which can inform the clarity of visualization.

This understanding of the processes involved in visual imagery seems to support the progression of long-term meditation training in the visualization-based practices that starts with low clarity of detail in the visualization and reliance on more abstract representations of what is being visualized. With repeated practice, the practitioner is able to visualize the deity image in increasingly more detail which might be supported by increasing involvement of early visual areas in creating the visualization supported by feedback loops from higher level visual representations of the visualized image. Based on this theory, it would be expected that the most advanced levels of proficiency in visualization-based meditation practices would be associated with patterns of activation in both high- and low-level visual areas which would be very similar to activations in response to viewing the visualized image. No research has so far evaluated this prediction.

Brain activation during mental imagery also closely overlaps with brain activation associated with visual working memory (Pearson et al., 2015). Indeed, studies have shown that whether research participants are instructed to hold an image in their memory or to create a mental image, both instructions lead to very similar activation in the V1 early visual area of the brain. This is perhaps not surprising given that most of us would use mental imagery as a tool in trying to remember an image, even though there are individual differences and some people may prefer using verbal descriptions to encode visual images in their memory. This highlights differences in individual propensities towards mental imagery with those who have clear preference for imagery memory encoding being perhaps more inclined to also engage in visualization-based meditation practices.

Given the overlap between mental imagery and visual working memory it might also be expected that extensive experience in visualization-based meditation practice would be associated with better performance in mental imagery tasks. Such performance enhancements could be either due to improvements in imagery processing or greater visual working memory capacity. An earlier case study with only one experienced meditator suggested that deity visualization is associated with enhanced right posterior gamma activity in the brain (Lehmann et al., 2001). In this study the meditator has been asked to engage in several different types of meditation including Buddha visualization, mantra recitation and dissolution of self. The gamma activity at 40 Hz frequency across the brain was measured during the meditation practices and the sources of the gamma activity were derived in further post-hoc analyses. The gamma activity was the target of the investigations because other researchers suggested that it is an index of conscious activity and, in case of visual processing, also of binding visual features into a meaningful representation of an object or scene. The findings of the study showed differential localization of gamma activity across the different meditation practice styles. The results in the visualization meditation suggested distinct activation in the right posterior areas which in comparison to mantra recitation was localized to the right middle temporal lobe. In line with the research evidence outside of meditation research the results of this study indicated that deity practice, just like other imagery tasks, results in activation of high-level visual processing areas.

The previous study provided interesting initial results, but also had limitations in terms of examining the effects of one participant rather than a group and measuring brain activity during meditation only. This does not allow for inferences about possible trait effects outside of meditation practice resulting from long-term visualization-based meditation training. These shortcomings were addressed in another study which investigated the performance of meditators in computerized mental imagery and visuospatial working memory tasks before and after deity meditation practice. The participants in the study were meditators experienced in deity practices, meditators with experience in other types of meditation (open presence) and meditation novices (Kozhevnikov et al., 2009). Specifically, the performance of participants in the groups was compared before and after the meditators engaged in 20 minutes of deity practice (first meditator group) or 20 minutes of open presence practice (second meditator group) and controls engaged in other imagery tasks for the same amount of time.

No differences in performance across the groups were found at the baseline, before the groups engaged in meditation practice. This is somewhat surprising because it could be expected that regular visualization-based practice would result in trait-like improvements in mental imagery or visual working memory capacity, which would be present within and outside of formal meditation. However, large differences between the meditators skilled in deity practice and the other groups were observed after the meditation practice. The meditators in the deity practice group showed large and significant enhancement in their performance on both the mental imagery task involving spatial rotation and the visuospatial working memory task. These findings were interpreted in terms of deity meditation resulting in temporary enhancements in the access to visuospatial processing resources. Such interpretation would perhaps be consistent with more efficient use of a greater capacity of visuospatial working memory. Given the absence of this effect before the deity meditation, it seems that the improved performance depends on state-induced enhancement, but this state shift is likely enabled by trait-like changes in the ability to recruit the resources in meditation since similar effects were not observed in the other groups of meditators or meditation novices.

The findings of increases in mental imagery and visuospatial working memory after deity meditation were replicated in another study with the same computerized tasks which compared the performance of experienced Theravada practitioners and Tibetan Buddhist practitioners (Amihai and Kozhevnikov, 2014). The practitioners of the Theravada tradition who did not train in deity practices did not show significant improvements in their performance after 20 minutes of either calm abiding or Vipassana practice. In contrast, the Tibetan Buddhist meditators showed improved performance on the two tasks after deity practice. In addition, the study assessed possible differences in heart-rate variability as an indicator of sympathetic and parasympathetic activity in the two groups of meditators. The findings revealed significant increases in parasympathetic activity in comparison to rest in the Theravada meditators and significant increases in sympathetic activity in comparison to rest in the Tibetan Buddhist meditators. These results were interpreted in terms of increased arousal in the Tibetan Buddhist meditator group possibly contributing to their enhanced performance on the mental imagery and visuospatial tasks.

Overall, the limited research evidence on the effects of visualization-based meditation suggests that this type of practice is associated with distinct patterns of brain activation in higher level visual areas of the brain which would be expected during any mental imagery task. More importantly, deity meditation has also been shown to significantly enhance performance in experienced meditators on mental imagery and visuospatial working memory tasks right after completion of the practice. No studies have so far assessed the progression of changes in the brain with increasing proficiency in visualization-based meditation. It could be expected that changes in the higher visual areas of the brain gradually propagate to lower visual areas as clarity of detail in the practice increases. Finally, no studies so far investigated the possible impact of these practices on the development of compassion or other wholesome emotional qualities and the cultivation of insight into the nature of self and reality.

Visualization-based meditation, self-regulation and well-being

As we have discussed earlier, visualization-based meditation seems to primarily impact attention and meta-awareness, but can also support development of emotional qualities and insight. Such changes are likely to have broad impact on the development of our self-regulation skills. Specifically, visualization-based practices aim to enhance the stability and clarity of attention with practitioners gradually able to sustain focus on the meditation for longer and with more attention to details of the visualized image. Just like other meditations training attention, the practitioner at the same time monitors distractions and redirects attention back to the visualized image – practice which aims to enhance meta-awareness and attention control as core aspects of the metacognitive self-regulatory capacity (MSRC) (Dorjee, 2016).

However, visualization-based meditation also aims to develop compassion, loving kindness, rejoicing and equanimity – qualities which are represented by the visualized images of deities. Many of these visualizations involve imagining the deity sending out light of compassion to all sentient beings which provides comfort and purifies afflictions as the root causes of their suffering. The practitioner also visualizes her own afflictions to be transformed or purified through such practice. In

this way, visualization-based meditations on the deity explicitly cultivate wholesome emotional qualities. Hence, training in these types of
meditation would also be expected to improve the emotional well-being
and the emotion regulation skills of practitioners, which are the second
dimension of the MSRC.

Visualization-based practices likely also significantly impact the conceptual systems which contribute to the MSRC. This is because this type
of meditation involves visual imagery and thus reduces the engagement
in ruminative verbal modes of thinking and speaking. The visualizations
may also prompt the development of new cognitive schemas which with
repetition may replace habitual schemas of the ordinary afflictive reality.
In addition, visualization-based practices are typically also accompanied
by recitation of mantras. This most likely further reduces the engagement
in ruminative thought given that both visual perceptual channels and verbal channels are highly active during such meditation, leaving very limited mental resources of working memory for ruminative thinking.

Depending on the proficiency and depth of engagement with the
visualization-based meditation, these practices can also support practitioners in the development of increasingly advanced MEA. For example,
deity meditations emphasize the illusory nature of ordinary afflictive
reality and the visualizations represent also illusory, but pure, representations of reality. In addition, with advancement in deity practice, the
practitioner may start focusing more closely on the wisdom (insight)
aspects of the deity and try to identify with their representations of the
nature of mind and reality. In this way, the deity meditations may loosen
up the conditioned notions of self and enable the practitioner to experientially understand its construed nature. At the most advanced levels, the
deity practice can be a catalyst for practitioners' recognition of pristine
awareness represented by the mind of the deity and from which the deity
visualizations ultimately arise and dissolve to. Thus deity practice can
provide multifaceted support for long-term practitioners of meditation
who can connect with different aspects of the practices depending on
their stage of progression on the path towards existential balance.

A day of visualization-based meditation

Whilst most of the previous discussion focused on the deity meditation in the Tibetan Buddhist context, visualization-based practices can
enrich long-term meditation practice of meditators across contemplative
traditions as well as religious and non-religious contexts. We will thus
consider how these types of meditation can be introduced into everyday

routines both as Buddhist practices and secular techniques. Starting early in the morning right after waking up, a Tibetan Buddhist practitioner would typically visualize the lineage of Buddhas and the accomplished master she has been following and in this way connect with their accomplishments and teachings as a way of motivating her engagement in meditation practice throughout the day. A secular practitioner could perhaps use visualization-based practice at the beginning of the day to imagine how they will go through the day by engaging in the daily activities mindfully, with meta-awareness and with qualities of compassion and loving kindness. Visualizations would also be used during morning routines when practicing Tonglen (giving and taking) such as imagining all sentient beings having a wholesome meal or not experiencing the difficulties we are experiencing.

While commuting, a Tibetan Buddhist meditator can practice the deity meditation by visualizing others as deities, which can serve as a reminder of the pure nature of mind that is present all the time in all sentient beings despite the lack of their connection with this aspect of their consciousness. The practice would also serve as a reminder of the illusory nature of the conventional reality and changeable nature of mental afflictions. This practice can be further enhanced by remembering the unconditional compassion qualities of the deity and trying to apply these when engaging with others throughout the day. A meditator practicing in the secular context could use visualization practices to enhance their meditation on compassion, loving kindness, rejoicing and equanimity by imagining themselves in a state of unconditional compassion and visualizing others experiencing the same state.

These visualizations can be continued through the morning and afternoon routines at work, combined with brief formal meditation sessions during which a Buddhist meditator can engage in a short deity practice following the steps outlined earlier. A very brief recollection of the image of the deity can also serve as a reminder of the qualities the practitioner is trying to develop themselves, whether it is compassion or aspects of existential insight. This can be particularly powerful since we know that mental imagery activates the same brain areas as actual visual perception and also given that imagery can be more powerful in impacting on our physiology than verbal descriptions. A similar practice can be used by a secular practitioner to remind herself of an image of themselves when they experienced a sense of tranquillity, compassion, contentment or expansion of their existential insight. This practice can be easily done during brief pauses and breaks throughout the day. In both Buddhist and secular contexts the visualization-based practice can also be applied as part of techniques such as working with antidotes. For example, when experiencing frustration or anger we can try to create an image of ourselves when we were calm and content or visualize a deity reminding ourselves of the illusory nature of ordinary experience, thus creating a broader, more spacious perspective on the current difficult situation.

We can keep on introducing these visualization-based meditations into the time we spend commuting from work and then also in the evening while interacting with friends and family. For instance, hearing about others' difficulties, whether in person or from the media, can become a prompt for us to remember the deity practice and visualize the difficulties easing for those who are suffering. This practice can also serve as a reminder for us to look deeper into the cause of suffering and opportunities we and others have in this moment to alleviate our suffering. With long-term practice, this way of thinking and visualizing can become for us habitual, instead of random mind-wandering and rumination or mindless engagement in daily activities. Finally, a Buddhist practitioner can apply visualization-based meditation as part of her formal evening meditation session to purify afflictions which arose during the day and to recollect positive situations to rejoice in these. A secular practitioner can also use mental imagery to connect with wholesome experiences during the day and use imagery rescripting as a coping strategy when recollecting any afflictive or difficult experiences.

Visualization-based meditation from a long-term practice perspective

While visualization-based meditation practices have been mostly neglected in research on meditation so far, they provide rich and multifaceted techniques which can boost progress in long-term meditation for meditators developing their practice in both traditional and secular contexts. These practices are applied across contemplative traditions (e.g., Christian Ignatian tradition), even though scientific knowledge of these meditations and their effects from psychological and neuroscientific perspectives is virtually absent. Broader applicability of these techniques as part of long-term meditation practice will likely depend on individual propensities of practitioners, with research in the general population showing that some people are naturally more inclined to rely on mental imagery in visual working memory tasks than others. However, this is likely the case for any meditation technique; that's why a variety of meditation practices can be helpful in tailoring long-term meditation training to practitioners' individual differences and preferences. Hopefully, future research will investigate visualization-based practices across traditions and degrees of proficiency with attention to their nuances and varied effects.

Summary

Chapter 5 discusses the theory and practice of visualization-based meditation techniques, which have been mostly neglected in previous scientific research on meditation, yet are broadly applied as part of contemplative training across traditions. The chapter starts with an explanation of scientific understanding of mental imagery and its role in mental health, and then proceeds onto an explanation of visualization-based meditation practices in the Tibetan Buddhist tradition. This is followed by an explanation of an example visualization-based practice – deity meditation – with particular focus on how this type of practice can enhance the development and sustaining of long-term meditation practice. The multifaceted impact of deity meditations on attention and meta-awareness as well as development of compassion and related qualities together with existential insight is of particular interest here. Research evidence on changes in the brain and cognitive processing associated with visualization-based meditation is presented in this context. We then explore how visualization-based meditation can impact all three dimensions of the MSRC, including conceptual processing, and we also highlight possible contributions of this type of meditation to the development of more advanced modes of existential awareness (MEA). The final section of the chapter integrates insights from the theoretical considerations with examples of how to introduce visualization-based meditation into everyday activities.

References

Amihai, I. and Kozhevnikov, M., 2014. Arousal vs. relaxation: A comparison of the neurophysiological and cognitive correlates of Vajrayana and Theravada meditative practices. *PLoS One*, *9*(7), p. e102990.

Cui, X., Jeter, C.B., Yang, D., Montague, P.R. and Eagleman, D.M., 2007. Vividness of mental imagery: Individual variability can be measured objectively. *Vision Research*, *47*(4), pp. 474–478.

Dahl, C.J., Lutz, A. and Davidson, R.J., 2015. Reconstructing and deconstructing the self: Cognitive mechanisms in meditation practice. *Trends in Cognitive Sciences*, *19*(9), pp. 515–523.

Dorjee, D., 2016. Defining contemplative science: The metacognitive self-regulatory capacity of the mind, context of meditation practice and modes of existential awareness. *Frontiers in Psychology*, *7*, pp. 1–15.

Hackmann, A. and Holmes, E., 2004. Reflecting on imagery: A clinical perspective and overview of the special issue of memory on mental imagery and memory in psychopathology. *Memory*, *12*(4), pp. 389–402.

Holmes, E.A., Arntz, A. and Smucker, M.R., 2007. Imagery rescripting in cognitive behaviour therapy: Images, treatment techniques and outcomes. *Journal of Behavior Therapy and Experimental Psychiatry*, *38*(4), pp. 297–305.

Holmes, E.A., Lang, T.J. and Shah, D.M., 2009. Developing interpretation bias modification as a 'cognitive vaccine' for depressed mood: Imagining positive events makes you feel better than thinking about them verbally. *Journal of Abnormal Psychology*, *118*(1), p. 76.

Kongtrul, J., 2002. *Creation and completion: Essential points of tantric meditation*. New York: Simon and Schuster.

Kosslyn, S.M., Ganis, G. and Thompson, W.L., 2001. Neural foundations of imagery. *Nature Reviews Neuroscience*, *2*(9), pp. 635–642.

Kozhevnikov, M., Elliott, J., Shephard, J. and Gramann, K., 2013. Neurocognitive and somatic components of temperature increases during g-tummo meditation: Legend and reality. *PLoS One*, *8*(3), p. e58244.

Kozhevnikov, M., Louchakova, O., Josipovic, Z. and Motes, M.A., 2009. The enhancement of visuospatial processing efficiency through Buddhist deity meditation. *Psychological Science*, *20*(5), pp. 645–653.

Laeng, B. and Sulutvedt, U., 2013. The eye pupil adjusts to imaginary light. *Psychological Science*, *25*(1), pp. 188–197.

Lehmann, D., Faber, P.L., Achermann, P., Jeanmonod, D., Gianotti, L.R. and Pizzagalli, D., 2001. Brain sources of EEG gamma frequency during volitionally meditation-induced, altered states of consciousness, and experience of the self. *Psychiatry Research: Neuroimaging*, *108*(2), pp. 111–121.

Mipham, J., 2007. *White lotus: An explanation of the seven-line prayer to Guru Padmasambhava*. Boston: Shambhala Publications.

Pearson, J., Naselaris, T., Holmes, E.A. and Kosslyn, S.M., 2015. Mental imagery: Functional mechanisms and clinical applications. *Trends in Cognitive Sciences*, *19*(10), pp. 590–602.

Tsogyal, Y., 1999. *Dakini teachings: Padmasambhava's oral instructions to Lady Tsogyal: Revealed by Nyang Ral Nyima Oeser and Sangye Lingpa*. Boudhanath: Rangjung Yeshe Publications.

Chapter 6

Existential insight and dream yoga

Buddhist teachings distinguish between two basic meditation styles: the calm abiding practices developing concentration (Shamatha) and practices cultivating insight into the nature of self and reality (Vipassana) (Wallace, 1999). Mindfulness and meta-awareness are the two main faculties developed in the practice of Shamatha, with meditation on the breath or visualization-based meditations being the main techniques applied. In contrast, Vipassana practices build on established mindfulness and meta-awareness foundations and use these faculties in investigating processes of the mind, the nature of self and the nature of reality. Practices developing compassion, loving kindness, rejoicing and equanimity as well as deity practices are sometimes singled out as other types of meditation outside of the categories of Shamatha and Vipassana (Lutz, Dunne and Davidson, 2007). However, as we have discussed in previous chapters they can also be considered as techniques developing attention and meta-awareness and some aspects of insight. This highlights the fact that Shamatha and Vipassana practices, while separable types of meditation, are typically both present in every meditation practice even though to different degrees. While Shamatha practices lead to only limited basic insight, Vipassana practices target the development of insight building on the pre-requisites of stable attention and enhanced meta-awareness cultivated in Shamatha. In this chapter, we will consider different gradients of existential insight and specific meditations particularly targeting its development.

The chapter starts by an in-depth exploration of the progression of cultivating existential insight with long-term meditation practice. This exploration is grounded in Tibetan Buddhist distinctions of three basic layers of consciousness with insight practices targeting access to and examination of increasingly deeper layers of consciousness. We will introduce the practice of dream yoga as a technique employed in cultivation of insight into the illusory nature of mind and reality. The chapter then progresses into a more detailed outline of how meditations developing contemplative insight are typically practiced and considerations about neuroscientific evidence regarding development of existential insight. This discussion will then be placed into the broader context of enhancing the metacognitive self-regulatory capacity (MSRC) of the mind and associated changes in modes of existential awareness (MEA) as the two main pillars of well-being. The final section of the chapter will outline how the practices of insight could be introduced into regular long-term meditation training as part of everyday activities including dream states during sleeping.

What is existential insight? The Western approach

In the Western scientific literature on meditation, open monitoring meditation (Lutz et al., 2008) has been closely linked to insight practice. Open monitoring involves vigilance, non-reactive noticing and examining the patterns of perceptions, thoughts and affect in the mind. In this framework open monitoring was primarily defined in terms of attention processes with particular focus on developing sustained attention and metacognitive awareness. Hence, the purpose of open monitoring practices is to gain familiarity with cognitive and affective patterns in our mind and with long-term practice to notice increasingly more nuanced habitual tendencies and reactions. The practice of open monitoring results in a less reactive awareness of mental processes and behaviour, and enables modification of mental habits which are not conducive to well-being. With further self-reflective inquiry, open monitoring can support the development of existential insight, this suggests that open monitoring and existential insight are not to be equated.

Indeed, a most recent and clearer categorization of meditation practices differentiated between open monitoring which could be considered a part of the attention family of meditations and a deconstructive family of meditations which refers to practices cultivating insight (Dahl, Lutz and Davidson, 2015). While both open monitoring and insight practices can look similar on the surface, they differ in terms of involvement of self-inquiry, which is a feature of insight practices only. Specifically, the deconstructive family of meditations applies self-inquiry in examining the processes and states of the mind, from perceptions, thoughts and affect to the more complex constructs of the self and reality. In this way, the deconstructive family can be differentiated from the attention family of meditation practices which primarily aim to develop attention focus and meta-awareness and in the traditional Buddhist terminology would fall under the label of Shamatha. In the same framework (Dahl, Lutz and Davidson, 2015) the deconstructive family also differs from a constructive family of meditation practices that aim to develop particular qualities such as compassion and loving kindness.

Importantly, the practices in the deconstructive family are further divided into three subgroups – object-oriented insight, subject-oriented insight and non-dual-oriented insight (Dahl, Lutz and Davidson, 2015). The object-oriented practices support self-inquiry of contents and processes of consciousness, for example, noticing and examining sensations of sound or bodily sensations. The subject-oriented practices can investigate the same content, but go further in the self-inquiry and question the nature of thoughts, sensations, affect etc. Finally, the non-dual practices examine the boundaries between the observer (the self) and the observed (object/subject of consciousness) which are closely linked to inquiry into the nature of self and at the most advanced levels also explore the nature of reality.

This framework (Dahl, Lutz and Davidson, 2015) is helpful in highlighting some of the subtle distinctions between inquiry practices and other meditations; for instance, as we have mentioned, it clearly states the similarities in the form of open monitoring practices and insight practices and also points to their deep differences in terms of the self-reflective processes and differences in results in terms of attentional/meta-awareness skills versus experiential insight. Furthermore, the distinctions between object-oriented, subject-oriented and non-dual insight practices clearly outline that insight practices differ in their focus and depth of resulting insight. However, there are also several aspects of the framework which could be questioned – for example, constructive family practices likely also support the development of contemplative insight, even though not to the same degree as the deconstructive family practices. So in some regards the distinctions between the families of meditation practices cannot be interpreted strictly.

In addition, the distinctions between the object-oriented and subject-oriented insight practices seem problematic. The framework suggests that the cognitive component in the mindfulness-based cognitive therapy (MBCT) could be considered an example of the object-oriented insight (Dahl, Lutz and Davidson, 2015). The insight aspect of MBCT is particularly related to the experience of decentring from thoughts, affect and also sensations in the body which arises as part of training in the MBCT. In this way, mental processes and contents are not perceived as solid facts, but as changeable events (Teasdale, 1999) characterized by lessening of emersion and identification with them. In comparison, the framework of meditation families also suggests that cognitive behaviour therapy (CBT) could be considered as an example of subject-oriented insight (Dahl, Lutz and Davidson, 2015), which is a more advanced level than object-oriented insight. This is surprising given that CBT encourages active changes in thinking and emphasizes modifiability of thoughts, but does not necessarily require the participant to inquire about the nature of thoughts. Decentring encouraged in MBCT actually seems to entail more advanced experiential understanding of the transient nature of thoughts, emotions and sensations.

Similarly, it is questionable whether the levels of insight arising from secular practices such as those implemented in MBCT and CBT could be comparable to the insight arising from meditations in the traditional Buddhist context. Here, for instance, the authors of the framework list Tibetan Buddhist Mahamudra Analytical Meditation and Dzogchen Analytical Meditation as well as Zen Koan practices in the same category of subject-oriented insight as CBT. However, the traditional Buddhist practices are grounded in a broader and much deeper understanding of the importance of phenomena and human suffering than CBT. These deeper analytical foundations directly feed into the insight which arises as a result of the traditional Buddhist practices in comparison to CBT. Moreover, the insight from CBT is mostly restricted to our own well-being whereas the insight in Mahayana Buddhist practices such as those mentioned in this category is intrinsically linked to the views about happiness and suffering of all beings. So while the categorization of meditation practices into the three families and the distinctions between subcategories of insight practices in the deconstructive family encourages more fine-grained differentiations amongst meditation types, these need to be carefully examined further.

What is existential insight? The Buddhist approach

An alternative approach to conceptualizing the different levels of insight can be based on Buddhist theories of consciousness. This is because the underlying assumption of insight practices is that they enable shifts in awareness towards increasingly more advanced experiential understanding of deeper layers of consciousness. Specifically, the Tibetan Buddhist tradition of Dzogchen describes three main layers of consciousness. The first one is often referred to as the ordinary mind; it is the layer of consciousness we are all familiar with, manifested by thoughts, sensations, perceptions, memories and affect. This is the layer of consciousness most of the research in psychology and neuroscience investigates.

Insight meditation practices working with the ordinary level of consciousness enable the practitioner to become more familiar with the patterns of conscious tendencies we have – the usual ways we respond to some triggers, the typical memories which arise in certain situations, the common themes that arise in our mind when we are faced with praise, criticism, boredom etc. Hence, the insight practices working with this level of consciousness enable us to gain more introspective metacognitive familiarity with how our ordinary mind works. This process of observing more closely the thinking and affective patterns in our mind is enabled by stabilization of our attention and enhancement of meta-awareness through the practices of Shamatha. If we get easily distracted and are unable to notice the processes in our mind for more than a couple of seconds, it would be nearly impossible for us to focus on the processes in our mind long enough to be able to derive any knowledge about how we usually think, feel and respond. This is why practices of Shamatha are indispensable in enabling insight into the processes and nature of the mind. Accordingly, we could claim that initial levels of insight in terms of familiarity with habitual patterns in our mind are developed as part of Shamatha practice.

As the stability of our attention and metacognitive skills improve further through continuous practice of Shamatha, we are able to apply insight-specific techniques to investigate the ordinary mind in more depth. We might be able to notice our habitual patterns in more detail and also notice more subtle tendencies of the ordinary mind. This can be further enabled by enhanced non-reactivity in our meditation – if reactions of anger, unhealthy attachment, jealousy and ego-centred pride arise in our mind easily, they may distract us from recognizing the typical patterns of reacting. In other words, a non-reactive attitude may allow us to let go of unhealthy defence mechanisms, which are strategies protecting our conditioned sense of who we are and why we value ourselves. In this way, we might be able to notice, perhaps for the first time, patterns in our thinking, reacting and functioning which were outside of our awareness previously. Practices of compassion, loving kindness, rejoicing and equanimity can be particularly helpful in loosening up the reactive tendencies of afflictions and developing a more balanced non-reactive perspective that may enable further insights into the patterns of our ordinary mind.

In the Buddhist context, such investigation is grounded in the contemplations on the impermanence of human existence and all phenomena together with contemplations on the nature of suffering etc. These contemplations prompt the practitioner to explore the impermanence and changeability of the processes and contents of our mind as well as their role in our experience of suffering. Similarly, meditations developing loving kindness, compassion and other qualities support the practitioner in cultivating initial insights into the role of afflictive mental states in our suffering and the beneficial effects of experiencing wholesome mental states. This further supports the insight into the impermanent and malleable nature of our thoughts, sensations, memories and affect.

Grounded in these initial insights, specific practices aiming to develop insight can then help the practitioner to investigate further the nature of the patterns arising in the ordinary mind. The meditator can, for example, engage in analytical meditations that aim to pinpoint the sources of the different emotions, thoughts, sensations etc. However, the analytical approach will provide only limited experiential understanding of the ways ordinary mind works. Some Buddhist schools, such as the Tibetan Buddhist tradition of Dzogchen, particularly emphasize the importance of experiential realization rather than analytical intellectual understanding. While the intellectual understanding is based on sound arguments, hence reliant on thinking, experiential understanding goes beyond ordinary ways of thinking and aims to access more holistic (non-propositional) modes of knowledge. These are typically associated with felt shifts in a sense of clarity, deep tranquillity and also associated with emotional qualities of contentment, compassion and sometimes bliss. The state of decentring which arises at the ordinary mind level can be considered one of the initial states of experiential insight characterized by a sense of healthy distancing from mental contents and processes, a sense of grounding and contentment.

As the practitioner progresses further in the training of Shamatha, the threshold for meta-awareness of mental contents and processes can slowly start shifting towards the next layer of consciousness. This layer is sometimes referred to as substrate consciousness (Sanskrit: ālayavijñāna; Tibetan: kun gzhi nams shes; Wallace, 2006; Ricard, 2003) and is typically not in the field of awareness if we are immersed in the ordinary mind most of the time and easily distracted. This is because the processes and contents of the ordinary mind automatically and robustly attract our attention unless we settle this layer of consciousness and develop advanced levels of non-reactive meta-awareness. The substrate consciousness stores more subtle patterns of tendencies and memories and could be described as an undercurrent of our behaviour and temperament. In the Tibetan Buddhist beliefs of reincarnation, the substrate consciousness stores memories and imprints of thoughts and actions across lifetimes.

When the practitioner starts working with this layer of consciousness in her practice, new patterns of emotions and thoughts can start emerging in the awareness after the ordinary mind had been well stabilized. This experience can come as a surprise to the practitioner because she may by now mostly abide in the tranquil states of Shamatha, so these new afflictive patterns might be initially perceived as a digression in the practice. This is why guidance of an experienced teacher is instrumental at this stage. The guidance is also essential after the practitioner stabilizes the appearances at the substrate consciousness level and starts accessing the ground of experience from which the ordinary mind arises. This can be associated with experiences of non-conceptuality, bliss and clarity that the practitioner did not experience before and therefore these experiences can be mistaken for abiding in the pristine awareness which is the deepest layer of consciousness.

There are three main differences between the substrate of consciousness and the pristine awareness. The first one relates to the non-dual aspect of insight which is a hallmark of pristine awareness, but is not present in the substrate consciousness. The difference, however, is quite subtle with the substrate consciousness still encompassing a residual sense of an individual separate self. In contrast, the distinction between the observer and the observed, between the subject and object of cognizing, dissolves at the level of pristine awareness. The second difference relates to how qualities of the substrate ground and pristine awareness manifest. It is important to emphasize here that both the ground of experience and the pristine awareness as experiential states are not associated with intellectual reasoning and analysis. So any conceptual descriptions of these states and their differences are inherently limited. Bearing this in mind, both the substrate ground and pristine awareness can be described in terms of their main features – of non-conceptuality, clarity, bliss and tranquillity. However, these qualities are separable in the state of substrate consciousness but are integral as part of a whole experience in the state of pristine awareness. In addition, the qualities of unconditional non-conceptual compassion and non-conceptual knowing are inherent in the state of pristine awareness, whereas they can appear separable and expressed to a limited degree in the substrate ground. Finally, the key hallmark of pristine awareness is that the practitioner 'recognizes' the nature of her mind, which means that there is no doubt in her mind about achieving the state. So there is an experiential certainty which does not need further questioning when one recognizes the nature of mind, even though moments of questioning the experience may arise when the practitioner does not abide in the state of pristine awareness anymore. The same quality of certainty does not arise in the substrate ground.

Insight at each of the three layers of consciousness is transient and needs to be stabilized. It is a common misconception that once a certain level of insight has been achieved, the practitioner can only progress further towards more advanced insights in the exploration of the layers of consciousness. This is often not the case; a beginner can sometime experience glimpses of the ground of substrate consciousness, but these experiences are only fleeting. Similarly, an advanced practitioner can fluctuate between experiencing ordinary mind and the substrate ground. In addition, at any level of long-term practice the meditator can develop unhealthy attachment to experiences of deeper layers of consciousness, particularly if these are associated with bliss, which can then hamper their further progress in the practice. This is where regular long-term practices and a broad perspective on the role of different meditation techniques is of the essence. For example, in a traditional Tibetan Buddhist training trajectory, the practitioner would progress onto targeted insight practices only after she has gained solid foundations in the motivational/ intentional aspects of the practice, contemplations on impermanence etc., stabilized her mind well through practices of Shamatha and developed an established practice of the four immeasurables. Of course, such foundations would already lead to initial glimpses of insight resulting from intellectual insight, stabilization of attention, development of meta-awareness and cultivation of compassion and other qualities together with equanimity. However, these glimpses do not challenge the ordinary perceptions, thoughts, emotion patterns and notions of self to the extent targeted practices such as deity meditations and the insight-specific practices applying self-inquiry and questioning the nature of reality do.

For those who have not sufficiently stabilized their mind before progressing onto these more advanced practices of insight such meditations may either not produce the effects they are intended for or can result in experiences the practitioner is not ready to work with. In the first instance, for example, the practitioner may engage in more advanced meditations but because of insufficient attentional stability and refinement of meta-awareness she will not be able to notice distinctive features of the different layers of consciousness. There are also further distinctions in gradients of experiential insight within each consciousness layer and all these nuanced aspects of insight may not be accessible if the ordinary level of the mind has not been settled sufficiently. As a result, the practitioner may conclude that these techniques do not work, or mistake mediocre experiences for advanced states of insight. The second consequence of starting to work with advanced insight techniques without sufficient stability can be further destabilization of the mind which can enhance pre-existing neurotic, anxious or anger tendencies. These can be managed through a guidance of an experienced teacher by going back to practices that stabilize the mind, but without proper guidance, such experience may result in mental health problems which need professional healthcare help.

This raises the questions whether secular meditation-based approaches are equipped for dealing with consequences of practitioners accessing deeper layers of consciousness and having more advanced experiences of insight. Within the typical training of the eight-week courses these experiences are likely to arise only rarely, but with long-term secular meditation practice their incidence may be more frequent. Indeed, possible adverse effects associated with going deeper into insight experience may occur more frequently with long-term secular meditation, similarly to long-term practice in at least some types of Buddhist meditation (Shapiro, 1992). In their current form, the secular meditation-based programmes do not have the motivational/intentional anchoring of meditation training in the traditional Buddhist context. They also do not have teacher training models which would take the whole meditation path into account and outline ways of working with the advanced aspects of insight. However, many of the secular meditation teachers at the same time receive support for development of their own meditation practice within their particular, often Buddhist, spiritual tradition. Given the increasing numbers of secular long-term practitioners and the popularity of these methods, it seems very timely for the field of secular meditation approaches to start addressing questions relevant to the development and managing of more advanced stages of insight in the secular context.

Developing existential insight in daytime and in dream yoga practice

There is a range of practices which are applied across contemplative traditions in order to cultivate insight. Some of these practices involve observing whatever thoughts, emotions, sensations, perceptions and memories spontaneously arise in the mind and inquiring about the process of arising and dissolving of mental phenomena back to the mind. The practitioner can also examine her own tendencies to stay with some of the mental contents and to let quickly go of others, basically explore the patterns of reactivity to whatever arises in our mind. Other inquiry practice may involve closer focus on particular sensations, perceptions, thoughts and affect, investigating them in detail such as examining where they come from, what they consist of and what their parts or aspects consist of etc. The process can continue further and further until the answers to the initial questions arise in the practitioner's mind as a sudden shift in understanding – as an insight.

Other practices turn the inquiry more directly onto the self and examine what the self consists of, what parts it may have and where it is. The practitioner may also invite specific thoughts about herself and examine how she reacts. She can, for example, think of praise and observe how her mind and body respond to this. Then she can bring to her mind thoughts of shame and disapproval, and watch how the mind reacts to that. Building on these practices she then turns to the notion of self and investigates what in the concept of self was causing the hurt or the ego-centred pride.

Another group of contemplative practices focuses more closely on the non-conceptual gaps between the thoughts, emotions, sensations and perceptions, rather than the contents themselves. The practitioner may try to sustain focus on the non-conceptual space and inquire about the nature of this space. This would be done by questions alternating with longer periods of staying with the non-conceptual space while monitoring for laxity or distraction. At the most advanced stages in the Tibetan Buddhist tradition of Dzogchen the practitioner can from this non-conceptual space turn the attention to the observer observing the non-conceptual space, and make the observer as such focus of the non-conceptual inquiry.

In Tibetan Buddhism, there is also a group of practices which aim to challenge the conventional grasping on our perceptions of reality. These practices examine the illusory nature of what we believe to be the reality outside of our mind. Dream yoga is one of the practices applied in this context and particularly focuses on examining the similarities and differences between the dream state and what we would consider the reality. As for any of the inquiry practices, the main pre-requisite for dream yoga is sufficient stability of attention and refined meta-awareness skills cultivated through Shamatha meditation. Without these skills the practitioner's mind might be too distracted and not malleable enough to allow for the development of lucid dreaming and then specific practices in the state of lucid dreaming.

Lucid dreaming is a state in which, while dreaming, we become aware that we are dreaming. In order to increase our chances of becoming lucid in a dream, it is recommended that throughout the day we develop the wish to become lucid during a dream state at night (Gyaltrul and Wallace, 1998). We would also reaffirm the wish before we go to sleep and a Buddhist practitioner would often also recite a particular mantra which can support the practitioner in becoming lucid during dreaming. In the Tibetan Buddhist context, the practitioner would also typically lie down in a certain body posture and create a visualization which aims to support the dream yoga practice.

Then during sleep, the practitioner can gradually develop the ability to become lucid in the dream. This is only a first step in the dream yoga practice. The next step involves manipulating the dream reality, for example, by trying to increase or decrease the size of appearances in the dream or change their colour. In the following steps, the practitioner can try to test the reality of their dream bodies etc. The meditator can also use the dream to practice deity visualization and connect with devotional practices. The investigations of the nature of self and reality would continue further during the awake state to compare the differences between the dream reality and the reality in a non-sleep state. Some of the difficulties that a practitioner may experience when attempting to develop lucid dreaming include waking up soon after they become lucid in a dream or not being able to recall dreams in the morning. The traditional Buddhist writings provide guidance on how to deal with such challenges, mostly through visualizations (Gyaltrul and Wallace, 1998).

As outlined in this section, there is a great variety of practices which can cultivate contemplative insight in the Buddhist context. Importantly, none of these techniques would be practiced in isolation – they would be embedded in a system of contemplative training and typically trained only after the practitioner has gained sufficient understanding of the motivational/intentional basis for meditation practice, stability of attention, improved meta-awareness and emotional balance. Each meditation session would also begin with connecting with the lineage of practitioners who achieved advanced levels of existential well-being and developing motivation/intention for engaging in the insight practice. This is often followed by other practices such as development of emotional qualities of loving kindness and compassion before progressing onto the actual practice of insight. At the end of the session the practitioner would dedicate the merit with the wish for their own progress in the practice towards existential balance and for other beings to achieve the same state.

Neuroscience of existential insight and dream yoga practices

Neuroscience investigations of insight practices seem to centre around three main types of effects. The first type comprises research on the effects of insight practices on attention and metacognitive monitoring skills. The second type focuses on the impact of insight practices on the default mode of brain function which describes random off-task brain activity. Finally, the third type, currently represented by very few studies, aims to investigate the associations between actual changes in awareness with insight practice and their brain correlates. We will now examine each of these three groups of studies in detail and at the end of this section also discuss physiological effects associated with dream yoga practice.

Most of the neuroscience research relevant to insight practice has so far focused on attention and meta-awareness processes associated with insight, rather than the states of intellectual and experiential insight as such. Researchers identified several regions in the brain based on the assumption that the state of open monitoring, which could be described as the attentional foundation of insight meditation, primarily involves vigilance and meta-awareness and also disengagement from distraction and shifting of attention back to the object of meditation (Lutz et al., 2008). In the context of monitoring bodily processes, these regions seem to consistently involve the anterior cingulate cortex, anterior insular cortex and secondary somatosensory cortex (e.g., Farb, Segal and Anderson, 2012). The anterior cingulate cortex supports voluntary attention control, disengagement from distractions and shifting of attention, whereas the anterior insula have been implicated in bodily awareness as well as awareness of emotional states and processes. Finally, the somatosensory cortex is activated during attention focus on the sensations in the body.

In addition to this research, some studies specifically investigated the differences in attention abilities between practices targeting focused attention and those developing open monitoring. This research, for example, showed that practitioners of open monitoring meditation are better able to detect unexpected stimuli than meditators mostly practicing focused meditation practice (Valentine and Sweet, 1999). This is perhaps not surprising given that differences in broad versus narrow focus of attention are inherent to open monitoring and focused attention, respectively, but these findings confirm that the distinction is reflected not only in meditation practice, but also in the actual performance of practitioner.

Another study of attention skills in insight meditators assessed changes before and after three months of Theravada insight retreat and found improvements in their efficiency of using attentional resources (Slagter et al., 2007). Specifically, the meditators were tested in an attention blink task which examined detection of simple stimuli such as letters or numbers during a very fast computerized presentation. The task is based on previous research which showed that within 500 milliseconds after detection of a target stimulus, we have a diminished capacity to detect another target. The three months of insight meditation retreat have been found to increase the detection rate of the second stimulus which suggests that the open monitoring capacity of meditators was enhanced. This pattern of findings was further supported by investigation of ERP responses to the targets which revealed less positive amplitudes to the first target of an ERP component (the P3b) sensitive to changes in attention resources. This decrease was interpreted as a lowered demand on attention resources, which enabled allocation of attention resources to the detection of the second target.

Aside from research on open monitoring, which can be considered a pre-requisite of insight practice, some studies aimed to link the changes in attention allocation to self-related processing. For example, one study compared brain responses of participants who completed an eight-week MBSR course with those new to meditation in a task that required participants to employ two different modes of self-referential processing (Farb et al., 2007). In both modes the participants were asked to respond to self-related adjectives such as 'confident', but in the narrative mode they were reflecting on the adjective in a story-like mode whereas in the experiential mode they were grounding their attention on the bodily sensations in the present moment. The findings revealed significant differences in brain activation in response to the two modes, which is not surprising given the differences in instructions and objects of focus. However, the MBSR group also showed stronger activation than the non-meditation group in areas such as the anterior cingulate cortex and secondary somatosensory cortex. While the differences were interpreted in terms of self-referential processing, a caution about such interpretation is warranted here given that the difference might simply be due to different attention focus and not relate directly to how the participants construed their sense of self.

The second group of studies aimed to investigate brain correlates of self-related processing by examining the default mode of brain function which assesses brain activity when participants are not instructed to do any particular task (other than resting or keeping their gaze fixated on a cross on the computer screen) (Raichle and Snyder, 2007). Previous research on the default mode suggests that off-task activity tends to activate a default mode network (DMN) of interconnected brain areas which has been linked to mind-wandering. Interestingly, some of the modes in the DMN, particularly those in the medial prefrontal cortex, have been directly linked to self-related processing – thinking about our own and others' mental states. Therefore, investigation of activation in the DMN, and particularly areas linked to self-related processing in meditators could more closely reflect changes in existential insight arising from meditation practice.

Building on this assumption, one study compared DMN brain activation of meditators during three meditation types and resting and compared the pattern to brain activation in meditation novices (Brewer et al., 2011). The three meditation types were focused attention, loving kindness and choiceless awareness as an insight practice building on open monitoring. The findings revealed distinct differences between meditators and novices across the four conditions with meditators consistently showing a deactivation in areas of the DMN linked to mind-wandering (medial prefrontal cortex) and increased connectivity between brain areas linked to attention control and monitoring including the dorsal anterior cingulate, posterior cingulate and dorsolateral prefrontal cortex.

Importantly, the pattern of DMN activation was very similar across the different meditation types, which the authors of the study interpreted as possibly reflecting changes in self-related processing (Brewer et al., 2011). However, this interpretation seems to assume that the three meditation types engage self-related processing equally whereas as discussed earlier in this chapter, it might be expected that their engagement of insight-related processing is differential. Specifically, focused meditation does not strongly engage insight-related self-reflective processing, whereas choiceless awareness targets it. Loving kindness could be expected to engage the self-related processes more than focused meditation but less than choiceless awareness practice. So an alternative interpretation of the similar findings across the practices might be that they reflect similar recruitment of attention resources associated with mindfulness and meta-awareness, since all three practices need to rely on these, rather than self-related processing.

Perhaps closer to the assessment of insight-related changes in the brain were recent studies that investigated different gradients of the self-boundaries (including differentiation between internal and external world and location in time and space) in experienced meditators and associated brain activation. The researchers first asked an experienced meditator to describe three different states of self-construal and then assessed whether these could be linked to dissociable brain patterns (Dor-Ziderman et al., 2016). When differences across the three states were obtained, the same instructions were applied in assessments of ten more advanced meditators to see if the same overarching pattern arises. The results across meditators revealed similar differences with increases in the right lateralized beta frequency generated by the temporo-parietal junction and the medial parietal cortex associated with more advanced levels of insight.

These two brain regions have been previously linked to thinking about self and others and to self-transcending experiences, respectively. This study was perhaps the closest so far to actually linking self-related experiential changes (rather than changes in attention processing) to modulations of activity in the brain.

Research into the neurocognitive correlates of dream yoga practices could possibly become a fourth type of meditation research targeting insight-related changes. However, research on lucid dreaming has over the last three decades mostly focused on the possibility of inducing such a state and its applicability in the treatment of problems such as nightmares. No studies so far particularly targeted the investigation of self-related processing changes with lucid dreaming and derivative practices. The research on lucid dreaming has shown that this state naturally occurs and is also trainable. For example, one study reported that in a sample of 919 participants 51% of them reported having a lucid dream previously (Schredl and Erlacher, 2011). Women were more likely to report the experience of lucid dreaming, however, this might be related to a better ability to recollect the lucid dream rather than a difference in the frequency of lucid dreams between women and men.

A similar pattern was confirmed in a recent meta-analysis (cumulative) study looking at the reports across studies which investigated frequency of lucid dreaming occurrence without training. The study found that 55% of participants reported having a lucid dream at least once and 23% reported experiencing lucid dreams once or more per month (Saunders et al., 2016). Over 30 studies have also shown that it is possible for participants (between half and two-thirds of them) without any meditation background to develop lucid dreaming within a few weeks of practice (Stumbrys et al., 2012). While most studies only focused on the development of the ability to have lucid dreams, some studies also investigated the possibility of transforming dreams in the context of therapy for nightmares with a moderate success. None of these studies investigated the more advanced practices of traditional dream yoga, which examine the nature of self and reality.

A few psychophysiological studies have also documented brain correlates of lucid dreaming. For example, an early study on lucid dreaming showed that lucid dreaming is associated with the REM (rapid eye movement) phase of sleep (La Berge et al., 1981). This was inferred from responses provided by five participants who were trained in lucid dreaming and were also able to signal to the researchers that they were in a lucid dream by their eye movements. This approach was further replicated by other researchers, for example, one recent study trained six participants in lucid dreaming and investigated their brain activity during lucid dreaming – they signalled to the researchers that they were lucid in the dream by horizontal eye movements (Voss et al., 2009). Their brain activation during lucid dreaming was assessed using EEG and compared to brain activation when awake and during non-lucid dreaming (usual REM sleep). The findings revealed that lucid dreaming is associated with a pattern of brain activation that shares some features of being awake and some features of a non-lucid REM sleep. Specifically, lucid dreaming produced similar patterns of coherence in brain activity as being awake. Lucid dreaming was also associated with distinct activity in frontal and fronto-lateral areas which may reflect the metacognitive aspect of the state. The findings were, however, not specifically related to the self-construal.

Overall, current understanding of changes in brain function and structure with insight practices is quite limited. Most neuroscience studies investigated changes in attention processes contributing to states (open monitoring) supporting self-inquiry from which insight can arise. Other studies investigated changes in the default mode of brain function as a result of meditation which are often interpreted in terms of changes in self-referential processing but without direct links to phenomenological modulations in self-construal. So both research on attention and DMN changes related to insight currently falls short of investigating insight-related processing as such. A few studies attempted to map detailed phenomenological changes in the construal of self (changes in self-boundaries); more research of this type is needed, particularly if it is grounded in an overarching theory of phenomenological changes with insight progression. Finally, research on lucid dreaming seems to present interesting, and so far untapped, opportunities in investigating insight shifts. This is because previous studies documented that the state is trainable and associated with distinct psychophysiological patterns, yet they did not investigate trainability of participants in more advanced practices of dream yoga linked to the testing of dream reality and awake reality. Such studies could be conducted with experienced meditators skilled in dream yoga to assess brain correlates of advanced insight states.

Existential insight, self-regulation and existential well-being

We will now examine the insight practices from the perspective of a framework outlined in Chapter 1 which proposes that the effects of meditation practices can be investigated in terms of changes in the metacognitive self-regulatory capacity (MSRC) of the mind and shifts in modes of existential awareness (MEA) (Dorjee, 2016). In this framework, practices targeting the development of meditative insight would be primarily considered as aiming to induce shifts in the MEA. The MEA define our overarching sense of self and construal of reality, hence only insight practice that impact on our sense of self-construal would be expected to lead to changes in MEA. For this reason, the term 'existential insight' referring more closely to the existential construal of self and reality seems appropriate in describing practices and states of this type. In addition, the term 'insight' has been applied in the psychological literature for a long time in reference to sudden shifts of understanding which is not related to the construal of self or reality in the contemplative sense, so it seems appropriate to distinguish it from existential insight.

The link between existential insight and MEA means that for a state to be described as existential insight it needs to be relevant to changes in the sense of self or reality. Based on this assumption, object-oriented insight (Dahl, Lutz and Davidson, 2015) would perhaps not be considered a type of existential insight, unless it can be shown how such object-oriented insight impacts on the self-construal. This further highlights that decentring, which was included in the category of object-oriented insight (see the first section of this chapter), is probably better classified as one of the beginning stages of subject-oriented insight. This is because decentring enables the participants to experience a MEA characterized by partial dis-identification with thoughts, sensations and feelings, which modifies the sense of self. This MEA could be considered one of the initial shifts in MEA resulting from meditation practice.

Starting with initial experience of decentring and up to the highest levels of existential insight in pristine awareness, long-term meditation practice can be associated with a range of progressively more advanced shifts in MEA. These shifts can also be described in terms of increasingly deeper access in terms of the three layers of consciousness: ordinary consciousness, substrate consciousness and the nature of mind (pristine awareness). Accordingly, the main shifts in MEA involve, as the first major step, existential insight into the construed, impermanent and changeable nature of our thoughts, sensations and feelings arising during progression from the ordinary mind into the substrate consciousness. This is followed by increasingly advanced shifts in MEA targeting the deconstruction of the conditioned notions of self at the level of substrate consciousness. This process culminates in a major shift from the ground of substrate consciousness into the level of the nature of mind when the construed sense of self dissolves. At the level of the nature of mind the final existential insight goes beyond this realization by experiential dissolution of the distinctions between the self and the other (the observer and the observed) into the state of cognizant non-duality experienced in pristine awareness. According to some Buddhist teachers, even within this state, gradients of extremely advanced non-conceptual states characterized by different degrees of existential knowledge can be distinguished (Gyaltrul and Wallace, 1998).

While existential insight meditation practices do not target the MSRC, shifts in MEA can only arise when the processes of the MSRC have been sufficiently refined. This is achieved mostly through practices training mindfulness and meta-awareness (Shamatha, see Chapter 3), practices cultivating emotional qualities such as compassion (e.g., the four immeasurables, see Chapter 4) and practices modifying conceptual processing including contemplations on existential topics (but also Shamatha practices and practices working with emotions). The visualization-based practices (see Chapter 5) seem to work across the range of the three main components of the MSRC (attention and meta-awareness emotion regulation and conceptual processing) and also cultivate existential insight. The refined MSRC processes create the conditions for shifts in MEA through the stabilization of attention focus, enabling effortless observation of deeper layers of consciousness. This also requires refined meta-awareness as a core aspect of the MSRC, so that the meditator can notice distraction and patterns of mental processes. Development of wholesome emotional qualities stabilizes the emotional processes of the mind further and also reduces fixations on distinctions between self and other through development of equanimity in cultivating loving kindness and compassion. Visualization practices train attention and meta-awareness, cultivate wholesome emotions and at the same encourage existential insight by developing experiential understanding of the illusory nature of mind and reality. They also support connection with advanced states of existential awareness through exemplification in the form of deity mind. Building on this overall stabilization and refinement of the mind, existential insight practices can further target inquiry towards the most-advanced experiential realization of the nature of mind and reality.

In the proposed framework, the enhancement of the MSRC as a prerequisite for practices cultivating existential insight together with increasingly more advanced shifts in the MEA is associated with improvements in overall well-being. This is because self-regulation and existential well-being are the core pillars of human well-being and existential insight practices further improve existential well-being (which can be cultivated in other practices only to a limited extent). This suggests that approaches aiming to prevent illness, enhance well-being or treat illness need to target enhancements in both self-regulation and existential well-being. Long-term meditation training initially mostly develops the self-regulatory skills and to a limited extent existential well-being. More advanced meditation training particularly targets improvements in existential well-being, via existential insight practices, after self-regulatory skills have been sufficiently enhanced.

Twenty-four hours of meditation practice

Insight practices, just like the types of meditation we have discussed previously, can be readily embedded into everyday activities. In the morning, after waking up and developing motivation/intention for the day, a practitioner can spend a few minutes (engaging in an insight practice of their choice. For beginners to meditation, this might be contemplation on impermanence and the nature of suffering, targeting the development of intellectual insight. More advanced practitioners can spend some time in self-inquiry observing and questioning the nature of thoughts, emotions and sensations as these arise and dissolve back into deeper layers of consciousness. More experienced practitioners can spend time in experientially examining the self: where it is, where it comes from etc. The most advanced practitioners may use the time to connect with the state of pristine awareness and develop motivation to sustain that state throughout the day. The session can end with a dedication for the day to deepen the existential insight for the practitioner and a wish to sustain a certain level of existential insight during the day.

Indeed, the main aim of introducing existential insight practices into the daily routine is to develop existential insight during brief formal sessions throughout the day and try to sustain the corresponding mode of existential awareness while engaging in active tasks. The latter is often the difficult aspect of the practice since engaging in everyday tasks requires our attention to be fully engaged with the tasks at hand, which limits the mind's capacity for monitoring and sustaining a MEA we are developing. Here, just like with any skill, repeated practice is the key element. While at the beginning shifting towards a certain MEA (e.g., decentring as one of the initial steps) might be effortful, with practice it will become much less challenging. Hence with practice, shifting towards a certain MEA can actually become fast and effortless, requiring minimal attention and meta-awareness resources and thus not interfering with a task at hand.

The gradual development of the ability to shift towards a certain MEA during daily activities can be considered in terms of the three layers of consciousness. Most of our daily activities require engagement at the ordinary level of consciousness whereas when we develop increasingly advanced levels of existential insight, we are shifting towards MEA associated with deeper levels of consciousness. As a result, we can perceive our experience at the level of the ordinary mind in daily activities as very different in comparison to our experience in a formal meditation session when our mind settles and we are able to access MEA associated with subtler levels of the ordinary mind or the surface level of the substrate consciousness. This sense of disconnection between MEA during daily activities and in formal practice can for some practitioners become a challenge and may prompt them to seek more time in retreat or, in the other extreme, they may abandon meditation practice. This is why integration of existential insight practices into everyday activities is particularly important.

Shifting towards more advanced MEA can be prompted in various ways depending on the type of existential insight practice a meditator is learning, the propensities of the practitioner and the circumstances of daily activities. For example, practitioners developing existential insight through contemplations on impermanence or other topics can use reminders in the form of a word or a phrase which can prompt them to briefly shift towards a more advanced MEA. Practitioners developing experiential existential insight can simply remember the state from their morning practice and try to connect with it as a prompt of experiencing it briefly in the moment. For practitioners in the Buddhist context, the prompt might be a memory of their teacher or a visualization of a deity with the focus on the existential awareness qualities associated with that image.

The speed of our everyday activities can become a particular practical obstacle to integrating increasingly advanced levels of MEA into our everyday life. This is because existential insight practices require a certain level of attentional stability and meta-awareness and if we are constantly bombarded by information we may not have enough cognitive capacity to employ in the insight practice. A reduction in distraction, slowing down and simplification of our lifestyle is required at any stage of the meditation training, but is a particular necessity when we are committed to developing focused meditative insight. This may require setting aside at least a brief time in the morning to develop existential insight and having brief formal existential insight practices throughout the day, perhaps at mid-morning, lunchtime, mid-afternoon and evening. These short formal practices can help sustain our focus on a particular MEA throughout the day and especially between the practices when we can combine moments of checking in and observing our mind with automatic shifting towards the MEA we are developing.

Retreat environment can be particularly helpful in supporting existential insight by providing the conditions for settling our attention, meta-awareness and consequently the ordinary mind. This may enable us to go deeper in our existential insight practice and experience gradually more advanced shifts in MEA. However, for this experience not to become restricted to the retreat environment, it can be helpful to come out of the retreat gradually, by introducing increasingly more everyday activities into the day whilst sustaining the MEA developed in deep meditation practice. Shorter weekly retreat sessions of a few hours, a half-day or a day may also support the practitioner in going deeper in their practice and at the same time keep integrating the contemplative insight into everyday activities. The combination of retreat experience and everyday existential insight can help the existential insight experience not to become isolated and restricted to particular conditions.

Integration of dream yoga practices can be especially helpful in this regard because it encourages the practitioner to check repeatedly during the day the dream-like quality of their experience. This in itself can become a prompt for a practitioner to shift to a more advanced MEA throughout the day. The practitioner would also develop a motivation to become lucid at night several times during the day. Briefly before going to sleep, the practitioner would do a brief formal practice in preparation for the dream yoga practice. In the Buddhist context, this can involve certain visualizations together with recitation of a particular mantra. Then once a practitioner becomes lucid in a dream, she can use the opportunity to test the nature of the dream reality and shift to a more advanced MEA. Most advanced practitioners can use this state to abide in the ground of substrate consciousness or pristine awareness. In the morning, the practitioner may try to recall the lucid dream experience before engaging in other activities, because this can interfere with recollecting the dream yoga experience. As with any meditation practice, a Buddhist practitioner would review the day of practice at the end of the day and dedicate any virtue and wholesome experience to attaining the highest level of existential balance and helping others on their path of existential insight.

Existential insight practice from a long-term perspective

As we have discussed in this chapter, long-term meditation practice is associated with increasingly more advanced levels of existential insight. These are linked to a progression of shifts in MEA, starting with deconstructing habitual patterns of thinking, sensing and affective feeling at the ordinary mind level. The more advanced MEA support existential insight into the construed nature of self in the substrate consciousness. At the most advanced level, the MEA is associated with existential insight into the nature of self and reality. It is essential for future research on meditation to carefully map the progression of MEA which might be conceptualized differently in different contemplative traditions. This understanding will also be instrumental in supporting applications of existential insight practices in well-being enhancement, and prevention and treatment of illness.

From the broad view of existential insight practices presented in this chapter, the current therapeutic application of existential insight practices seems to be very limited. The development of therapeutic techniques which more fully embrace the progression of shifts in MEA towards increasing existential well-being will also bring with itself many challenges. These include the need for a firm grounding in motivational/intentional contemplative training, attention training and development of wholesome emotional states before progressing onto more advanced existential insight practices. Current secular meditation-based programmes cannot provide such grounding, so we are left with the options to either develop such comprehensive meditation-based training in the secular context or enable long-term practitioners to connect with more advanced training in their respective contemplative traditions as part of supporting their well-being. Perhaps the latter option seems more viable at the current stage of meditation-based training development. Such an approach would require establishing links between health services and contemplative training providers and guidelines for their interactions as well as working with clients.

Summary

While the majority of previous research on meditation focused on mindfulness and practices cultivating loving kindness and compassion, our understanding of the effects of meditations developing existential insight is very limited. Chapter 6 provides an in-depth examination of this type of meditation, starting with an initial overview of insight practice categories and conceptualizations. Building on this discussion, the following section outlines practical aspects of cultivating existential insight as part of long-term meditation training. The potential of dream yoga in supporting the development of existential insight is also highlighted in this section. This is followed by an outline of neuroscience evidence relevant to existential insight practices which can be considered in four categories:

attentional foundations of existential insight, changes in the default mode network (DMN), investigations of neural correlates of self-construal and psychophysiological studies of dream yoga. The discussion about existential insight practices is then placed into a broader framework of changes with long-term meditation practice, particularly in relation to shifts in modes of existential awareness (MEA) which determine our existential well-being. The theoretical discussion is finally applied in practical considerations about how to integrate practices cultivating existential insight into everyday life as part of daytime and night-time (dream yoga) meditation practice.

References

Brewer, J.A., Worhunsky, P.D., Gray, J.R., Tang, Y.Y., Weber, J. and Kober, H., 2011. Meditation experience is associated with differences in default mode network activity and connectivity. *Proceedings of the National Academy of Sciences*, *108*(50), pp. 20254–20259.

Dahl, C.J., Lutz, A. and Davidson, R.J., 2015. Reconstructing and deconstructing the self: Cognitive mechanisms in meditation practice. *Trends in Cognitive Sciences*, *19*(9), pp. 515–523.

Dorjee, D., 2016. Defining contemplative science: The metacognitive self-regulatory capacity of the mind, context of meditation practice and modes of existential awareness. *Frontiers in Psychology*, 7, pp. 1–15.

Dor-Ziderman, Y., Ataria, Y., Fulder, S., Goldstein, A. and Berkovich-Ohana, A., 2016. Self-specific processing in the meditating brain: A MEG neurophenomenology study. *Neuroscience of Consciousness*, *2016*(1), pp. 1–13.

Farb, N.A., Segal, Z.V. and Anderson, A.K., 2012. Mindfulness meditation training alters cortical representations of interoceptive attention. *Social Cognitive and Affective Neuroscience*, *8*(1), pp. 15–26.

Farb, N.A., Segal, Z.V., Mayberg, H., Bean, J., McKeon, D., Fatima, Z. and Anderson, A.K., 2007. Attending to the present: Mindfulness meditation reveals distinct neural modes of self-reference. *Social Cognitive and Affective Neuroscience*, *2*(4), pp. 313–322.

Gyaltrul, R. and Wallace, B.A., 1998. *Natural liberation: Padmasambhava's teachings on the six bardos*. New York: Simon and Schuster.

La Berge, S.P., Nagel, L.E., Dement, W.C. and Zarcone, V.P., 1981. Lucid dreaming verified by volitional communication during REM sleep. *Perceptual and Motor Skills*, 52(3), pp. 727–732.

Lutz, A., Dunne, J.D. and Davidson, R.J., 2007. Meditation and the neuroscience of consciousness. In P. Zelazo, M. Moscovitch and E. Thompson (Eds.) *Cambridge handbook of consciousness*, pp. 499–555. Cambridge: Cambridge University Press.

Lutz, A., Slagter, H.A., Dunne, J.D. and Davidson, R.J., 2008. Attention regulation and monitoring in meditation. *Trends in Cognitive Sciences*, *12*(4), pp. 163–169.

Raichle, M.E. and Snyder, A.Z., 2007. A default mode of brain function: A brief history of an evolving idea. *Neuroimage*, *37*(4), pp. 1083–1090.

Ricard, M., 2003. On the relevance of a contemplative science. In B. Alan Wallace (Ed.) *Buddhism and Science: Breaking New Grounds*, pp. 261–279. New York: Columbia University Press.

Saunders, D.T., Roe, C.A., Smith, G. and Clegg, H., 2016. Lucid dreaming incidence: A quality effects meta-analysis of 50 years of research. *Consciousness and Cognition*, *43*, pp. 197–215.

Shapiro, D.H., 1992. Adverse effects of meditation: A preliminary investigation of long-term meditators. *International Journal of Psychosomatics*, *39*(1–4), pp. 62–67.

Schredl, M. and Erlacher, D., 2011. Frequency of lucid dreaming in a representative German sample. *Perceptual and Motor Skills*, *112*(1), pp. 104–108.

Slagter, H.A., Lutz, A., Greischar, L.L., Francis, A.D., Nieuwenhuis, S., Davis, J.M. and Davidson, R.J., 2007. Mental training affects distribution of limited brain resources. *PLoS Biology*, *5*(6), p. e138.

Stumbrys, T., Erlacher, D. and Malinowski, P., 2015. Meta-awareness during day and night: The relationship between mindfulness and lucid dreaming. *Imagination, Cognition and Personality*, *34*(4), pp. 415–433.

Stumbrys, T., Erlacher, D., Schädlich, M. and Schredl, M., 2012. Induction of lucid dreams: A systematic review of evidence. *Consciousness and Cognition*, *21*(3), pp. 1456–1475.

Teasdale, J.D., 1999. Metacognition, mindfulness and the modification of mood disorders. *Clinical Psychology & Psychotherapy*, *6*(2), pp. 146–155.

Valentine, E.R. and Sweet, P.L., 1999. Meditation and attention: A comparison of the effects of concentrative and mindfulness meditation on sustained attention. *Mental Health, Religion & Culture*, *2*(1), pp. 59–70.

Voss, U., Holzmann, R., Tuin, I. and Hobson, J.A., 2009. Lucid dreaming: A state of consciousness with features of both waking and non-lucid dreaming. *Sleep*, *32*(9), pp. 1191–1200.

Wallace, B.A., 1999. The Buddhist tradition of Samatha: Methods for refining and examining consciousness. *Journal of Consciousness Studies*, *6*(2–3), pp. 175–187.

Wallace, B.A., 2006. *The attention revolution: Unlocking the power of the focused mind*. Boston: Wisdom Publications.

Chapter 7

The state of existential balance

The most advanced states of existential insight and corresponding shifts in modes of existential awareness (MEA) are virtually unexplored in the Western scientific literature. These shifts in MEA which are the culmination of long-term meditation practice are rarely discussed in current meditation research and accordingly are poorly understood. This is perhaps partially due to difficulty in translating the Buddhist conceptualizations of the most advanced MEA into terms of Western psychology and neuroscience. Looking deeper into this translational challenge, it appears that it might be at least partially due to the fact that Western psychology has been mostly pre-occupied with the investigation of the ordinary mind whereas the advanced shifts in MEA occur at deeper levels of consciousness. As a result, the Western science does not even have terms which could describe advanced MEA. In addition, the focus of Western research of the mind has been primarily on the disruptions in mental functioning rather than different levels of mental balance. So considerations about trainability and gradients of mental balance, particularly in the context of existential well-being, are a new subject in the Western psychological context.

In contrast, Buddhist psychology has placed equal, if not greater, emphasis on nuanced states of mental balance rather than the afflictive states. Indeed, Buddhist literature and teachings contain elaborate descriptions of stages of accomplishment on the path of meditation training (Sanskrit: Bhūmis; Tibetan: byang chub sems dpai sa), which are likely associated with increasing progression of MEA. The Mahayana tradition describes 11 such stages whereas in the teachings of Dzogchen 16 stages are described. These stages are outlined not as examples of unachievable ideals; they specify states which have been repeatedly accomplished by long-term meditation practitioners over many centuries. The highest levels outline stages of exceptional well-being both in terms of self-regulation and existential well-being – states of existential balance. In this chapter we will examine some aspects of these advanced MEA and explore their implications for Western scientific understanding of well-being.

What is the state of existential balance?

Perhaps closest to the theories and concepts in Western psychology is the conceptualization of advanced MEA in terms of changes in three types of consciousness (see Chapter 6). These can be further subdivided into eight types of consciousness based on the work of the 19th-century Tibetan Buddhist master Mipham Rinpoche (1997). The first six of the eight types of consciousness can be considered as arising at the level of the ordinary mind. They include the eye consciousness, ear consciousness, nose consciousness, tongue consciousness and body consciousness, and roughly correspond to Western notions of the four senses together with proprioception. The sixth consciousness is called 'mind consciousness' and is the main type of consciousness employed in meditation training during contemplations, cultivation of mindfulness and meta-awareness and development of emotional qualities of loving kindness and compassion. These six types of consciousness are called 'unstable' types because they fluctuate, arise and dissolve at the level of the ordinary mind and are not always present.

In contrast, the two remaining types of consciousness are considered stable because they are constantly present in the mind until the final levels of existential balance are achieved. The first of the two (seventh type of consciousness) is called the 'afflictive consciousness' and refers to clinging to an independent notion of 'self' or 'I'. This unhealthy attachment to a construed notion of self can manifest with varied intensity ranging from very gross to very subtle. Long-term meditation training gradually deconstructs the different gradients of construed self towards the most subtle ones. The afflictive consciousness is rooted in the second of the two stable types of consciousness, which is the substrate consciousness.

As we have described in the previous chapter, the substrate consciousness enables storing and retrieving of overarching patterns underlying our tendencies, temper, cognitive habits and behaviour patterns. In long-term meditation practice the first six types of consciousness are stabilized to enable examination and further settling of the stable types of consciousness in practices of existential insight. However, even after the practitioner works through the mental patterns of the substrate consciousness and reaches its ground, the most subtle sense of an independent self, arising from the afflictive consciousness, remains.

Pristine awareness, as the most advanced MEA, is not included amongst the eight types of consciousness. However, abiding at the level of pristine awareness is enabled by changes in the eight types of consciousness and also modifies them. Access to pristine awareness is supported by enhancements in mindfulness and meta-awareness, which are trained as part of the mind consciousness. These enhancements together with training in the wholesome states enable the development of non-reactive awareness and settling of the reactive responses of the eight types of consciousness and the mind consciousness. In this way, the meditator is able to work with subtle patterns of mental habits at the level of substrate consciousness and then access the pristine awareness. In turn, abiding at the level of pristine awareness eliminates the afflictive consciousness and further purifies the substrate consciousness. This then removes the sources of afflictive perceptions in the ordinary mind because those arise from the afflictive consciousness and substrate consciousness.

Abiding at the level of pristine awareness means that we recognize the nature of our mind and at the most advanced levels also the nature of reality – how the conventional reality arises and dissolves dependent on the eight types of consciousness. The distinction between the observer and observed is no longer present at this level of existential insight – that's why pristine awareness is sometimes described as a non-dual state. Importantly, pristine awareness is a non-conceptual MEA, so any descriptions of it are mere approximations of the actual phenomenological state. These descriptions typically mention clarity, compassion, non-conceptual knowing, tranquillity and subtle joy as the aspects of pristine awareness integrated into a holistic unidimensional experience without subject–object differentiation. So even though the state of pristine awareness is non-conceptual, it is not a state of vacuum – it is a state transcending the afflictive affirmation of self and reality by the afflictive mind and the ordinary consciousness, but at the same time the pristine awareness transcends nihilistic notions of emptiness as non-existence. Hence, the state of pristine awareness is often also described as being free of the extremes of existence and non-existence.

Abiding in pristine awareness as the highest level of existential insight also does not mean that the meditator remains isolated in a state which is out of touch with the reality as it arises for others who haven't accessed the pristine awareness. Tibetan Buddhist teachings explain that a practitioner who reaches this highest level of existential balance transforms the eight types of consciousness into two types of primordial awareness (Mipham, 2009; Longchenpa, 2011). The first type of primordial awareness is the awareness of dharmadhātu (Sanskrit: dharmadhātu; Tibetan: Chosyang).

Dharmadhātu can be described as the non-conceptual space from which all appearances, both mental and physical, arise and the awareness of dharmadhātu is no different from the pristine awareness. The second type of primordial awareness enables the meditator to perceive the illusory reality as it arises for those who have not accessed pristine awareness, but not from a perspective of the eight types of consciousness. These are instead transformed into five kinds of enlightened wisdom.

The first kind of enlightened wisdom is called mirror-like awareness and it arises from a transformation of the affliction of anger and substrate consciousness into their pure forms. The mirror-like wisdom enables the practitioner to perceive the afflictive experience and construed reality from the perspective of others without afflictive aversion, while at the same time understanding the illusory nature of these appearances. The second kind of enlightened wisdom is the awareness of equality which arises from transformation of the affliction of ego-centred pride and the afflictive consciousness. The awareness of equality enables the practitioner to help sentient beings without the impedance of ordinary perceptions of like and dislike. The third enlightened wisdom is the discriminating awareness which manifests from transformation of unhealthy attachment and the mind consciousness. This type of awareness enables the practitioner to recognize the needs of sentient beings and effectively help them. Finally, the fourth kind of enlightened wisdom, termed 'the primordial awareness that accomplishes all actions', is the result of transforming the affliction of jealousy and the first five types of consciousness (associated with senses) arising in the ordinary mind. This awareness underlies the tireless striving of enlightened practitioners to be of help to others and support them on their spiritual paths. These five kinds of primordial awareness can be considered the most advanced MEA and together form the highest level of existential balance.

Each of the five kinds of enlightened wisdom aims to provide the practitioner with means to be of true help to sentient beings. The mirror-like wisdom provides the platform for the practitioner to see with clarity the suffering of others and its sources without being overwhelmed by emotional reactions. The awareness of equality further enhances this knowledge by eliminating the biases of ordinary preferences and rejections. The discriminating awareness does not simply see the superficial needs of others, but the deeper trajectory of spiritual development of beings and from this deeper perspective enables one to decide how to best help others. Finally, the awareness that accomplishes all actions supports the enlightened practitioner in staying unwaveringly on course with her efforts to help all sentient beings to reach existential balance.

Buddhist teachings say that without these very advanced cognizant kinds of awareness, our ability to help others is very limited because our perception of what they need is limited by what we see on the surface and know in the moment without understanding their full potential and the deeper obstacles they face. This is the case even if our motivation is truly compassionate; without the guidance of primordial wisdom we are not able to see clearly how to help. This of course should not stop any practitioner from engaging in the genuinely compassionate activities; on the contrary, development of authentic compassion is instrumental in long-term meditation training and progression towards the advanced MEA.

From the descriptions of the advanced MEA in this section we can see that these are not characterized as mystical and unreachable states. These states are the natural culmination of long-term meditation training and need to be sustained with further practice. The qualities of these states involve both cognizant elements of wisdom and emotional qualities such as unconditional compassion. However, in discussing and describing these states, we need to remember that their qualities are beyond conceptual descriptions and can be fully understood only at the phenomenological level – experientially.

Whilst keeping in mind that the nature of the five kinds of primordial awareness cannot be fully grasped conceptually, it would be helpful for the field of meditation research to include these advanced MEA in its considerations without oversimplification or trivialization. The current lack of discussion about these states is perhaps one of the reasons why terms traditionally describing pristine awareness and its aspects are relatively often used in descriptions of initial existential insights arising in the context of secular meditation training. For example, the term 'direct perception' is in the Tibetan Buddhist tradition of Dzogchen applied in descriptions of the perception of reality (through the five kinds of enlightened wisdom) which is not clouded by the ordinary illusory notions of self and conventional reality. The direct perception arises when the ordinary mind, the afflictive mind and the substrate consciousness have been transformed into their pure forms. In contrast, in the context of secular mindfulness the same term is often used to describe non-reactive perceptions which are not heavily impacted by habitual patterns of thinking and emotional reactivity (e.g., Shapiro et al., 2006; Brown, Ryan and Creswell, 2007). While shifts towards this non-reactive way of perceiving can be supportive to the practitioners' well-being, these states arise from the level of the ordinary mind with the afflictive awareness and substrate awareness present and contributing to the experience. This and similar conceptual confusions in the field of meditation research (e.g., Dorjee,

2010; Rosch, 2007) can only be clarified if we take a full view of the long-term meditation path and its goals.

Developing the state of existential balance

Practices supporting the highest levels of existential insight build on the foundations of meditations which develop motivation/intention for the practice, mindfulness, meta-awareness and qualities of compassion, loving kindness, rejoicing and equanimity together with progressively more advanced levels of existential insight. Only when sufficient stability of the ordinary mind and the substrate consciousness has been achieved through these practices is the meditator able to turn to deep self-inquiry and inquiry into the nature of reality. This process expands the previously established existential insight into the transient nature of habitual patterns of thinking, behaviour, emotions etc. together with initial insights into the construed nature of the self. The transition from these insight practices into the most advanced ones can be supported by visualization-based meditations with emphasis on abiding in pristine awareness as the source of the deity visualization and by focusing on the deity as an embodiment of the five kinds of enlightened wisdom.

The actual practices which enable insight into the nature of mind and reality can have different forms. In the tradition of Dzogchen the practitioner closely relies on the guidance of a realized master who himself/ herself has experience with abiding in the pristine awareness. Such a teacher is able to introduce the practitioner to pristine awareness directly, by sharing in the experience of pristine awareness or by providing the student with teachings pointing to experiential realization of pristine awareness. After the initial glimpse of pristine awareness, the practitioner is encouraged to practice accessing pristine awareness on their own. The practitioner is encouraged to practice increasingly more frequent glimpses of abiding in pristine awareness and also gradually try to increase the duration of abiding in that experience. There are also further meditation practices enabling the practitioner to deepen their realization and fully manifest the five kinds of primordial awareness (Gyaltrul and Wallace, 1998). However, these practices are only taught to practitioners who have strongly stabilized their mind in previous meditation training and have the right motivation/intention for the practices.

Another group of practices which enable the practitioner to develop the realization of pristine awareness comprises meditations of dream yoga and practices preparing the practitioner for the process of dying. As explained in the previous chapter, the practice of dream yoga can be instrumental in facilitating increasingly advanced levels of existential insight into the nature of self and reality through testing similarities and differences between the dream and awake states. This can create the basis of another type of dream yoga practice which targets the experience of falling asleep. Tibetan Buddhist teachings outline the progression of dissolution of energies in the body followed by dissolution of levels of consciousness when we are falling asleep (Dalai Lama, 2002). According to these teachings, this dissolution process while falling asleep mimics the actual dissolution of bodily energies and consciousness at the time of death. Obviously, the process of falling asleep does not represent the full dissolution and is reversible when we are awakening from sleep, but it presents an excellent opportunity to recognize the pristine awareness. This is because at the end of the dissolution process pristine awareness is revealed.

However, for a practitioner whose mind has not been sufficiently stabilized the experience of pristine awareness when falling asleep may be too brief to notice and they may not have developed sufficient levels of meta-awareness to be able to notice the dissolution process in the first place. Yet, for experienced practitioners who are aware of the dissolution process as it is happening, this can present a valuable opportunity to abide in pristine awareness, which further enhances their existential insight. This is because during the consciousness dissolution process the layers of the ordinary mind and substrate consciousness gradually subside and the pristine awareness is revealed. In addition to experiencing pristine awareness during the process of falling asleep, the practitioner has another opportunity to abide in pristine awareness before waking up when the dissolution process progresses in the reverse order.

The dissolution of bodily energies followed by dissolution of consciousness fully unfolds only as part of the process of dying. Accordingly, meditation training in the Tibetan Buddhist tradition emphasizes the importance of gaining familiarity with the dissolution process so that the practitioner can face it without fear or attachment and embrace it as an opportunity enhance their existential insight. In the final stage of consciousness dissolution the dharmadhātu space is fully revealed with more clarity and intensity than while falling asleep. A practitioner can use this opportunity to recognize the dharmadhātu as the nature of her mind and through this fully manifest the pristine awareness. The dream yoga practices preparing the practitioner for this process, as well as daytime practices in which the practitioner is able to abide in pristine awareness, increase the likelihood that the practitioner will recognize his/her nature of mind at the time of death. The teachings suggest that the time a practitioner is able to spend in pristine awareness while alive is multiplied by seven when abiding in pristine awareness at the time of death.

One of the common misconceptions about the advanced MEA including pristine awareness is that once the meditator achieves one of these advanced levels of existential insight, they abide at this level and can only progress further towards even more advanced MEA. This is not the case for the vast majority of practitioners; sometimes glimpses of the more advanced states are experienced by relative beginners to meditation. However, they are not able to sustain the advanced MEA because of insufficient motivational/intentional and self-regulatory foundations of their meditation practice. Accordingly, the main task for advanced practitioners who experienced glimpses of pristine awareness is to repeatedly experience the state for increasingly longer periods of time until it is maintained all of the time, during their daytime and sleep hours.

Neuroscience of the state of existential balance

Very few studies investigated neural correlates of the most advanced states of existential awareness. This is perhaps not surprising given that there is very little theoretical research in the Western scientific literature which would build the basis for empirical research on such states. In addition, it is very difficult to find practitioners who are able to produce such states at will in laboratory environments. We also don't know what the best way might be to assess different levels of these advanced MEA and how to ensure comparability of the states across meditators.

However, the main challenge of research investigating the neural correlates of MEA, and particularly the most advanced MEA, is the need for dissociating the brain activity specific to MEA from other support processes such as attention control, regulation of emotions or conceptual processing. This is very difficult to do in practice because abiding at different levels of MEA is intertwined with differences in employing these other, more basic cognitive processes. For example, abiding in the ground of substrate consciousness might be for some practitioners easier than abiding in pristine awareness, so the resulting brain activity will be inevitably 'contaminated' by more attentional effort in the latter case. A similar argument can also be made in the opposite direction: a practitioner who is accustomed to abiding in pristine awareness may find it difficult, possibly even uncomfortable, to switch to the substrate or any 'lower' MEA. This in itself would modify the brain activity and make it difficult to distinguish changes due to MEA and due to the other cognitive processes. So the findings of studies investigating MEA will need to carefully control for the contribution from processes non-specific to MEA to the resulting brain patterns.

Only one study so far aimed to directly assess the state of non-dual awareness (Josipovic, 2014). Over 20 advanced Tibetan Buddhist meditators in the study were asked to practice focused attention in one part of the study and to abide in the state of non-dual awareness in another part of the study. Their brain activity was recorded during the meditations using fMRI with particular focus on patterns of connectivity between different brain areas. The results revealed a clearly different pattern of brain activity in focused meditation and in the state of non-dual awareness. One of the main distinctive features of brain activity during the non-dual state was increased functional connectivity between the central precuneus and dorsolateral prefrontal cortex. The author of the study suggested that the connectivity between these two regions might index the different gradients of non-dual awareness.

This study is a valuable first step in further investigation of non-dual awareness, yet lack of information on the phenomenological aspects of the non-dual MEA experienced by meditators in the study makes it difficult to specifically assess what type of advanced MEA they experienced and to what extent the results may have been impacted by attentional effort. The comparison between focused attention and non-dual state surely also includes differences in attentional focus in the two types of meditation, so the specific findings regarding the pattern for non-dual state are perhaps more pertinent in this regard. Yet, they may still have been impacted by participants' experiential understanding of MEA and the degrees of meditators' expertise in this type of meditation. These factors have been previously highlighted in theoretical considerations about research into non-duality using EEG (Josipovic, 2010).

Another study measured brain activity and levels of autonomic nervous system (ANS) arousal while Tibetan Buddhist meditators engaged in the pristine awareness (rigpa) meditation (Amihai and Kozhevnikov, 2014). However, the study focused on attentional and ANS correlates of this type of meditation in comparison to the same practitioners engaging in deity meditation, and also in comparison to Theravada practitioners practicing two other meditation types. The findings suggested that the pristine awareness meditation was associated with similar levels of arousal to deity practice, but somewhat distinct pattern of brain activity measured using EEG. However, the study included very limited information on the actual state participants induced and their proficiency in this type of practice. The primary focus of the research was on differences between the Tibetan Buddhist and Theravada practices. So the findings do not provide clear pointers to what specific brain correlates could be indicative of the pristine awareness state.

The important next step for further research on advanced MEA including pristine awareness will be clear theoretical mapping for possible experiential distinctions which could be applied in research on neural correlates of these states. Collaboration with meditators experienced in advanced MEA will be essential to such work. The 'map' of MEA could then be used in guiding instructions for meditators in neuroscientific studies which would measure brain patterns associated with these states. Assessment of proficiency in inducing such states will be an essential aspect of this research given the likely impact of experience and proficiency on recruitment of cognitive resources while inducing and sustaining the MEA. Another aspect of the research should control for differences in basic levels of attention control and emotion regulation in practitioners which can also skew the brain pattern findings (Josipovic, 2010).

No previous research assessed possible neural correlates of the other five types of primordial awareness (the primordial awareness from the perspective of others) we have described. It would be intriguing to assess whether advanced practitioners would be able to distinguish between abiding in pristine awareness and a state which also includes other types of pristine awareness. In addition, no previous studies investigated possible brain correlates of pristine awareness during dream yoga, while meditators are falling asleep. It might be possible for experienced meditators to signal to researchers, for example using eye movements, when they finish abiding in the state of pristine awareness and the time preceding the signalling could be analyzed for patterns which could be linked to abiding in pristine awareness. Signalling after the state might be necessary because the process of monitoring and signalling during pristine awareness would interfere with the state and associated brain correlates.

Whilst further research into advanced MEA including the states of primordial awareness has the potential to provide very interesting new insights into these states, it is important to also keep in mind the limitations of neuroscientific research. Currently, the reports from neuroscience studies are often given higher weight, particularly by non-experts in this type of research, even when the findings may not be stronger than other types of research evidence (Weisberg et al., 2008). All neuroscience methods, despite their advantages, also have limitations in terms of measurement as such, as well as signal processing techniques and interpretation of findings. They may also not be sensitive to some subtle distinctions between meditative states, particularly MEA, due to these being masked by other cognitive activities or unsuitable types of assessment. So despite the excitement about evidence from neuroscientific methods, we also need to keep in mind their drawbacks and use various types of converging assessments in investigating advanced MEA, with feedback from expert meditators being of primary weight.

The state of existential balance, self-regulation and existential well-being

As with all the advanced MEA, refinement of the metacognitive self-regulatory capacity (MSRC) is a necessary pre-requisite enabling existential insight, including the insight into pristine awareness. Importantly, the state of existential balance requires maintaining the glimpses of pristine awareness, which places further demands on the stability of the MSRC. In this process, mindfulness supports the continuity of pristine awareness and meta-awareness monitors for subtle divergence from the state. The need for mindfulness and meta-awareness is no longer there when the pristine awareness is completely stabilized and a state of existential balance, which is irreversible, is achieved.

Since abiding in pristine awareness eliminates the afflictive mind and the afflictive pattern sources in the substrate consciousness, in the state of pristine awareness there is no longer any need for applying emotion regulation strategies of actively cultivating emotional qualities of compassion, loving kindness etc. These are continuously present in their most advanced form as an integral part of the state of pristine awareness. Abiding in this state also most likely results in a radical shift in the functioning of the conceptual systems, since this state is beyond conventional ways of thinking. One way to consider this change in conceptual processing is in terms of a shift from propositional meanings to implicational meanings (Dorjee, 2016). The distinction between these two meaning systems has been postulated by Teasdale (1999) and in his theory propositional meanings are associated with typical ways of language-based reasoning whereas implicational meanings describe more holistic meanings which are not language-driven. There are other features of meaning processing at the most advanced levels of MEA which have not been so far examined in Western research.

The state of existential balance is the ultimate adaptive expression of the existential instinct as the primary drive of our mind motivating our behaviour. In the first chapter we have discussed various ways misplaced existential drive can result in psychopathology. In contrast, well-being arises if the existential drive finds its adaptive expression in thinking patterns, emotional qualities and behaviour which support our progression towards increasingly more advanced MEA. Contemplative practices particularly target adaptive manifestation of the existential drive and aim to support practitioners in stabilizing their mind to enable shifts in MEA. Other adaptive expressions of the existential drive can take on various forms of pro-social behaviour driven by unconditional compassion.

Once the state of existential balance is achieved and the state of pristine awareness fully manifests, the existential drive is extinguished, there is no need for it anymore. The manifestation of the second type of primordial awareness which enables the practitioner to provide unparalleled help to all sentient beings could also be considered as the most advanced expression of the existential drive. The practitioner is now able to help sentient beings without impediment and is most effectively informed by the knowledge of primordial awareness and supported by the highest levels of self-regulation. As such, this is the state of the ultimate existential balance, the most advanced state of well-being.

Interestingly, the state of existential balance is not necessarily linked to physical health. Tibetan Buddhist teachings describe 'case studies' of practitioners who despite abiding in pristine awareness showed physical signs of illness. These practitioners, however, were mentally not affected by the physical difficulties. I have personally had an opportunity to witness at least one such case. However, the Dzogchen tradition also describes cases of practitioners who by abiding in pristine awareness and progressing on further states of existential manifestation were able to transform their physical bodies, either at the time of death or during life. These cases are referred to in the Tibetan Buddhist tradition as the achievement of the rainbow body.

There are different levels of the rainbow body, from those manifested by gradual shrinking of the physical body at the time of death with the body not showing signs of decay, through disappearance of the body at the time of death, to manifestation of a light body instead of a physical body. Whilst these descriptions may sound very exotic in the Western culture, such manifestations have been part of the Tibetan culture for the last 12 centuries, with some cases of the initial manifestations of rainbow body documented recently (Dorjee, 2013). Even though Western scientific understanding of such states is virtually absent, there is the possibility that they represent the highest levels of accomplishment in terms of human potential for existential balance and transformation. Any investigation into such states will require close collaboration with advanced meditation practitioners combined with respect for and deep understanding of associated ethical and cultural factors.

The state of existential balance in everyday life

Just as in the case of other advanced types of existential insight, there are two main principles which support the practitioner in introducing the state of existential balance into everyday life. The first principle highlights the importance of brief formal meditation sessions throughout the day in which the practitioner repeatedly connects with the state of pristine awareness. Obviously, the meditator is only able to do this if she has previous experience of abiding in pristine awareness, possibly developed in retreat or longer formal sessions. Then building on the short formal sessions, the practitioner can try to reconnect with the state during brief moments throughout the day. This very advanced way of combining formal and informal practice will require great stability of the mind and excellent command of self-regulatory abilities as its basis, with both grounded in the motivational/intentional foundations of the meditation training.

The experienced practitioner may start the practice during the state of awakening from sleep in the morning, by connecting with the state of pristine awareness and observing the reverse process of consciousness dissolution. This can be followed by returning to the state of pristine awareness while awake and sustaining the state of a brief or longer period of time depending on the practitioner's level of proficiency in the practice. The practitioner will then aim to sustain the state while engaging in routine activities throughout the day. This is supported by the second type of primordial awareness which, while abiding in the state of pristine awareness, enables the meditator to see the conventional reality from the perspective of others yet without the identification with afflictions associated with it. Advanced meditation masters often describe this state as being able to perceive at the same time two sides of the same coin – while abiding in the pristine awareness also seeing the reality from the perspective of others without this causing cognitive or emotional disturbance to the state of pristine awareness. With further practice, the meditator aims to stabilize this state continuously without interruption throughout the day.

Obviously, such an advanced MEA which equals to the state of existential balance is currently very rarely achieved in the West and is the final culmination of the path. Most practitioners will work with less advanced

MEA as they are progressing towards this ultimate state of existential balance. These practitioners may find it helpful to contemplate on the five kinds of primordial awareness as a way of connecting with approximations of these states first intellectually and then experientially. At the experiential level, the practitioner may for example practice insight meditations in which he or she experientially investigates afflictive states of anger, unhealthy attachment, jealousy and ego-centred pride and particularly focuses on the qualities which arise as these afflictions dissolve back to their ground. In this way, the practitioner might be able to experience glimpses of the five kinds of enlightened wisdom arising as a transformation of the underlying energy of the afflictions. Subsequently, the practitioner can train throughout the day, during brief moments of pausing in addition to formal sessions.

One possible impediment of progress in practice with the more advanced MEA is 'fossilization' of insight – a state when practitioners intellectually know that they have experienced advanced MEA, but instead of repeatedly experientially connecting with the state to increase the frequency of the initial glimpses and their continuity, the practitioners slip into intellectual ascertaining. In other words, instead of repeatedly connecting with the non-conceptual experiential MEA, the practitioner may engage in propositional thinking at the level of the ordinary mind, reassuring themselves that they are abiding at the MEA. This way of thinking may be linked to brief experiential glimpses of the state itself which can further solidify the stagnation. Deeper and more extensive inquiry into the MEA combined with a guidance of an experienced teacher can help practitioners to deal with this obstacle in their progress. This further highlights the importance of support from a qualified and experientially realized meditation teacher at these advanced stages of long-term meditation training.

The state of existential balance from a long-term practice perspective

The state of existential balance, which has been described in this chapter in terms of pristine awareness and four other types of primordial awareness, is the culmination of the path of long-term meditation practice. It is a state free from afflictions and existential confusion about the reality of 'I' and what is perceived as the external world. This state can be considered as the final point of accomplishing the human potential for well-being at the cognitive, emotional and existential levels. From the perspective of the Tibetan Buddhist tradition of Dzogchen, the state of pristine awareness is the ultimate goal of striving for humans and all sentient beings because it is a state free from suffering and a state of unwavering genuine happiness.

In contrast, the goal of secular meditation-based approaches is to alleviate more obvious forms of suffering such as physical illness and stress while developing initial levels of mindfulness and meta-awareness together with non-reactivity which may become a platform for further self-inquiry. This may support the development of decentring as one of the initial MEA which can be possibly deepened and stabilized further with long-term practice. While the secular meditation-based programmes do not foster further levels of insight, the initial experience of settling the ordinary mind together with some pre-dispositions may result for some practitioners in deeper self-inquiry. In the very rare case that this further process of self-inquiry would spontaneously lead to glimpses of dharmadhātu, the practitioner would most likely not be able to contextualize the experience and recognize it as the nature of her mind. It is also possible that the experience might be incorrectly interpreted as vacuity and be a source of existential distress for the practitioner.

Importantly, a secular meditation practitioner would probably not find relevant guidance on how to work with such experience if she shared it with secular meditation teachers. This is why familiarity with the progression of MEA including the more advanced MEA can be relevant to both Buddhist and secular practitioners of meditation. It also highlights the importance of secular meditation teachers working together with experienced meditation teachers in established contemplative traditions in supporting secular practitioners who progress towards more advanced MEA. It is essential that guidance on such advanced states is received from teachers who have a grounded experiential understanding of the advanced MEA. Hence, it seems that support of long-term meditation practitioners of secular meditation-based approaches will at the more advanced stages of MEA necessitate involvement of experienced non-secular meditation teachers.

Summary

Chapter 7 examines the highest level of existential insight, the state of existential balance arising when a practitioner realizes the nature of their mind and reality. In the Tibetan Buddhist tradition of Dzogchen, this state is described in terms of abiding in pristine awareness which eliminates afflictive sources of self-construal together with afflictive perceptions of reality. At the same time, the practitioner's mind manifests five kinds of enlightened wisdom, which arise from transformation of anger, unhealthy attachment, jealousy and ego-centred pride. These enable the practitioner to perceive the reality from the perspective of others without afflictive reactions and cognitive patterns. Detailed explanation of the five kinds of enlightened wisdom is followed by an outline of practices which support the practitioner in accessing the state of existential balance. The chapter then discusses neuroscientific findings of brain activation associated with non-dual awareness whilst acknowledging their limitations and providing recommendation for further research. The next section further elaborates these considerations by discussing possible modulations in the MSRC and MEA associated with the state of existential balance. The implications of this state for our understanding of adaptive expressions of the existential drive and human potential for existential well-being are also considered. The last two sections outline possible ways of incorporating meditation practices targeting the development and maintaining of the state of existential balance into everyday activities. The chapter concludes with considerations about the implications of learning about the state of existential balance for development of long-term meditation practice, particularly in the secular context.

References

Amihai, I. and Kozhevnikov, M., 2014. Arousal vs. relaxation: A comparison of the neurophysiological and cognitive correlates of Vajrayana and Theravada meditative practices. *PLoS One*, *9*(7), p. e102990.

Brown, K.W., Ryan, R.M. and Creswell, J.D., 2007. Mindfulness: Theoretical foundations and evidence for its salutary effects. *Psychological Inquiry*, *18*(4), pp. 211–237.

Dalai Lama, 2002. *Sleeping, dreaming, and dying: An exploration of consciousness*. New York: Simon and Schuster.

Dorjee, D., 2010. Kinds and dimensions of mindfulness: Why it is important to distinguish them. *Mindfulness*, *1*(3), pp. 152–160.

Dorjee, D., 2013. *Mind, brain and the path to happiness: A guide to Buddhist mind training and the neuroscience of meditation*. London: Routledge.

Dorjee, D., 2016. Defining contemplative science: The metacognitive self-regulatory capacity of the mind, context of meditation practice and modes of existential awareness. *Frontiers in Psychology*, *7*, pp. 1–15.

Gyaltrul, R. and Wallace, B.A., 1998. *Natural liberation: Padmasambhava's teachings on the six bardos*. New York: Simon and Schuster.

Josipovic, Z., 2010. Duality and nonduality in meditation research. *Consciousness and Cognition*, *19*(4), pp. 1119–1121.

Josipovic, Z., 2014. Neural correlates of nondual awareness in meditation. *Annals of the New York Academy of Sciences*, *1307*(1), pp. 9–18.

Longchenpa, 2011. *Guhyagarbha Tantra*. Ithaca, NY: Snow Lion Publications.

Mipham, J., 2009. *Luminous essence: A guide to the Guhyagarbha Tantra*. Ithaca, NY: Snow Lion Publications.

Rinpoche, G. and Wallace, B.A., 1999. *Natural liberation: Padmasambhava's teachings on the six bardos*. New York: Simon and Schuster.

Rinpoche, M.J., 1997. *Gateway to knowledge*, vol. 1. Trans. Erik Pema Kunsang. Hong Kong: Rangjung Yeshe Publications.

Rosch, E., 2007. More than mindfulness: When you have a tiger by the tail, let it eat you. *Psychological Inquiry*, *18*(4), pp. 258–264.

Shapiro, S.L., Carlson, L.E., Astin, J.A. and Freedman, B., 2006. Mechanisms of mindfulness. *Journal of Clinical Psychology*, *62*(3), pp. 373–386.

Teasdale, J.D., 1999. Metacognition, mindfulness and the modification of mood disorders. *Clinical Psychology & Psychotherapy*, *6*(2), pp. 146–155.

Weisberg, D.S., Keil, F.C., Goodstein, J., Rawson, E. and Gray, J.R., 2008. The seductive allure of neuroscience explanations. *Journal of Cognitive Neuroscience*, *20*(3), pp. 470–477.

Chapter 8

The potential of contemplative science

The fast growing interest in meditation, both in the secular and traditional contexts, raises many wider questions about the potential and implications of long-term meditation practice for our well-being and understanding of meaning and purpose in life. As we have discussed throughout the book, self-regulation and existential well-being can be considered the core pillars of our overall well-being. From the perspective of a long-term trajectory of meditation training, the initial stages mostly develop self-regulatory skills through mindfulness and meta-awareness practices whereas the more advanced meditation practices of existential insight particularly enhance existential well-being. Contemplations developing motivational/intentional foundations for meditation practice, meditations on compassion, loving kindness and other wholesome qualities, and visualization-based practices are relevant throughout the path and contribute to development of both self-regulation and existential insight.

Whilst each chapter focused on a different type of meditation practice, each of these were discussed in terms of an overarching framework for research on meditation which explains the impact of meditation on the mind and brain in terms of the metacognitive self-regulatory capacity (MSRC) of the mind and modes of existential awareness (MEA) (Dorjee, 2016). The MSRC consists of systems and processes enabling attention control and meta-awareness of contents and processes of the mind together with emotion regulation and conceptual processing. Hence, the MSRC supports reflective meta-awareness of our behaviour and mental processes and also our ability to adaptively modulate these. The MEA build on the refined self-regulatory abilities which stabilize the mind and refine our metacognitive awareness. Specifically, the MEA refer to our phenomenological (experiential or felt) sense of self and reality. From a long-term practice perspective, initial stages of meditation training particularly aim to improve the processes of the MSRC, which then enable shifts towards more advanced MEA as the meditation training progresses further. The existential drive, as the need for understanding of existential meaning and purpose in life, can be considered the primary motivational force of the mind, which is adaptively expressed through engagement in practices leading to realization of the more advanced MEA.

The explanatory potential of the MSRC, MEA and the existential drive in building up a theory of how meditation impacts on the mind suggests that they could become central to meditation research as a scientific discipline. The term 'contemplative science' is now increasingly more often used to describe this emerging field of research, which has been so far mostly understood as a study of particular meditation practices. However, such conceptualization seems limiting in many regards (see Dorjee, 2016) including terminological confusions about definitions of meditation practices (e.g., mindfulness; see Williams and Kabat-Zinn, 2011) and a lack of emphasis on unique aspects of meditation research such as the role of meditation training in the development of existential well-being. If we highlight these unique features of contemplative science in its definition, the potential of this discipline in broadly contributing to our understanding of the human mind, brain and well-being will be much more visible. Following this approach, one possible way of defining contemplative science is as an interdisciplinary study of the MSRC of the mind and associated MEA which are both modified by the motivational/ intentional and contextual (secular or non-secular, lay or ordained etc.) factors of meditation practice (Dorjee, 2016).

Defining contemplative science in terms of the MSRC and the MEA together with motivational/intentional and contextual factors has implications for further research and application of this framework in psychology, psychotherapy, neuroscience, education, healthcare and society more broadly. This chapter explores these implications with a particular focus on the development of long-term meditation practice as a means for adaptive expression of the existential drive supporting human potential for well-being across the life-span. The existential aspect of human well-being has been particularly neglected across the board in the Western society, which might be one of the core contributing factors to the current mental health crisis in the West. The main argument of this chapter suggests that contemplative science can play a central role in a paradigm shift in relevant scientific disciplines and our society towards a long-term sustainable view of human well-being. Long-term meditation training has a pivotal role to play in this shift not only because it can enhance our self-regulatory skills, but perhaps even more importantly because it develops our sense of existential connection and purpose and thus enables realization of our existential drive.

Contemplative psychology

Psychological research on meditation has so far almost exclusively focused on the effects meditation practices have on different attention functions and emotion processing. Studies have, for example, found improvements in orienting attention (e.g., Jha, Krompinger and Baime, 2007) and sustained attention (e.g., Jensen et al., 2012) after the mindfulness-based stress reduction (MBSR) programme. Other research reported improvements in affect after loving kindness training (Hutcherson, Seppala and Gross, 2008). However, research on changes in conceptual processing with meditation and motivational/intentional factors of meditation is scarce. Similarly, studies investigating shifts in MEA are mostly limited to the state of decentring from mental processes and contents (the ability to observe them as fleeting rather than solid facts, Fresco et al., 2007) (e.g., Hoge et al., 2015). This means that the current understanding of psychological processes underlying meditation is mostly restricted to the attentional and emotion regulation aspects of MSRC.

In addition, most of previous research examined immediate (after a short meditation session) or short-term (up to several weeks) effects of meditation. Any follow-up investigations, ranging from a few months, and in rare cases a couple of years, focused on whether the initial gains in reductions of illness symptoms, or enhancements in well-being, were sustained later on. They were not examining whether with long-term practice the MSRC further improved or whether participants experienced shifts towards more advanced MEA. Accordingly, our understanding of the long-term trajectory of psychological changes resulting from continuous meditation practice is minimal. This is the case not only for experimental research, but also for theory of long-term meditation practice.

For the next phase of psychological research on meditation it seems necessary to address these shortcomings, starting with development of scientific theories of MEA, intentional/motivation factors and their progression with long-term meditation. Such theoretical research will hopefully lead to development of psychological measures which will enable assessment of MEA and intentional/motivational aspects of meditation practice. This work will also need to pay closer attention to the context of meditation training, particularly whether it is secular or traditional, with further subdivisions within each type. This is because the context of meditation practice modulates the intentional/motivational factors, the progression and types of meditation training and guidance a practitioner receives during long-term meditation training. All these aspects of meditation training will in turn modulate the resulting changes in MSRC and MEA.

Finally, further advancement of psychological research on meditation will require stronger reliance on introspective research methods which are unique to the field of contemplative science and enable measurement of changes in phenomenological experience in both formal and informal meditation practice. This is because, unlike other psychological approaches, meditation training particularly targets the development of meta-awareness of mental contents and processes which builds a basis of all meditation practices. This necessitates the assessment of meta-awareness skills as well as phenomenological (first-person) experience in meditation research, most importantly shifts in MEA, which are enabled by enhanced meta-awareness. In addition, these introspective abilities as well as phenomenological shifts need to be captured both within formal meditation sessions and during meditation 'on the go', with the latter providing particularly powerful understanding of the impact of meditation training in everyday life. Experiential sampling methods prompting meditators to record their experience at random points during the day are now more often used to capture changes in meditation within and outside of formal meditation practice. Refinement of these methods and other new approaches will further enhance our understanding of such effects.

Contemplative psychotherapy

Application of meditation practices as possible therapeutic techniques has been the primary area of fast growth within applied contemplative science over the last three decades. The most broadly implemented and investigated meditation-based programmes include the mindfulness-based stress reduction (MBSR), mindfulness-based cognitive therapy (MBCT) and a range of programmes developing compassion and loving kindness such as compassion-focused therapy (CFT). This trend is perhaps not surprising given that in the traditional contemplative context meditation practices are applied as tools enhancing mental stability and supporting existential insight to enable the practitioner to manifest increasing levels of existential well-being. However, the current secular therapeutic applications of meditation almost exclusively focus on self-regulation, not the existential well-being. For example, there is strong evidence on the effectiveness of mindfulness-based approaches in reduction of symptoms of anxiety (Hofman et al., 2010) and depression

(Kuyken et al., 2015). In contrast, very few studies investigated the impact of secular meditation training on existential well-being as the sense of meaning and purpose in life (e.g., Labelle et al., 2015); and aside from research on decentring, our understanding of the impact of secular meditation training on the MEA is absent.

The lack of focus on existential well-being in current therapeutic applications of meditation is perhaps the result of the need to demonstrate that these programmes have clear symptom-reducing effects and thus have a solid place in mainstream healthcare. However, this is based on the prevailing, and limited, view of health which only focuses on adaptive self-regulation and leaves existential well-being out of the picture. Yet, existential well-being itself has been highlighted as a major determinant of health and well-being. Indeed, there is mounting evidence suggesting that higher existential well-being is likely to reduce the risk of depression (Maselko, Gilman and Buka, 2009) and improve coping with life-changing diagnoses (Edmondson et al., 2008). Accordingly, there have also been repeated calls to include spiritual care supporting existential well-being as a basic aspect of healthcare across the board (Davidson, 2008; Mueller, Plevak and Rummans, 2001). Such recommendations seem closest and particularly pertinent to psychotherapeutic applications of meditation.

The humanistic psychological and psychotherapeutic tradition has long recognized existential well-being as a main contributor to health and well-being and this tradition has an established connection to approaches which target existential well-being as a part of therapy. This is best exemplified by the existential psychotherapy work of Viktor Frankl (1985). The current interest in meditation-based approaches provides an opportunity to build on this long-standing focus on existential aspects of well-being in therapy and expand it further within the context of contemplative psychotherapy. The postulation of the existential drive as the primary motivational force of the mind is particularly pertinent in this regard. As we have discussed in the first chapter, maladaptive expression of the existential drive can lead to psychopathology manifesting as anxiety disorders, depression, addictions etc. This means that supporting clients in finding adaptive ways of expressing their existential drive is one of the main tasks of psychotherapy. Meditation-based practices, particularly those targeting the development of existential insight (including meditations on compassion and loving kindness and visualization-based meditations), can play a central role in new therapeutic approaches supporting the development of existential well-being.

Further interest and broader implementation of meditation-based techniques in the secular context may also necessitate greater focus on existential well-being. Glimpses of existential insight may arise as a result of shorter meditation training even in the secular context. However, no research studies have so far investigated the frequency of such experiences and their impact on the well-being of participants in the secular meditation-based courses. Importantly, secular meditation training currently does not provide guidance on how to support practitioners in dealing with such experiences and in guiding them towards deepening their existential insight beyond the experience of decentring. This is perhaps one of the consequences of outrooting meditation techniques from their traditional systems which support the whole path of contemplative existential exploration.

The need to address questions about supporting participants of secular meditation courses in developing existential well-being is becoming more pertinent with the increasing numbers of participants trained and taking on long-term practice. In addition, if meditation-based programmes are not to become only methods for a quick temporary fix of certain pathological symptoms, development and support of long-term meditation practice will need to be a central focus of the teaching and implementation of such programmes. In long-term meditation training practitioners are much more likely to work with self-inquiry which will target their existential insight. This again highlights the importance of secular meditation-based approaches embracing the whole path of meditation training.

There seem to be two main routes which secular meditation approaches may take as they expand the scope of secular meditation training. The first one involves the ambitious project of building up a secular version of the whole contemplative path. Such approach might be attractive for reasons of religion-neutral possibilities of implementation and resulting in broad reach. However, whether development of such an approach is viable in principle is questionable. One of the core aspects of traditional contemplative approaches supporting their effectiveness is the time-tested lineage of practitioners who accomplished the highest levels of insight. For example, a meditator taking on training in an authentic Buddhist tradition builds on the experience of previous practitioners, and is guided by current teachers who have accomplished the highest levels of existential insight. Given that secular approaches have not targeted development of higher levels of existential insight so far, these aspects of teaching are absent from the training of teachers in these methods and there isn't a lineage of practitioners accomplished in higher levels of existential insight to build on. Based on the precedent from traditional contemplative systems, development of such a lineage would take a very long time if it is at all possible in a secular context. There are also other reasons which make a secular approach to the whole path of existential exploration unlikely, including the currently unmet need for a firm grounding in deep ethical principles and motivational/intentional qualities of meditation.

The second approach to expanding the scope of secular meditation-based approaches to support practitioners in development of their existential well-being involves close collaboration between secular and traditional meditation-based training. One result of such collaboration can be better understanding of the progression of MEA from the perspective of long-term meditation practice in the secular context, informed by traditional approaches where the MEA are clearly described. This knowledge can in turn support teachers of secular meditation-based approaches in recognizing cases where attendees of their courses may need further support in developing existential balance. This support may for some involve working with therapists specializing in existential therapy; for others it may require further guidance by experienced meditation teachers. In some cases initial existential exploration can be facilitated in the secular context, provided that more experienced secular meditation teachers train further in skills which enable them to experientially understand levels of existential insight beyond the initial levels of decentring.

However, if a practitioner progresses beyond the initial levels of MEA, this will likely require that secular meditation teachers refer practitioners to well-qualified traditional contemplative teachers, depending on the contemplative preferences of the practitioner. For such referrals to be possible, establishing reliable and professional links between providers of secular meditation training and teachers across contemplative traditions will be needed. This will be necessary to accommodate a wide variety of contemplative backgrounds and preferences which practitioners bring to their secular meditation training. Development of such links will also require effort on the part of traditional contemplative teachers, so that they develop basic understanding of the principles and practices applied in secular meditation programmes and are able to build on this foundation in further contemplative training. There will also be a need for familiarity with basic concepts of contemplative science, particularly those relevant to the progression of MEA, to allow for informed exchanges about supporting existential insight and existential well-being of practitioners across contemplative traditions.

Another platform for supporting long-term meditation practitioners could arise within psychotherapy itself, provided by contemplative psychotherapists who aside from the necessary psychological training also have experiential understanding of MEA. The development of contemplative psychotherapy would also bring with it unique requirements regarding transparency about the contemplative tradition a particular contemplative psychotherapist follows and their qualifications in terms of experiential and intellectual understanding. Contemplative psychotherapy as an established approach could build on the common principles outlined in contemplative science theory in terms of MSRC, MEA and existential drive. These constructs would then be adapted within a particular contemplative context. In this way, contemplative science can provide the platform and focus needed for contemplative psychotherapy to establish itself as a rigorous and effective psychotherapeutic approach.

Contemplative neuroscience

Research in neuroscience of meditation attracted a lot of scientific and public attention over the last decade. It demonstrated that meditation practices reliably induce tangible changes in brain function and structure. However, this line of research has been also subject to the same limitations as psychological research on meditation, and in some regards even more so. These limitations include primary focus of neuroscience studies on short-term effects of meditation training and dispositional associations. No longitudinal neuroscience studies using fMRI or EEG have so far investigated effects of meditation beyond four months. While there are also interesting studies with advanced long-term meditators, these applied cross-sectional designs where we are not able to assess brain activity of practitioners before they started meditation. In cases of very advanced practitioners this may simply not be possible because their meditation training may span over 20 years. However, in other cases, particularly in studies which assess effects of secular meditation programmes from before to after the program, follow-ups of at least a year or a couple years would significantly enhance our understanding of longer-term effects.

Another drawback of neuroscientific, just like psychological, studies on meditation is their nearly exclusive focus on self-regulation abilities of practitioners. Indeed, most studies have so far investigated brain changes resulting from meditation training which are associated with attention or emotion processing. In contrast, our understanding of neural correlates linked to MEA is virtually absent. Only a couple of studies investigated brain activity modulations resulting from decentring and there are less than a dozen studies which examined more advanced MEA. In addition, most of these studies still focused on changes in attention and emotion processing as consequences of shifts in MEA, rather than on unique neural correlates of MEA as such (see examples in Dorjee, 2016).

The current lack of contemplative theory to guide research in contemplative neuroscience also results in difficulties when it comes to comparing and integrating findings from studies. This is because descriptions of meditation techniques, programmes or traditions often do not contain enough detail to allow for clear predictions of similarities and differences in expected brain patterns. In addition, researchers sometimes combine studies to make inferences about overarching patterns in ways which seem driven more by similarities in brain activation than similarities in practices and expertise of meditators. For example, a recent review combined findings from studies with participants in secular mindfulness courses with results of studies with Zen, Vipassana and Tibetan Buddhist meditators (Tang, Hölzel and Posner, 2015). Despite the differences in practices and levels of proficiency of practitioners, the authors attributed similarities in findings as indicative of neural correlates of mindfulness relevant to enhancements in self-regulation.

Building on the initial findings of neuroscientific studies on meditation, the next phase of research in contemplative neuroscience will need to be driven by stronger theoretical foundations and finer distinctions between meditation practices. Increasing numbers of studies now target more nuanced classifications of meditation types (e.g., Dahl, Lutz and Davidson, 2015) and more studies are trying to relate subtle phenomenological descriptions of MEA with associated neural correlates (e.g., Dor-Ziderman et al., 2016). The framework of contemplative science proposed in this book (and in Dorjee, 2016) suggests that conceptualizing contemplative neuroscience research in the terms of MSRC and MEA can further support development of comprehensive contemplative science theory. This is because this theory would allow for comparison of similarities and differences in modulations of the MSRC resulting from various contemplative practices and enable targeted investigation of neural correlates of shifts in MEA with long-term meditation training (rather than attention or emotion processes associated with it).

Contemplative neuroscience research possibly also offers further, largely unexplored opportunities to investigate some of the most persistent questions of science. One of these is the mind–body problem, which asks how an immaterial mind and a material body interact. Perhaps this is where meditation research has further untapped potential to make a contribution. Meditation training, unlike any other type of mental training, aims to further enhance our ability to be aware of processes and states of our mind, and of the 'what it is like' phenomenological aspects of experience. Such training makes meditators experts at distinguishing subtle shifts in their minds and knowledge of these can then guide researchers in linking these more closely to the associated brain changes (Lutz, 2002; Lutz and Thompson, 2003; Ricard, 2003; Wallace and Hodel, 2009). Hence, research into long-term effects of meditation is likely an instrumental next step in furthering our knowledge of how phenomenological shifts in the mind relate to brain activity.

Contemplative science in healthcare

If self-regulation and existential well-being can be considered the core pillars of human well-being, the research in contemplative psychology, contemplative psychotherapy and contemplative neuroscience has direct implications for healthcare. Aside from psychotherapeutic applications, which we have discussed in one of the preceding sections, contemplative approaches have a significant potential to contribute to prevention of illness and enhancement of well-being and resilience more broadly. This is because previous studies outside of meditation research documented clear links between improvements in self-regulation and better health, and initial research shows that meditation training can enhance attention (Jha, Krompinger and Baime, 2007) and emotion regulation skills (e.g., Goldin and Gross, 2010). In addition, meditation-based approaches have largely untapped potential in supporting existential well-being, which is another factor associated with resilience and better coping skills (Maselko, Gilman and Buka, 2009).

However, to fully harness the potential of meditation-based approaches in public health, more rigorous long-term investigations of their effects across the life-span are needed. The number of studies on possible protective effects of meditation is limited and the effects reported are relatively short-term. Future research needs to assess the impact of long-term meditation training on illness prevention. Such research also needs to go hand in hand with an expansion of the repertoire of meditation techniques investigated since majority of previous studies examined only the effects of mindfulness-based approaches. Meditation-based programmes developing compassion, loving kindness and existential insight which build on the foundations of self-regulation developed through mindfulness-based approaches may have particularly strong impact on enhancing both self-regulation and existential well-being. In addition, access to continuous support in developing and sustaining long-term meditation practice, both in formal and informal formats, will most likely be instrumental in maintaining and further enhancing the initial gains. Finally, further research is needed regarding tailoring of meditation-based training to particular dispositions of course participants to reduce dropout rates and increase the likelihood of practitioners developing long-term meditation practice. For example, very preliminary evidence suggests that participants with high rumination levels may benefit more from mindfulness training than loving kindness meditation whereas those with low rumination may benefit more from loving kindness practices (Barnhofer et al., 2010).

Another underexplored area of contemplative science application is in palliative care. Initial research highlights the potential of mindfulness-based approaches in reducing symptoms of anxiety and depression in those faced with life-threatening diagnosis (Piet, Würtzen and Zachariae, 2012). However, very few studies examined the effects of meditation-based approaches on existential well-being with initial research providing some encouraging results (Labelle et al., 2015). However, this research particularly looked at the effects of mindfulness-based approaches, and in the palliative context meditation techniques targeting more closely the development of MEA might be of most relevance. This includes compassion and loving kindness meditations, visualization-based practices and existential insight practices. Here the evidence of effects is particularly limited, together with the lack of research on long-term effects of meditation for existential well-being at the end of life. Furthermore, meditation-based approaches have virtually untapped potential in informing care during the process of dying, since they provide very detailed accounts of associated changes in the mind and ways of supporting practitioners during this process (Dalai Lama, 2004).

Aside from the potential role of contemplative practices in prevention and treatment of illness, contemplative science can also make a significant contribution to the support of care staff. A compassionate approach to patients is together with competent care the main expectation of professional healthcare. Yet, care staff typically does not receive training in experiential aspects of compassion, which would give authentic grounding to compassionate relating to others, even though they are expected to behave compassionately. Initial research on empathy and compassion suggests that we can respond to others' suffering either with empathic distress linked to negative affect or with compassion associated with positive affect (Singer and Klimecki, 2014). Thus, being able to compassionately relate to others seems to be not only an expected part of caring, but can also have protective effects on the carer's own well-being. With the high rates of burnout in healthcare professions (e.g., Glasberg, Eriksson and Norberg, 2007) meditation-based training, particularly programmes cultivating compassion, has the potential in both improving the care provided by and well-being of care staff. This, together with possible preventive effects of meditation-based approaches, points to a powerful potential of contemplative science in meaningfully contributing to healthcare.

Developmental contemplative science

Possible applications of meditation-based programmes in education have over the last decade attracted a lot of attention from educators, policy makers and researchers primarily because of the potential of meditation training in enhancing self-regulation of children and adolescents (Davidson et al., 2012; Roeser and Zelazo, 2012). This could have longer-term protective effects given that self-regulation in childhood predicts health, levels of education and even income in adulthood (Moffitt et al., 2011). The initial evidence in support of enhancements in self-regulation is encouraging even though limited by the weak methodological quality of the available studies. Nevertheless, recent meta-analyses suggest that cumulative evidence on the effects of mindfulness-based approaches shows improvements in cognitive performance and reductions in stress in children and adolescents (Zenner, Herrnleben-Kurz and Walach, 2014).

Most of the available studies on the effects of meditation training on self-regulation and well-being of children and adolescents did not include follow-ups longer than three months. So it is currently not clear whether exposure to meditation-based practices in young age can have protective effects later on. Nevertheless, there have been arguments made that teaching meditation-based techniques to children may have long-term protective effects on their health and well-being. This is particularly pertinent given the increasing rates of mental health problems in children, adolescents and young adults. There is no evidence currently available which would support such claims, but these arguments highlight the need for both long-term follow-ups and for supporting children in cultivating long-term meditation practice. This may require development of programmes for children and adolescents which follow the developmental trajectory and gradually build a progression of meditation training. Such training will most likely need to include a variety of meditation practices which may also provide a broader repertoire for children to choose from based on their preferences and propensities.

No studies so far investigated possible impact of meditation training with children and adolescents on their spiritual development. Such investigations could target assessments of MEA, particularly with adolescents who are more able to provide introspective reports because of more advanced meta-awareness than children. Given that decentring is the most investigated MEA and seems to be the central mechanism underlying therapeutic effects of mindfulness-based training on anxiety in adults (Hoge et al., 2015), examining shifts in MEA with meditation training in adolescents seems particularly relevant to the possible impact of these methods on the well-being of young people. In addition, no studies so far investigated possible links between changes in self-regulation and shifts in MEA from the developmental perspective; these investigations could provide valuable understanding of developmental mechanisms of meditation practice. Such knowledge from a long-term developmental perspective would be particularly helpful in guiding decisions of educators and policy makers about introducing meditation-based techniques into education.

Contemplative science and society

Aside from possible applications of meditation-based techniques in psychotherapy, healthcare and education, there has been growing interest in introducing meditation-based programmes in the context of the workplace, in prisons, in developing sustainable behaviour and across sectors more broadly. In the workplace context these programmes are considered as ways to support well-being of employees which in turn could also enhance their productivity. Meditation-based programmes also have potential to contribute to the well-being and rehabilitation of offenders who have very high rates of mental health problems. In the sustainability context, meditation-based techniques may have the potential for supporting behaviour change because of their emphasis on the meta-awareness of mental processes, which may result in the lessening of non-sustainable reactive and automatic behaviour.

However, these wide applications of meditation-based techniques, particularly mindfulness, have also attracted a lot of criticism. For example, there is the concern that in the workplace context these methods could primarily become the means of increasing productivity without employers looking at actual causes of productivity decline such as long hours or unrealistic demands. There isn't sufficient research to support or reject these concerns yet, but the obvious temporary solution might be to apply these techniques in contexts such as the workplace with the intention of both supporting the well-being of employees while at the same time also trying to address work conditions which could negatively impact their well-being. Nevertheless, the criticism of applying meditation techniques in the workplace is perhaps particularly rooted in a deeper concern about these methods being introduced as a means to a goal which isn't consistent with the intention behind these practices in the traditional contemplative systems. In these, meditation techniques are practiced with the goal of progressing towards increasingly higher levels of existential insight whereas secular applications of meditation have been separated from this intention.

This is again where contemplative science may provide a platform for the development of a long-term view of meditation practice which is grounded in exploration of motivational/intentional factors for engaging in meditation training and also involves exploration of ways we express our existential drive in our work and everyday activities. Are our responses from the broader perspective and purpose and meaning in our life adaptive or maladaptive? Are meditation practices in whatever context we are training improving our existential well-being? Are we by our actions supporting others in developing their existential balance? If we start perceiving meditation training not only as a means to a short-term superficial goal but also focus on the development of long-term meditation practice, these existential explorations may become natural. They may possibly lead to authentic transformation in our thinking and behaviour, which may facilitate wider societal change towards a sustainable and pro-social way of living.

Challenges facing contemplative science

The potential of contemplative science also highlights many challenges which will need to be addressed in order for this potential to fully manifest. One of these challenges is the current, rather narrow focus of meditation research and applications. As we have discussed in this book, contemplative traditions contain a wide range of meditation practices targeting different aspects of contemplative training, from the development of stability of attention and enhancement of meta-awareness, through cultivation of qualities of compassion and loving kindness, to supporting shifts in MEA in order to enhance the practitioner's existential well-being. So far most of these meditation techniques have not been explored in research or wider applications. Moving towards such an expansion of the field of contemplative research will require the firm grounding of a contemplative science theory and focused considerations about how such contemplative training can be implemented in different contexts.

Another challenge is linked to a shift towards a long-term view of meditation training in the secular context. Currently, secular meditation training is mostly viewed in terms of its short-term self-regulation effects. This builds a very good foundation for the next phase in the application of meditation-based approaches which can take a longer-term view of meditation and its lasting impact on the well-being of practitioners. This long-term perspective will necessitate introducing existential well-being dimensions of meditation practices into secular meditation training, which will bring up the need for investigating the ethical and motivational/intentional foundations of secular meditation training. This process will create new demands on the training of secular meditation teachers and the development of connections between secular and traditional contemplative approaches.

Finally, the broader vision of contemplative science will also encourage investigation of meditation practices and contemplative training trajectories across contemplative traditions. Most of the current research and applications of meditation have focused, both in secular and traditional contexts, on mindfulness as a core practice of Buddhism or derived from Buddhism. However, contemplative traditions involve a variety of meditation practices, which at least to some extent cultivate mindfulness and meta-awareness (perhaps conceptualized differently from Buddhist accounts) as the foundations for further contemplative training. In the same way, different contemplative traditions will apply different techniques in supporting practitioners in developing contemplative insight. However, it can be expected that across the multitude of traditions the basic mechanisms of the mind targeted by meditation practices will be very similar. Specifically, all meditation practices are likely to impact the processes of the MSRC and shifts in MEA while being grounded in motivational/intentional factors and a particular context of meditation practice. However, the specific constellations of modifications in MSRC and forms of MEA may differ across contemplative approaches. The core task of contemplative science is to investigate these similarities and differences with the aim of developing a comprehensive, discipline-specific theory which can systematically guide further investigations and applications.

Conclusion

This book aimed to highlight the wide-reaching potential of meditation in supporting the development of our self-regulation and existential well-being. In order for us to fully grasp this potential, we need to expand our view of meditation in terms of the range of meditation practices and traditions investigated, long-term trajectory of meditation training and contemplative science theory. To encourage this broader perspective on meditation, this book considered several types of meditation practices including mindfulness, compassion and related qualities, visualization-based practices, existential insight practices and the state of existential balance. These were explored from a long-term meditation point of view with regard to their underlying theory, practical guidance, neurocognitive changes and applicability in everyday life. Throughout the book, these considerations were grounded in the understanding of contemplative science as a new discipline which investigates changes in the metacognitive self-regulatory capacity (MSRC) of the mind and modes of existential awareness (MEA). These discussions particularly highlighted the need for research and applications of meditation-based techniques to embrace the existential dimension of meditation training, which is particularly pertinent to long-term meditation practice. These considerations have implications for further developments in secular applications of meditation techniques as well as ways they approach interactions with traditional contemplative approaches. Overall, the considerations in this book show that despite the exponential increase in research and applications of meditation-based approaches over the last three decades, we are still only scratching the surface of the potential that these techniques have for transforming our sense of meaning and purpose in life with broad societal implications.

Summary

Chapter 8 introduces a framework of contemplative science as a new discipline investigating changes in the metacognitive self-regulatory capacity (MSRC) of the mind and shifts in modes of existential awareness (MEA) resulting from meditation training. Building on this framework, the following discussion introduces the subdisciplines of contemplative psychology, contemplative psychotherapy, contemplative neuroscience and developmental contemplative science. Implications of contemplative science research and applications of meditation techniques are then considered in the context of healthcare and other societal contexts. Finally, the chapter highlights challenges which the field of contemplative science will be likely facing as it grows and expands, including a broadening of the range of meditation practices investigated, a focus on the long-term perspective of meditation and investigations of meditation across contemplative traditions. The chapter concludes with an emphasis on the much wider than currently grasped potential of contemplative training in contributing to human well-being, particularly with regard to our sense of meaning and purpose in life.

References

Barnhofer, T., Chittka, T., Nightingale, H., Visser, C. and Crane, C., 2010. State effects of two forms of meditation on prefrontal EEG asymmetry in previously depressed individuals. *Mindfulness*, *1*(1), pp. 21–27.

Dahl, C.J., Lutz, A. and Davidson, R.J., 2015. Reconstructing and deconstructing the self: Cognitive mechanisms in meditation practice. *Trends in Cognitive Sciences*, 19(9), pp. 515–523.

Dalai Lama, H.H., 2004. *Advice on dying: And living a better life*. London: Random House.

Davidson, R.J., 2008. Spirituality and medicine: Science and practice. *The Annals of Family Medicine*, *6*(5), pp. 388–389.

Davidson, R.J., Dunne, J., Eccles, J.S., Engle, A., Greenberg, M., Jennings, P., Jha, A., Jinpa, T., Lantieri, L., Meyer, D. and Roeser, R.W., 2012. Contemplative practices and mental training: Prospects for American education. *Child Development Perspectives*, *6*(2), pp. 146–153.

Dorjee, D., 2016. Defining contemplative science: The metacognitive self-regulatory capacity of the mind, context of meditation practice and modes of existential awareness. *Frontiers in Psychology*, 7, pp. 1–15.

Dor-Ziderman, Y., Ataria, Y., Fulder, S., Goldstein, A. and Berkovich-Ohana, A., 2016. Self-specific processing in the meditating brain: A MEG neurophenomenology study. *Neuroscience of Consciousness*, *2016*(1), pp. 1–13.

Edmondson, D., Park, C.L., Blank, T.O., Fenster, J.R. and Mills, M.A., 2008. Deconstructing spiritual well-being: Existential well-being and HRQOL in cancer survivors. *Psycho-Oncology*, *17*(2), pp. 161–169.

Frankl, V.E., 1985. *Man's search for meaning*. New York: Simon and Schuster.

Fresco, D.M., Moore, M.T., van Dulmen, M.H., Segal, Z.V., Ma, S.H., Teasdale, J.D. and Williams, J.M.G., 2007. Initial psychometric properties of the experiences questionnaire: Validation of a self-report measure of decentering. *Behavior Therapy*, *38*(3), pp. 234–246.

Glasberg, A.L., Eriksson, S. and Norberg, A., 2007. Burnout and 'stress of conscience' among healthcare personnel. *Journal of Advanced Nursing*, *57*(4), pp. 392–403.

Goldin, P.R. and Gross, J.J., 2010. Effects of mindfulness-based stress reduction (MBSR) on emotion regulation in social anxiety disorder. *Emotion*, *10*(1), p. 83.

Hofmann, S.G., Sawyer, A.T., Witt, A.A. and Oh, D., 2010. The effect of mindfulness-based therapy on anxiety and depression: A meta-analytic review. *Journal of Consulting and Clinical Psychology*, *78*(2), p. 169.

Hoge, E.A., Bui, E., Goetter, E., Robinaugh, D.J., Ojserkis, R.A., Fresco, D.M. and Simon, N.M., 2015. Change in decentering mediates improvement in anxiety in mindfulness-based stress reduction for generalized anxiety disorder. *Cognitive Therapy and Research*, *39*(2), pp. 228–235.

Hutcherson, C.A., Seppala, E.M. and Gross, J.J., 2008. Loving-kindness meditation increases social connectedness. *Emotion*, *8*(5), pp. 720–724.

Jensen, C.G., Vangkilde, S., Frokjaer, V. and Hasselbalch, S.G., 2012. Mindfulness training affects attention: Or is it attentional effort? *Journal of Experimental Psychology: General, 141*(1), p. 106.

Jha, A.P., Krompinger, J. and Baime, M.J., 2007. Mindfulness training modifies subsystems of attention. *Cognitive, Affective, & Behavioral Neuroscience, 7*(2), pp. 109–119.

Kuyken, W., Hayes, R., Barrett, B., Byng, R., Dalgleish, T., Kessler, D., Lewis, G., Watkins, E., Brejcha, C., Cardy, J. and Causley, A., 2015. Effectiveness and cost-effectiveness of mindfulness-based cognitive therapy compared with maintenance antidepressant treatment in the prevention of depressive relapse or recurrence (PREVENT): A randomised controlled trial. *The Lancet, 386*(9988), pp. 63–73.

Labelle, L.E., Lawlor-Savage, L., Campbell, T.S., Faris, P. and Carlson, L.E., 2015. Does self-report mindfulness mediate the effect of Mindfulness-Based Stress Reduction (MBSR) on spirituality and posttraumatic growth in cancer patients? *The Journal of Positive Psychology, 10*(2), pp. 153–166.

Lutz, A., 2002. Toward a neurophenomenology as an account of generative passages: A first empirical case study. *Phenomenology and the Cognitive Sciences, 1*(2), pp. 133–167.

Lutz, A. and Thompson, E., 2003. Neurophenomenology integrating subjective experience and brain dynamics in the neuroscience of consciousness. *Journal of Consciousness Studies, 10*(9–10), pp. 31–52.

Maselko, J., Gilman, S.E. and Buka, S., 2009. Religious service attendance and spiritual well-being are differentially associated with risk of major depression. *Psychological Medicine, 39*(06), pp. 1009–1017.

Moffitt, T.E., Arseneault, L., Belsky, D., Dickson, N., Hancox, R.J., Harrington, H., Houts, R., Poulton, R., Roberts, B.W., Ross, S. and Sears, M.R., 2011. A gradient of childhood self-control predicts health, wealth, and public safety. *Proceedings of the National Academy of Sciences, 108*(7), pp. 2693–2698.

Mueller, P.S., Plevak, D.J. and Rummans, T.A., 2001. Religious involvement, spirituality, and medicine: Implications for clinical practice. *Mayo Clinic Proceedings, 76*(12), pp. 1225–1235.

Piet, J., Würtzen, H. and Zachariae, R., 2012. The effect of mindfulness-based therapy on symptoms of anxiety and depression in adult cancer patients and survivors: A systematic review and meta-analysis. *Journal of Consulting and Clinical Psychology, 80*(6), p. 1007.

Ricard, M., 2003. On the relevance of a contemplative science. In B. Alan Wallace (Ed.) *Buddhism and Science: Breaking New Grounds*, pp. 261–279. New York: Columbia University Press.

Roeser, R.W. and Zelazo, P.D., 2012. Contemplative science, education and child development: Introduction to the special section. *Child Development Perspectives, 6*(2), pp. 143–145.

Singer, T. and Klimecki, O.M., 2014. Empathy and compassion. *Current Biology, 24*(18), pp. R875–R878.

Tang, Y.Y., Hölzel, B.K. and Posner, M.I., 2015. The neuroscience of mindfulness meditation. *Nature Reviews Neuroscience*, *16*(4), pp. 213–225.

Wallace, B.A. and Hodel, B., 2009. *Contemplative science: Where Buddhism and neuroscience converge*. New York: Columbia University Press.

Williams, J.M.G. and Kabat-Zinn, J., 2011. Mindfulness: Diverse perspectives on its meaning, origins, and multiple applications at the intersection of science and dharma. *Contemporary Buddhism*, *12*(01), pp. 1–18.

Zenner, C., Herrnleben-Kurz, S. and Walach, H., 2014. Mindfulness-based interventions in schools: A systematic review and meta-analysis. *Frontiers in Psychology*, *5*, p. 603.

Glossary

Abhidharma (Pāli: Abhidhamma; Sanskrit: Abhidharma): Buddhist texts containing philosophical considerations about the mind and taxonomies of mental phenomena.

Affect: in the context of cognitive psychology and cognitive science an overarching category which includes emotions, moods, impulses and stress.

Amygdala: almond-shaped brain structures located in the medial temporal lobes and involved in affective reactions such as fear.

Anterior cingulate cortex (ACC): area of the brain involved in regulation of emotions and decision making.

Arousal: in the context of emotion research reflects the intensity of emotional experience.

Attention blink: describes the limited attentional capacity of the mind to detect stimuli occurring too close together in time (within 500 milliseconds) which often results in the second stimulus of a sequence not being noticed.

Bhūmi (Sanskrit: Bhūmi; Tibetan: byang chub sems dpai sa): levels of accomplishment in contemplative training on the path to complete enlightenment; the Mahāyāna tradition usually describes 11 Bhūmis; teachings of Dzogchen often discuss 16 Bhūmis.

Bodhicitta: a quality of the mind which directly links contemplative mind training to the goal of enlightenment. It is often divided into relative and absolute bodhicitta. Relative bodhicitta is the mental state of a strong aspiration to attain enlightenment and help all sentient beings achieve this state, which translates into dedicated engagement in mind training leading to it. Absolute bodhicitta is the state of recognizing the nature of the mind and stabilizing consciousness in this mental state, which is the same as enlightenment.

Cognition: a broad category encompassing mental processes involved in perception, thought, language, decision making and affective processing.

Cognitive neuroscience: a branch of neuroscience examining the links between mental processing and brain structure and functioning in humans.

Cognitive science: an interdisciplinary science of the mind integrating research in cognitive psychology, cognitive neuroscience, philosophy of mind and science, linguistics, computer science and cognitive anthropology.

Contemplative: referring to contemplative practice, which involves a range of mind training methods, mostly meditation, used in spiritual philosophies and religious traditions.

Contemplative science: an interdisciplinary study of the metacognitive self-regulatory capacity (MSRC) of the mind and associated modes of existential awareness (MEA) modulated by motivational/intentional and contextual factors of contemplative practices.

Default mode network (DMN): a network of brain areas which are active when people are resting with eyes closed or focusing on a fixation point. DMN activation is a marker of interconnectedness in activation across brain regions in a resting state.

Defence mechanisms: mental strategies such as rationalization protecting the self from feelings of guilt or shame.

Dharmadhātu (Sanskrit: dharmadhātu; Tibetan: Chosyang): In Dzogchen, the space or root of existence from which all phenomena arise.

Dorsolateral prefrontal cortex: area of the brain involved in functions of executive control, particularly working memory, aspects of attention monitoring and decision making.

Dzogchen: a tradition of Tibetan Buddhism which focuses on direct understanding of the innate pristine nature of awareness; within the system of Tibetan Buddhism, Dzogchen is classified as the highest of the teachings (Ati-yoga). It is often described as a group of practices focusing on non-duality.

Electroencephalography (EEG): neuroscientific research method which records electrical activity of the brain (on the scale of microvolts) in the form of oscillations reflecting the firing of neural assemblies.

Emotion regulation: the ability to modulate processing and expression of emotions.

Emotions: one of the subcategories of affect experienced for a shorter amount of time than moods, often in response to a specific event.

Eudaimonic happiness: found in the pursuit of something worthy in the deeper sense; this type of happiness comes from accomplishing our highest potential, from looking for meaning in life and experiences beyond the self-centred perspective.

Event-related potentials (ERPs): averaged brain wave patterns elicited by a certain type of stimuli (e.g., affective pictures or words); ERPs have excellent temporal resolution – are able to record the brain's activity with millisecond accuracy, but do not provide very specific information about the brain structures producing the electrical signal.

Existential instinct: the search for meaning and purpose in life postulated as the fundamental driving force of the human mind; meditation approaches suggest that the ultimate sense of meaning and purpose arises from experiential understanding of the nature of self and reality.

Existentialism: philosophical tradition and psychotherapeutic approach explaining how attribution of meaning determines the direction of human life.

First-person methods (introspective methods): methods investigating functioning of the mind in which the research participant observes mental processes in their own mind and reports on this.

Five types of primordial wisdom: describe the enlightened mind. They include primordial awareness of dharmadhātu, mirror-like awareness, primordial awareness of equality, discriminating primordial awareness and the primordial awareness that accomplishes all actions.

Frontal lobes: large areas of the brain located in the frontal parts of the two brain hemispheres; their functioning mediates complex mental processes including planning, decision making, working memory, attention control and monitoring, and coordination of complex movement.

Functional magnetic resonance imaging (fMRI): brain imaging method based on metabolic changes in the blood (blood-oxygenation-level-dependent (BOLD) signal) in response to cognitive demands. This method has very good spatial resolution (in terms of millimetres), but relatively poor timing specificity.

Grey matter of the brain: mainly contains brain cell bodies and receptive branches of neurons.

Hedonistic happiness: derived from pleasure, typically short-lived and bound to particular pleasurable stimuli or circumstances.

Insula: area in the cortex of the brain involved in awareness of emotions and sensations in the body.

Introspection: method of exploring the mind based on observation of our own mental processes.

Mahāyāna: set of Buddhist teachings emphasizing the Bodhisattva ideal which are predominant in Tibet, China, Vietnam and Japan.

Meta-awareness (Pāli: sampajañña; Sanskrit: samprajanya; Tibetan: shizhin): the monitoring element of attention, which checks the quality of focus on the object of meditation and notices distraction.

Metacognitive self-regulatory capacity of the mind (MSRC): a natural propensity of the mind which enables introspective reflective awareness of mental processes and behavior, and is a necessary pre-requisite for effective self-regulation supporting well-being. It consists of interacting systems and processes of metacognition and attention, emotion regulation and conceptual processing.

Mindfulness (Pāli: sati; Sanskrit: smṛti; Tibetan: trenba): in the Buddhist context it is a faculty of the mind which enables the practitioner to sustain attention on the object of meditation; in Buddhism mindfulness is associated with prospective memory – remembering to pay attention to the object of meditation. In secular approaches mindfulness is described more broadly as non-judgmental awareness focused on the present moment.

Mindfulness-based approaches: a group of secular programmes and therapeutic approaches in which mindfulness is the central component; these most notably include mindfulness-based stress reduction (MBSR) and mindfulness-based cognitive therapy (MBCT). There are other approaches such as dialectic behaviour therapy and acceptance commitment therapy in which mindfulness is a therapeutic element.

Mindfulness-based cognitive therapy (MBCT): an eight-week secular programme combining mindfulness training with elements of cognitive behavioural therapy; MBCT was specifically developed for treatment of recurrent depression.

Mindfulness-based stress reduction (MBSR): an eight-week secular programme developed by Jon Kabat-Zinn which involves a variety of mindfulness practices, education about stress, group discussions about conscious experience and yoga-based practices. The MBSR laid the foundation for other mindfulness-based approaches.

Modes of existential awareness (MEA): overarching, phenomenologically distinct, state shifts in the awareness of self and reality; they are enabled by cumulative changes in the metacognitive, attentional, affective and conceptual aspects of the MSRC modulated by motivational/intentional and contextual factors of meditation practice.

Mood: in comparison to emotions a more general emotional state lasting for days or weeks.

Neural plasticity: describes the modifiability of neural connections, and more broadly brain function and structure, by experience.

Orbitofrontal cortex (OFC): area in the prefrontal cortex of the brain involved in decision making and particularly in reward-related processing imbalance, which may contribute to development of addictions.

Ordinary mind: in the context of Dzogchen one of the three levels of consciousness which includes sensations, perceptions, thoughts, memories and affect we typically experience and can mostly become aware of if we observe the mind. These mental processes enable us to learn new skills, make decisions and function efficiently in everyday life.

Precuneus: a brain structure implicated in conscious experience.

Prefrontal cortex: the most frontal part of frontal lobes of the brain excluding motor cortex of the frontal lobes.

Pristine awareness (Sanskrit: vidyā; Tibetan: rigpa): in Dzogchen it is the most subtle aspect of consciousness; the final goal of Dzogchen practices is to access and experientially recognize this type of consciousness and sustain awareness at this ever-present level of ultimate mental balance.

Self-regulation: the ability to notice and effectively manage thoughts, emotional responses and behavior; typically described as consisting of attention regulation and emotion regulation.

Shamatha (Pāli: samatha, Sanskrit: śamatha or shamatha; Tibetan: shiyné): aspect of Buddhist mind training concerned with cultivation of stability, monitoring and redirecting qualities of attention; sometimes referred to as calm abiding.

Substrate consciousness (Sanskrit: ālayavijñāna; Tibetan: kun gzhi nams shes): the second out of the three layers of consciousness described in the Dzogchen tradition. This layer of consciousness contains more subtle tendencies of behaviour, mental habits and temper which influence the ordinary mind. It contains the roots of mental frameworks which underlie our construed notions of 'self' or 'I'.

Theravāda: considered the oldest school of Buddhism and predominant in Southeast Asia.

Vajrayāna (Tantrayāna): a branch of Buddhism prevalent in Tibet which focuses on practices involving sacred visualizations, mantra recitation and work with energies of the body.

Valence: places an emotion on a scale from positive to negative (pleasant to unpleasant).

Vipassana (Pāli: vipassana; Sanskrit: vipasyana; Tibetan: lhaktong): practices in which the meditator watches as thoughts, perceptions and emotions arise and fade away, and gradually explores the source of mental activity and its characteristics.

Index